Thinking Together
At The Edge Of History:

A Memoir Of The Lindisfarne Association

THINKING TOGETHER AT THE EDGE OF HISTORY:
A Memoir of the Lindisfarne Association, 1972-2012

WILLIAM IRWIN THOMPSON
© Copyright Evan and Hilary Thompson, 2016

Book design by Jeremy Berg

ISBN-13: 978-0-936878-86-7

Thompson, William Irwin
Thinking Together At The Edge Of History: *A Memoir Of The Lindisfarne Association, 1972-2012*/William Irwin Thompson

Library of Congress Control Number: 2016935747

First Edition: March 2016

Printed in the United States of America, the United Kingdom and Australia

Thinking Together At The Edge Of History:

A Memoir Of The Lindisfarne Association

William Irwin Thompson

Lorian Press
6592 Peninsula Dr
Traverse City MI 49686

Table of Contents

Photographic Credits

Pg	Photogapher	Pg	Photogapher
3	W.I. Thompson	81	Unknown
17	W.I. Thompson	82	W.I. Thompson
21	W.I. Thompson	85	Mind Life Institute
22	W.I. Thompson	86	Nina Hagen
23	W.I. Thompson	87	W.I. Thompson
25	W.I. Thompson	88	Unknown
26	Nina Hagen	89	Unknown
27	Nina Hagen	91	Nina Hagen
28	Nina Hagen	92	W.I. Thompson
30	Nina Hagen	93	Nina Hagen
31	W.I. Thompson	94	W.I. Thompson
32	Nina Hagen	95	Nina Hagen
33	Nina Hagen	98	W.I. Thompson
35	Nina Hagen	99	Unknown
36	Nina Hagen	101	Nina Hagen
37	Sandy Lovelock	102	W.I. Thompson
38	Evan Thompson	103	Evan Thompson
39	Evan Thompson	105	W.I. Thompson
46	Nina Hagen	110	San Francisco Zen Center
47	Nina Hagen	111	Nina Hagen
48	Nina Hagen	112	Nina Hagen
52	Nina Hagen – Top	115	Hanne Strong
52	W.I. Thompson – Bottom	116	Nina Hagen
53	W.I. Thompson	117	Nina Hagen
53	W.I. Thompson	119	W.I. Thompson
55	Nina Hagen	120	Nina Hagen
56	Nina Hagen	121	Unknown – Top
57	Nina Hagen	121	Hanne Strong – Bottom
59	Nina Hagen	122	Marianne Marstrand
62	Nina Hagen	124	Marianne Marstrand
63	Nina Hagen – Top	125	Marianne Marstrand – Top
63	W.I. Thompson – Bottom	125	W.I. Thompson – Bottom
68	W.I. Thompson	126	W.I. Thompson
69	W.I. Thompson	127	W.I. Thompson
71	W.I. Thompson	128	W.I. Thompson
72	W.I. Thompson	129	W.I. Thompson
73	Beatrice Rudin Thompson	130	Amyas Ames – Top
74	Unknown – Top	130	W.I. Thompson – Bottom
74	Unknown – Bottom	132	Nina Hagen
78	Unknown School Photo	133	W.I. Thompson
80	Unknown	136	Nina Hagen

Chapter 1
Pilgrimage to Lindisfarne, 1972

In the slalom of humanity's descent into time, we seem to lean alternately from Left to Right as we hope to steer away from imagined disasters. Today the Libertarian counterculture is on the Right, but in the days of the Viet Nam War the counterculture was on the Left. One generation will envision a return to nature in an effort to escape spirit-killing bureaucracies, and the next will dream of a return to White Protestant small farms and towns, simple markets, and Libertarian values in an effort to escape metropolitan cultures, intellectual experts, and Big Government. More recently, the global Occupy Wall Street movement indicated that the New Left was reawakening—thanks to Obama's abandonment of the liberal-progressives and his orientation to Wall Street, so effectively implemented by Timothy Geithner and Larry Summers. And yet neither shift in our inclinations, Right or Left, seems to affect the general direction of humanity's descent into the strange attractor of a global catastrophe bifurcation.

The generation that came of age in the sixties and seventies had an apocalyptic sensibility that expressed itself in radical Left political movements, millennial cults, and popular science fiction mythic art forms in novels and films. The artistic imagination is much like the hypnogogic state of mind that separates the waking from the dreaming consciousness; in this transitional state in which the muscle inhibitors kick in to prevent us from moving while we sleep, we can sometimes see things in the room that aren't really there—even with our eyes open—as diverse sensory signals are converted into imagery and then into the enacted imagery of the dramas we call dreams. This state of imaginary perception also seems to occur during fevers. In the nineteen-sixties, a whole generation seemed to be living at a fevered pitch. Myths, millennial movements, popular art forms such as the science fiction movie *2001: A Space Odyssey* took an indistinct and slower cultural transformation and compressed it into events in the imagery of a mythic narrative that was much like a waking dream.

The Lindisfarne Association that I founded in New York in 1972 was very much a seventies kind of cultural movement in that it sought to avoid the sixties-style mass movements of drugs and revolutionary violence to seek out a more spiritual and intellectual third way to effect the transformation of culture. As a student of cultural history, I had a sense that our Western civilization was at the edge of its kairos and that a newly emerging planetary

1

culture called out for a new formation with which to realize itself, so I sought out others in what became the Lindisfarne Fellowship that seemed to embody this third way. Paradoxically, such a gathering together is very much in the ethos of Western Civilization, from the Axial Age to the Renaissance and the Enlightenment.

I chose to call this new emergent domain a planetary culture rather than a planetary civilization with a mind tuned to complex dynamical systems. A civilization has a single imperial capital and a monocrop mentality of dominance. A culture can be polycentric and composed of competing ideologies, such as those of science, art, and religion. Lovelock and Margulis's Gaia theory is a vision of planetary dynamics in which ocean, continent, and atmosphere create an emergent domain through energizing diversity. Our planet is not a primal sludge in which earth, air, and water are one common medium. From the early eighties, this Gaian theory, therefore, became basic to Lindisfarne's philosophy. With the addition of chaos dynamics and complex dynamical systems at the end of the eighties through the influence of Ralph Abraham, Susan Oyama, and then, Stu Kauffman, Lindisfarne's work took a further step toward the articulation of this new culture of science and a post-religious spirituality.

Because of my personal background in university teaching, Lindisfarne in the nineteen-seventies was aimed at university students and drop-outs, but the Lindisfarne conferences soon proved to be attractive to professors, artists, scientists, and scholars, and we found ourselves described as what *Harper's Magazine* called "a summer camp for intellectuals." Like Trabuco College, Black Mountain, Bennington, or Esalen before us, Lindisfarne's identity was not really based on its institutional structure. We were more of an atmosphere than a physical location—a cloud more than a clod. For those of us inside this nebula it felt as if a Zeitgeist were trying to condense and form into a stellar body. But this Zeitgeist was definitely an ephemeral manifestation of the spirituality of the seventies, and with the onset of the Reagan eighties it felt as if America had voted a resounding No! to whatever intercessionary angel was seeking to manifest its mysteries in historical time.

After a generation of this countercultural work to articulate a new planetary culture, Courtney Ross's visit to the Lindisfarne Mountain Retreat in 1995, accompanied by the Lindisfarne Fellow Ralph Abraham, and her request that I design the curriculum for her new private school in East Hampton, New York provided me with an opportunity to extend my vision from adults to the education of children for a post-national world. Although the Lindisfarne Association ceased to be a formal not-for-profit educational foundation in

2009, the Lindisfarne Fellows continued to meet to think together about ecology, planetary culture, and issues of global concern up to the year 2012, but the Ross School still continues to develop internationally in an effort to transform education so that it may express a new global consciousness for a new planetary civilization.

Lindisfarne Mountain Retreat, Crestone, Colorado 1995

I did not know why I had picked Lindisfarne out of all the monastery schools of the Dark Ages, and I did not know what I would do when I got there, but I went on all the same. When, after traveling around the world for three months in 1972, I finally came to Holy Island off the coast of Northumbria in early autumn, I had only a few minutes to cross before the tide flooded the channel.[1] I was glad that I had followed my hunch not to stop on the way down from Edinburgh, for now I would have the whole afternoon on the island until the channel again opened at dusk. I crossed over quickly, parked the car, and began a slow ambulation in search of whatever was left, suspended in the ether of another era. I circled around the castle on the high rock, went down to the shore, paced in the enclosed garden, and came back to the ruin of the twelfth-century priory and the modern chapel. Nothing of the original seventh-century monastery remained; after the sacred power of the founding saints had gone, the profane power of the Vikings had come in like the tides. Since there was no other place in which to pause and meditate

3

on the tides of history, I went into the modern chapel.

In all the sacred places I had visited in my journey around the world, I had constructed an imago: a spiral in a new planetary space in which all the religions of the past were circulations in a single hypersphere. And to match this uniqueness of space, I envisioned a uniqueness of our present moment in time, a *kairos*, in which it was appropriate to look back at all the religions of the past, and then move beyond them in the next turn of the spiral into a new post-religious and scientific planetary spirituality.

Once I had concluded my meditation, I had only to wait until the tide went out to return to Edinburgh. In the chapel I saw and bought a little pamphlet that told of the life of St. Aidan, the founder of Lindisfarne, and of St. Cuthbert, his greatest successor. One of the hagiographic fables seemed to connect the ethos of Lindisfarne with ancient esoteric traditions of the Essenes and the Judaism of the desert. According to several esoteric traditions — among them the Anthroposophy of Rudolf Steiner as well as the kriya yoga of Paramahansa Yogananda — John the Baptist was said to be the reincarnation of Elijah, and Jesus was said to be the reincarnation of Elijah's disciple, Elisha. When Elisha asks his departing master that a double part of his spirit descend upon him, he is asking for an acceleration of his spiritual evolution. Elijah cannot grant this to him, for it can only take place if Elisha himself can stand to receive such powers all at once. And so Elijah tells him that if he can so control his consciousness so as to be able to see all the planes of consciousness, the *lokas*, through which Elijah will ascend as he departs, then Elisha's inheritance of what the Zen Buddhists call the "mind to mind transmission" of his master will be achieved. Elisha does indeed see Elijah ascend to heaven "in a fiery chariot"; he picks up the mantle of Elijah and returns to the esoteric community on Mt. Carmel and all the followers recognize that Elisha now wears the power and mantle of Elijah. A similar kind of prophetic succession is expressed in the hagiography of Aidan and Cuthbert.

> On the night of St. Aidan's death an athletic lad of 17, whose dust is now the prized possession of Durham Cathedral, where his name—Cuthbertus— is engraved on a great stone slab behind the high altar, was watching sheep in the Leader valley on the lower slopes of the Lammermoor hills. Awake while other shepherds were sleeping, he had a vision of angels bearing a great soul to paradise; and when a few days later news came of the death of the beloved Aidan, he took the vision as a call to the services of God.[2]

It would seem that something of the esoteric was transmitted through archaic Celtic Christianity; or, perhaps, it would be closer to the truth to say that in Ireland two streams met to create the river that sustained life in Western Europe in the Dark Ages. One was the ancient stream of esoteric thought that had been centered in Ireland since megalithic times; the other was the Christian monastic tradition which had its source in that other fountainhead of esoteric traditions, Egypt.[3] With Druid Ireland on one side, and syncretistic Egypt on the other, one can see that there have been times in the past, much like our own, in which one esoteric tradition comes into contact with another. The Sufis claim that their knowledge predates Islam and goes back to Egypt, but this claim to have a source of authority that does not derive from orthodox centers of priestly power can create trouble for mystics, Gnostics, or Nestorian heretics, as both Sufis and Celtic Christians discovered at different times.

Initiates of certain inner experiences can recognize in the imagery of another tradition different metaphoric systems for similar experiences. Fundamentalist zealots, who have not experienced these inner illuminations and transformations, are both full of fear and then rage that they have been excluded from some mystery, so they reify religious belief into textual literalisms and then use these as a license for persecution and murder of their rivals. An initiate of these inner experiences recognizes that whether it is the case of the Egyptian serpent rising out of the forehead, or the Indian snake of kundalini, or the Mexican serpent turning into a plumed Quetzal bird, or the winged snakes of the caduceus of the god Mercury, or the snake worship of the Druid priests that St. Patrick drove out of Ireland, that a single experience of illumination has been encoded in the imagery. What is common to them all is human physiology, with its energies, both physical and subtle.

Of course, most scholars, especially those who have not experienced this physiologically based process of illumination, would object to such global theories of transcultural communication and see them as some form of Pynchonesque conspiracy network. But imagine that our civilization were to be wiped out and that scholars thousands of years from now were trying to reconstruct its activities. No archaeologist would be willing to accept the fact that pieces of things as different as Volkswagens, Cadillacs, and buses represented, not artifacts of isolated cultures, but parts of one industrial civilization that covered the face of the Earth. The specialists would split up the civilization into pieces and talk about how the Volkswagen I people conquered the Ford II people until both were replaced by an empire which moved troops around in large vehicles. Other experts would argue that no one could possibly have crossed the great oceans, and that the Volkswagen and Ford cultures could have had nothing to do with one another but were separate and independent technologies of isolated cultures.

Humans traveled in the past as they do now, carrying their culture with them in their heads. Pythagoras was not the first or last man to travel and bring the mysteries of the East to the West. Strange as it may seem, St. Cuthbert seemed to know the yoga of body heat and knew how to match the waves of inhalation and exhalation with mantras and waves of the sea.

> A spying monk recorded how he watched him descend the cliff while others were sleeping, cross the slippery rocks, enter the sea, and chant psalms while the waves lapped around him; and how on his return to shore two small creatures, otters or young seals, came and rubbed themselves upon his chilled feet.[4]

It is sad to think how little of the esoteric and initiatic has survived in modern Christianity, but given our Western history of the Albigensian Crusade, the Inquisition, and the witch trials, it is not surprising that those seekers of illumination and enlightenment now must go to Japan or India to find something as simple as a breathing technique for quieting the noisy inner dialogue of the mind so that the aspirant may enter states of consciousness deeper than egocentric prayers of God give-me-this and give-me-that. Americans have to go to the "New Religions" because our old religions of Catholic, Protestant, and Jew tend to give us the institutional culture of priests and not the experience of the divine.

Christianity once contained specific instructions on the cure of our malaise, but these instructions about techniques of inner consciousness opened doors that were not doors of the Church with its clergy and sacraments, so the doors to the mind were slammed shut in a campaign carried on over centuries of persecution to wipe out "heretics." No doubt, the Princes of the Church were able to terrorize monks and nuns with the examples of a few religious psychotics, and, perhaps, a few of these delusional heretics were truly evil; but if Christianity had kept its esoteric tradition alive, there would have been, as well as Popes and Cardinals, a few adepts who knew the inner geography of the soul sufficiently well enough to tell the spirit of the Lord from possession by the devil.

But it is now pointless to argue over whose fault it was that Christianity lost its way and became the religion about Christ and not of Christ. We have to accept the fact that we now live in a time when the esoteric traditions of Christianity are barely alive, found only occasionally in a few scattered individuals, and that the esoteric traditions that served to inspire Western science are fast dying off in our age of technological idolatry. The whole light of the civilization that came out of Christian Europe is flickering toward a new age of darkness. Now we live in a culture in which the Rosicrucian Enlightenment of Kepler, Boyle, and Newton has been reduced to a new electronic version of what Whitehead called scientific materialism. The Celtic Christianity of Columba, Aidan, and Cuthbert has been reduced to the soporific pieties of the clergy—be they Roman Catholic or Anglican. The esoteric is not a visible presence in Christianity any longer.

If you wish to go back to the point at which Christianity took the wrong turn, so that you can find the other road at the fork, you must go back to Lindisfarne to see the clash between the Celtic Christianity that identified itself as the Church of John and the Roman imperial Christianity that identified itself as the Church of Peter.

The clash had been developing during the episcopate of Finan, who succeeded Aidan at Lindisfarne; and it became unavoidable when Oswy in 655 slew Penda of Mercia, the last defender of heathenism, who had stood between the stream of Christianity coming down from Iona and the stream pressing northwards from Canterbury. Colman, the third bishop, inherited the dispute when Finan died in 661. King Oswy's sympathies were with the Celtic Church in which he had been brought up at Iona, but his queen and her chaplain followed the usages they had been familiar with in Kent. The confusion in the royal household was such that Easter was kept twice...The king's long reign (642-670) and religious zeal gave the Church the opportunity to become deeply rooted in his extensive kingdom; but which Church and which customs was he to support? Aware that the Easter divergence in 665 would be greater than usual, Oswy summoned the Synod of Whitby in 663 or 664 at the monastery ruled by Hilda, pleading that all who served the one God should agree to observe one rule of life. Colman claimed that the Celtic traditions went back to St. John; but Wilfrid, a former disciple of Aidan, who had visited Rome and adopted Roman usages, laid emphasis on the folly of resisting the unique authority of St. Peter: "The only people who are stupid enough to disagree with the whole world are these Scots and their obstinate adherents the Picts and the Britons, who inhabit only a portion of these two islands in the remote ocean." The king had evidently already made up his mind, with a view to unity and peace in his own house, and with a smile he announced his decision in these words: "If Peter is the guardian of the gates of heaven, I shall not contradict him. I shall obey his commands in everything to the best of my ability: otherwise, when I come to the gates of heaven, he who holds the key may not be willing to open them.[5]

Two roads diverged at Lindisfarne; one went to Rome through Wilfrid, the other went to Iona through Colman. Aidan had come to Lindisfarne from Iona, and it was at Iona that Aidan's teacher, St. Columba, had created a center of esoteric Christianity. It is small wonder that after the failures of the Synod of Whitby, Colman and his monks left Lindisfarne and went back to remote Iona.

From contemporary sciences of ecology, we have learned that a rich biological diversity is a healthier way to maintain an ecosystem or a planet. Imperial modes of thinking, however, demand and command a monocrop that destroys wetlands with dams and turns prairies into single crop factories forcefully maintained by center-pivot irrigation, fertilizers, and pesticides. The industrial farm, the modern corporate university with its aluminum and glass business-containers, and the drive-in, parking lot super-churches of Dallas are all embodiments of this imperial mentality. One can only look back to the Synod of Whitby and speculate how much richer Western Christianity would have been if Rome and the Papacy had not triumphed, if Celtic, Roman, Greek, Armenian, Coptic, Ethiopian, Maronite-Syriac, and Nestorian Christianities had all flourished and prospered. After all, there is no Pope for Buddhism, and Hinayana, Mahayana, Tibetan, Chan, Shin, and Japanese Zen Buddhisms have managed very nicely around the world without an imperial standardization. But the West chose the Roman model, and in taking on the form and thinking of empire, it was easier to move toward the politics of empire in the Albigensian Crusade and the permanent establishment of the Inquisition.

Since the esoteric has been often forcefully eliminated from Christianity, and had only survived in prophetic sects in which, unfortunately, the personality of the founder also became part of the message, I felt in the nineteen-seventies that the only way for a healthier diversity to re-establish itself was to back-propagate Christianity with living esoteric seeds from other traditions. Influenced by the Hindu-Christian syncretism of Yogananda, I thought that in a planetization of the esoteric, Yoga, Sufism, Tibetan Buddhism, Zen, and native American traditions could be brought into communion with a new form of post-religious Christian spirituality and Western science.

Both the Church and the university, as narrowly politicized institutions, were inseparable from the values and world view of the modern postindustrial corporation; their clergy and faculty lacked the imaginative capacity to effect the shift from the ecological crisis of our postindustrial global civilizaton to a new planetary culture with a more profound understanding of our biospheric condition. Education had been captured by industry, science had been taken over by a technological idolatry based upon a narrow linear reductionism, and religion had been taken hostage by mind-numbing rituals and emotionally infantilizing forms of worship. What was needed was a new kind of educational community in which the individual was empowered through meditation to connect the *unique* to the *universal* without the mediation of clerical ritual and collectivizing worship, and in which a more holistic science that recognized complexity could work toward the design of architectural forms that were more symbiotic with our new biospheric understanding of ecology. A new kind of educational association would need to be created in which the transformation of individual consciousness and the redesign of human settlements could be brought together in meta-industrial villages and more symbiotic cities—not to preserve the old in a monastic museum or pre-industrial commune, but to articulate an emergent evolution to carry us forward into a new historical landscape. Such was to be my project in returning from my pilgrimage to the historical Lindisfarne, quitting my professorship in Toronto, and working to establish the Lindisfarne Association in New York City in December of 1972.

---

[1] An earlier version of this essay was published in Passages about Earth: an Exploration of the New Planetary Culture (New York: Harper & Row, 1974).

[2] Henry Kelsey, *St. Aidan and St. Cuthbert* (Berwick on Tweed, no date), p. 23.

[3] See Maire and Liam De Paor, *Early Christian Ireland* (London: Thames & Hudson, 1958); also "Ireland and the East" in G. T. Stokes, *Ireland and the Celtic Church* (London: Hodder and Stoughton, 1886), pp. 166-170.

[4] *Kelsey, loc.cit.*

[5] Ibid.

For further reading, see Jean Markale, *Le Christianisme celtique et ses survivances populaires* (Paris: Editions Imago, 1983).
Brendan Lehane, *The Quest of the Three Abbots* (New York: Viking Press, 1968).
Celtic Chrsitian Spirituality : An Anthology of Medieval and Modern Sources, Ed. Oliver Davies and Fiona Bowie (New York: Continuum Books, 1995).
Celtic Christianity: Ecology and Holiness, Ed. Christopher Bamford and William Parker Marsh (Great Barrington, MA: Lindisfarne Press, 1982).

Chapter 2: The Founding of the Lindisfarne Association in New York, 1971-73

A book made the founding of the Lindisfarne Association possible, so the story of Lindisfarne is entwined with the story of this curious little book that did not follow the usual path to publication, nor the usual road to post-publication success. The book was *At the Edge of History* and was published by Harper & Row in 1971. It arrived at the editorial offices in the mail, without the representation of an agent, because I was naïve enough not to know that the chances of a book being accepted through the mail were 1 in 7500. For unexplainable reasons, the young editorial assistant, Christie Noyes, whose task it was to deal with the towering dead weight of all those manuscripts dumped on her desk, turned the pages quickly, asking for the manuscript to give her a signal to put it in the rejections list, but she kept getting little signs that asked her to grant it a stay of execution. Like Sheherazade postponing her fate with another interconnected story, the manuscript caught her interest. The stay of execution turned into a full pardon, and the manuscript was carried to the senior editor's desk, Buz Wyeth, and from there to acceptance and the contracts department. While the manuscript was moving from what were then called galleys to page proofs, Arthur C. Clarke was visiting the editorial offices on one of his visits from Sri Lanka. Since the concluding chapter had a riff on his book and the movie, *2001: A Space Odyssey,* he was shown the pages, and was delighted. As Clarke moved about Manhattan, from Harper & Row to *The New Yorker,* he shared his enthusiasm and talked about the book everywhere. There was a murmuring buz around the book—not just Wyeth—even before it was published. The reviewer for *The New York Times,* Christopher Lehmann-Haupt, decided to review it, which, considering the hundreds of books he had to choose from, was no small act of intercessionary grace in itself. Lehmann-Haupt gave the book a rave review, but as rave reviews were not uncommon, what truly astonished everyone in Manhattan was that three days later, in the middle of reviewing another book, he stopped mid-column, and admitted that he could not get *At the Edge of History* out of his mind and had been haunted by it. "Read Thompson," he said, "a silver thrush among pterodactyls." Harper & Row was delighted and took out an ad in *The New York Times* that proclaimed: "so extraordinary –*The New York Times* raved twice!"

Now everyone in Manhattan was talking about the book. It became a bestseller, but only in Manhattan, but that was good enough to make the top ten list in *Time* magazine for the week. Since many of those people who were talking about the book in the city were executives, these were going to be the very people I would have to see in, first, incorporating Lindisfarne as a not for profit corporation, and then seeking foundation grants.

Away from the talk of Manhattan, up in suburban Toronto, I began to receive phone calls to appear on David Frost and the Dick Cavett Show. To the horror of Harper & Row, I declined both and tried to explain to them that I was not a television celebrity but a writer, one more interested in creating a lifetime's oeuvre than becoming a celebrity or a narcississtic habitué of talk shows. As I focused in my mind on my high school heroes of Whitehead, Yeats, and Thomas Mann, I held to an image of culture that had disappeared with them. I simply did not understand that there was no longer any such thing as a successful writer who was not a TV celebrity—with the single exception of Thomas Pynchon. With more than 32,000 books published a year then, it was impossible for a book to survive simply on its literary merits. Gore Vidal, Norman Mailer, and Susan Sontag understood this only too well, but I did not.

On the basis of the book, the editor of *The New York Times*, Harrison Salisbury, asked me to do several OpEd page essays, and as these too stirred up talk around town— one was even read aloud by an actor before a play on Off-Broadway—the book continued to sell well in Manhattan, but nowhere else in the country; so the sales began to dwindle. Fortunately for me, while the book was still hot, I was able to get a good advance for my next book, *Passages about Earth*, and these funds enabled me to finance a trip around the world, one that ended with my visit to the ruined abbey of Lindisfarne on Holy Island in Northumbria. The book took another upward turn in its life, when it was a finalist for the National Book Award in early 1972. And when the award went to the *Whole Earth Catalogue*, one of the judges quit in protest to giving a literary award to a hippie Yellow Pages catalogue. The next day the American historian Max Lerner protested in his column in the *New York Daily News* and said that the award should have gone to *At the Edge of History*.

Although Frank Sinatra had hymned "New York, New York! If you can make it there, you can make it anywhere," those sentiments proved to be truer of the forties than the seventies. The book became a bestseller only for a season in Manhattan and nowhere else. In Chicago, Dallas, and L.A., people watched TV to find out what people were talking about, and since I wasn't on TV, I was under the edge of their history.

Although the book received good reviews in Manhattan and the *Los Angeles Times*, it was not universally well received, and more conservative reviewers in more solidly academic journals, such as the *Virginia Quarterly* and the *Partisan Review*, dismissed the work as apocalyptic and more a symptom of the decline of Western Civilization than a description of its end. These august and Augustan defenders of the dominant Neo-Roman imperial culture were suspicious of wild, mystical, and otherworldly Celts, and my particular re-visioning of history—and their elitist position at its center—was simply unacceptable. They were, of course, right about me; I was apocalyptic, but I had good reason to be, and in my writings I strove to be reasonable about why I did not place much faith in reality.

One good reason for becoming paranoid is to grow up in an environment in which the news never tells the real truth while your peripheral senses pick up on an invisible environment of menace. I grew up in the age when America itself was paranoid and broadcast news of the global threat of communism. In my parochial elementary school, the nuns taught us how, at the sound of the single command "*Drop!*" to leap under our desks to seek the protection of a one inch thick slab of wood from a Hydrogen bomb. The government, however, offered us no protection from American atom bombs and continued their open air atomic explosions in Nevada; and when the Santa Ana desert winds would blow the contaminated dust into the air and onto the grazing lands around the city, no one said that the contaminated milk should be destroyed rather than given to the children, whose thyroid glands absorbed the Iodine 131. At ten, I would rise at dawn to witness the marvel of the eastern sky lighting up from atomic bombs in man's preemptive strike at dawn; at eleven, I had cancer of the thyroid.

If I was sick, the environment was also sick. The air was brown with smog. Everyone smoked everywhere. The shoe stores were filled with Xray machines in which I could play as a child and look at my bones in an eerie green light. At my Catholic parochial school we were warned to be suspicious of cultured intellectuals who were more likely to be communist sympathizers, and on the new medium of television we were taught by our Hollywood producers to dislike unruly Arabs and revere Israelis. This was not hard, as the Israeli dessert frontier seemed to be another sort of Western with a Cowboys and Indians conflict. (Small wonder that Sharon tried to break up the West Bank into reservations.) I can still remember the United Jewish Appeal's image on TV and in newsreels of Ben Gurion on a hill in Israel, with a new wind lifting his white hair in the Promised Land.

When you can't really know what is truly going on around you, you begin to grow up with a sense of unease and dread. I looked to books to deliver me from the media, so I had a vague distrust of television. I wanted to grow

13

up to become a writer and not a television star or politician. But I was not strong enough in my youth to be completely immune to the new political medium. I could see at once how repulsive Senator Joe McCarthy was, but like most of my generation I was taken in by the media manipulations of the Kennedys and when I came of age and exercised my first vote, it was for the appealing JFK over the dour and droning five o'clock-shadowed delusionary Richard Milhous Nixon.

But what had been a nebulous atmosphere of unexpressed menace in the nineteen-fifties became a clear and distinct threat in the sixties in the days of the Cuban Missile Crisis—which we now know was indeed a time when we hung by our fingernails above the abyss of thermonuclear war. In 1962, I was a first year graduate student at Cornell. My friends from Pomona College, Leon Leeds and Linda Thompson, were with me as we examined our apartment and realized that the only place we could escape the imploding glass of the windows was in the closet under the stairs. Leon, then a graduate student from Indiana, was visiting his girl friend Linda—later to become his wife—who was also a graduate student with me in the English department at Cornell. As we listened to the news, we talked about places where one could live, far away from the cities, in some imaginary communal "return to nature."

The Cuban missile crisis came and went, but there was no let-up on the environment of hidden menace and public lies as JFK and Martin Luther King were assassinated, and the country shifted from its fifties postwar culture of consumerism to race riots in Detroit, Newark, and Watts, and radical left bombings and open talk of revolution. A new youth culture appeared, whose avatars were Bob Dylan and the Beatles, and no one believed what the political leaders were saying anymore, not simply about the War in Viet Nam and the global communist menace, but about the nature of reality itself. Reality was broken and needed fixing.

In those unstable times, studying literature and following the deconstructionist leadership of Paul De Man at Cornell seemed too nihilistic and valueless. Of course, at that time I did not know that De Man had written fascist and anti-Semitic articles for Belgium newspapers in the early forties; I was simply repelled at his way of reading Yeats and the whole aura around him when he lectured. I turned away from the approaches of all my professors of English and Comparative Literature at Cornell to return to my own anthropological approach of my Pomona College days and began to study another time of insurrection in Ireland. I didn't want to decenter authorial narratives in the post-modernist thinking of Paul De Man and Roland Barthes, I wanted to study the role of the artist as a prophetic figure who rearticulated the relationship between myth and history. I wanted to understand the role of the imagination in the transformation of culture. The Ireland of radical Patrick Pearse on the one side, and conservative William Butler Yeats on the other, seemed the perfect place to pursue this line of inquiry.

Although I never knew my maternal grandmother, Margaret Mary O'Leary—since she had died when my mother was a child—I had listened to my mother in Chicago talk about her Irish mother and grandmother, so these invisible beings became mythical ancestors for me. My colleagues in my graduate seminar on James Joyce were drawn to study *Ulysses* or *Finnegans Wake* as if they were verbal crossword puzzles to be solved, but I was drawn to the historical horizon behind Joyce. I shifted away from studying to become a literary critic to becoming a cultural historian and chose to write my dissertation on the insurrection in Dublin in 1916, the Easter Rising. As I was finishing my dissertation, and getting ready to take my first teaching job in the Department of Humanities at MIT, Los Angeles went up in flames in the insurrection in Watts of 1965.

In the winter of 1966-1967, I received an MIT Old Dominion faculty fellowship that allowed me to take off a semester from teaching to do research. I thought of going back to Dublin and London, but I felt this strong pull back to California. From L.A. to San Francisco and Berkeley it seemed as if history was happening out there, so studying history in the libraries of Dublin and London seemed too antiquarian for my years, as I was still in my twenties.

I flew to L.A., and then in the summer of '67 drove up to Esalen in Big Sur, where I met Alan Watts, Joan Baez, and Esalen's founder, Michael Murphy. There are times in history when to be at the right place at the right age is to feel a state of exaltation. Wordsworth felt it in France in the early days of the Revolution, before the Terror: "Bliss was it in that dawn to be alive,/But to be young was very Heaven!"

I didn't take acid, because as a child of four I had experienced yogic samadhi while listening to classical music, and, as an adolescent of eighteen, I had experienced Daimonic transmissions, the spontaneous elevation of kundalini, and the opening of the third eye while listening to Beethoven's Ninth string quartet. In one of these transmissions, I was warned against taking the path of drugs; however, at that moment in Esalen—unlike President Clinton—I did inhale when Alan Watts passed me his joint as we soaked in the tubs, and I passed it on to the gloriously beautiful naked woman on my right.

I was able to resist losing myself in sex, drugs, and rock and roll at Esalen, but what really took possession of me during my conversations at the wine bar with Michael Murphy was the idea of the countercultural institution—of completely breaking away from academe and creating a completely different sort of institution. I didn't cheat on my wife, but held on tightly to my weakening grasp of monogamy, but I did cheat on MIT and the muse I became embedded with was not Erato but Clio as I used my research fellowship to shift away from purely academic research to begin writing what became *At the Edge of History*.

The more I worked on the book, the harder it became to endure MIT, especially during the Viet Nam War when the faculty was polarized between the Defense Industry Hawks and the Marxist Doves under the aggressive bird of prey leadership of Noam Chomsky and Louis Kampf.

Under Louis Kampf's direction, the Literature Division took a radical Left turn and he hired several Maoist-inspired radicals who argued in faculty meetings that we should stop teaching works like Wordsworth's *Prelude*,[1] because the self was a bourgeois-personalist fiction, and that we should teach Eldridge Cleaver's *Soul on Ice* instead.

Since I was interested in the evolution of consciousness, and the coeval emergence of phenomenological models for the growth and development of the mind in Hegel, Wordsworth, and Coleridge, this forceful eliminativism of the Leftist radicals took away the literary and philosophical classics and cultural history I was interested in exploring. In the spirit of Foucault, the humanities at MIT became focused exclusively on power, technology, and the means of production. The third way that Esalen was exploring, and that I would continue to develop through Lindisfarne in the Seventies and Eighties became impossible at MIT.

On one side, MIT was an instrument for the enforced modernization of traditional cultures in Viet Nam and the traditional Humanities; and on the other, it was a suburban revolutionary cabal lost in fantasies about Mao—whom we now know was responsible for the deaths of more people than either Hitler or Stalin. Like the I. M. Pei building for the Earth Sciences that stood on pylons to bestride the world like a colossus, both the Right and Left sides of MIT took the earth for granted, and ecology there was all about the domination of nature.

The Earth Sciences Building and Calder Stabile at MIT

I quit MIT and went off to Toronto, and certainly Toronto in the age of McLuhan and Canada in the age of Trudeau was a good place to be, but my brand new suburban drive-in university was not Esalen. Leon Leeds, now an archaeologist, joined me to teach in the Humanities Division of York University, and in the spirit of the times we went back to our discussions of rural communal life, and he and his wife Linda joined my family on a rented fifteen acre farm in Bradford, Ontario and from there we commuted to campus, which was at the northernmost edge of suburban Toronto.

I kept at work on my book, and when invited to the 1969 Lake Couchiching conference in Ontario, I shared the first draft of my chapter on MIT with the audience. At that conference was Ivan Illich. He was the most charismatic speaker I had ever encountered, and when he spoke of the need for creating "counterfoil institutions," I knew that it was not simply MIT I had to leave, but the institution of the university itself. Michael Murphy's Esalen in Big Sur and Ivan Illich's CIDOC in Cuernavaca began to appear as morning stars on the horizon at the dawn of the seventies.

I finished my book in 1970 and sent it off in the mail to Harper and Row in New York. But while I was writing, I also began to experience another mode of artistic expression in lecturing.

At Cornell and MIT, my classes had been small, so teaching was simply talking to a close and familiar group and lecturing was only needed on occasion. But York was a public university, and there I found myself asked to give lectures to classes of 200 and supervise a team of five to six teaching assistants. At first, I was inexperienced and afraid of so large an audience. Because I had acted in six plays in college, this exposure to dramatic stage fright had given me some experience in getting past it, so I worked at steadying myself and overcoming my anxiety. And then, after a few lectures, something peculiar happened. I began to feel a different presence inside myself; actually, I began to feel a whole new sense of self. A larger kind of mind took over the field of my consciousness, and I would begin to say things I didn't know, or didn't realize I knew. I can remember the first time it happened, when I said to myself as I was lecturing, "Oh, that's interesting. I didn't know that."

Along with the shift in my sense of self, came a shift in the general feeling-tone of the audience. Restless students became listeners. I seemed to be able to conjure an atmosphere in the room. There is something about public lecturing that forces you to think intensely. When you are writing, you can let your mind wander, or take a break, or look out the window; but public lecturing is like playing improvisational jazz before a live audience. You have to be absolutely present, and yet, paradoxically, know how to get out of the way to let the *Daimon* take over. Undoubtedly, the kriya yoga I was doing for three and a half hours each day aided this process of ego/Daimon restructuring.

I remember the first time I listened to the pianist Keith Jarrett's seventies classic, *Köln Concert*, how I realized in a shock of recognition that he played the piano in the same way that I thought, spoke, and improvised in a lecture. Unconsciously, I had stumbled into a new art form, one that wasn't an academic lecture or a poetry reading. So I called this new form "mind jazz."[2]

I was told by one of my teaching assistants that some of the more psychedelic students would sit in the back row, smoke dope, and exhale: "Wow! that is vintage Thompson, man; he's really wailing today!" Another of my graduate teaching assistants— who himself had dropped acid scores of times—insisted he could pick out the word in which my mind went "clunk" as I shifted gears from a racing third to psychic overdrive. Faculty members began to sit in on my lectures. Some producers at CBC downtown heard about me and also began to sit in. People began to drive in from neighboring towns. And then, in 1971 after the rave reviews for my book in the *New York Times*, an advertizing executive from New York flew up to sit in on one lecture, and then continued to fly up every week. His name was Gene Fairly and he would be the one responsible for Lindisfarne moving, instead of onto a rural commune in Ontario or New England, to the Big Apple itself.

It was certainly unusual to have someone fly up every week from New York to sit in on my lectures for my freshman humanities class, so when Gene Fairly asked to have coffee with me after a lecture I agreed. Over the weeks remaining in the term, the after-lecture coffee became a habit. We talked of many things, and he shared his interests in cultural history and the works of Spengler. Gene had been in military intelligence at the very end of World War II, had learned German, and after the war gone into advertizing. He lived in Manhattan, and also in East Hampton, and said he was at a turning point in his life when he saw the rave reviews for *Edge* and decided to read the book, and then to sit in on one of my lectures. I responded by saying that I too was at a turning point and was getting ready to leave the university and together with my wife Gail and my college friends Leon and Linda Leeds to set up what Ivan Illich called a counterfoil institution. At that, Gene's ear's picked up, his eyes brightened with interest, and he began his own slow and charming advertizing campaign to get me to think of establishing Lindisfarne, not on some farm in rural Ontario, but more in proximity to New York—in the Hamptons where he lived, or around Litchfield in Connecticut. As an advertizing executive, Gene was more habituated to the postwar fifties culture of success in Manhattan and the Hamptons and had absolutely no feeling for or experience with the sixties counterculture, so our world-views were quite divergent from the start.

I confess to never having heard of "the Hamptons" at that time, so the area held out no caché to me at all. Since I had a lecture to give in New York, Gene offered to put me up at his apartment on the upper Eastside and drive me out to the East End of Long Island. I was impressed with this for me hitherto unknown enclave, but the splendor of the Hamptons—especially East Hampton—put me off. I liked the New England whaling town ethos of Sag Harbor, and the woods around it, but the mansions of the rich and famous did not seem to me to be the right place to locate Lindisfarne, so I continued to think of the Berkshires.

But Gene knew that a promotional campaign was not simply a single ad, so he put off lobbying for one place over another and concentrated instead on offering to be of help in the difficult process of legal incorporation for a not-for-profit corporation. He had a wealthy friend in the person of John Upjohn, so he convinced me we should fly together to see Mr. Upjohn at his home and headquarters in Kalamazoo, Michigan. Mr. Upjohn obliged Gene, and donated the funds for the legal fees for our incorporation as what the I.R.S. calls a 501(c) 3 not-for-profit educational corporation. In keeping with Gene's knowledge of what law firm the best people used in Manhattan, he chose the very expensive firm of Paul Weiss.

Now it began to be my turn to do the commuting to Manhattan by air, and over the weeks and months I began to be introduced to a whole new world of fund-raising lunches at the Century Association, the University Club, the Knickerbocker Club, the Harvard Club; and in most cases my little book had gone ahead of me, so people were willing to meet me and become interested in Lindisfarne. Harrison Salisbury, the Editor of *The New York Times*, Harry Hollins of the World Law Fund, Amyas Ames, the Chairman of Lincoln Center, and his wife Evelyn Ames, James Morton, the newly appointed Dean of the Cathedral of St. John the Divine, Nancy Wilson Ross, Jean and Sydney Lanier, all became part of a new circle that gathered around the founding of the Lindisfarne Association in New York, and many of them agreed to serve on Lindisfarne's founding Board of Advisers.

When I returned from Lindisfarne in Northumbria to our rented farm in Bradford, Ontario, the time had come to quit my professorship and choose the land and location for the establishment of the Association. The property of the Theosophical Association in Ojai, California was on the market, and this facility was singularly appropriate as it had been the site of the counterfoil institution of the previous generation in the Trabuco College of the philosopher Gerald Heard, but I vetoed going to California as I felt there was too much gravitational pull toward making Lindisfarne into another Esalen. Large houses and farms in Connecticut didn't offer us enough rooms for students, so once again Gene campaigned for the Hamptons, and since our constituency had developed over the year in New York City, there was a stronger case now for being close and distant to New York at the same time. So Gene and I went out to look at two properties on the market in Southampton.

The first was an elegant, if run-down, great estate in the village in walking distance from the beach. This Stanford White mansion had recently been a private school, and as we inspected its grand wood paneled ballroom, Gene loved it, but its F. Scot Fitzgerald atmosphere of wealth and privilege turned me off. The price was close to a million dollars, so I felt it was out of the question. The second property was the old Fish Cove Inn, which had been built in the Depression. With its 29 half-log cabins and main Lodge overlooking Fish Cove, adjacent and connected to Peconic Bay, the facility looked like a Boy Scout camp. Its small thirteen acre site had fourteen hundred feet of private beach and a large open field surrounded by scrub oaks. Gene disliked it intensely, but I loved it for its simplicity and lack of pretention, and its much lower price tag of $270,000—a figure I still found daunting.

Fish Cove as seen from our beach in front of the main Lodge

The 29 cabins and the Fish Cove Inn in Southampton, New York

I firmly refused to go along with making an offer on the grand Stanford White estate and told Gene that I wanted the Fish Cove Inn. Gene was deeply disappointed, but as he also deeply wanted Lindisfarne to locate in the Hamptons where he had a rental place and many friends, he reluctantly agreed. And so we made a down payment, established a mortgage held by the owner, and I prepared to move down from rural Ontario to Southampton and set to work full time with my first wife Gail on turning a summer's inn into a winterized year-round facility for Lindisfarne.

Gail Thompson, Office Manager, doing KP duty with Maureen O'Shea

Gail became the office manager who held the whole project together, but we could not hold our marriage together as the glue that holds an intentional community together is often extracted from the nuclear family. As happened particularly in Findhorn and San Francisco Zen Center, and generally throughout intentional communities and spiritual centers in the seventies and eighties, the sexual liberation of the sixties became applied to the communal living experiments of the seventies. The solid containing cube of the nuclear family became the complex geometry of the tesseract in which unseen geometries and facets of relationships proved to be fascinating but unstable in the three dimensional space of ordinary human time.

It seems that at the same time humanity was growing beyond the simple Copernican model of the solar system, the family was also growing beyond the patriarchal model of the solar father Zeus. Feminism was on the rise, and many intentional communities became caught up in projects of cultural retrieval of the matristic culture of the early neolithic era. Homosexuality was coming out of the closet after the Stonewall riots, and monogamy was becoming challenged by an eroticization of culture in the seventies in which multiple partners embodied its own chaotic dynamical system

Gene Fairly had his own hidden agenda in wishing to work for Lindisfarne, but without Gene's help, I would never have come to know all the people in New York who would become part of Lindisfarne's twenty-five years of cultural activity. I would have pursued a rural vision of escape in a millenarian fantasy of waiting for the edge to become the end. I did not understand at that time that these sorts of historical visions express the imagination's ability to pick up on multiple and diffuse signals and compress them into images, dreams, and visions that the narrower field of consciousness can recognize and react to. For example, in Hieronymus Bosch's painting, "The Temptation of St. Anthony," he presents a vision of the end of the world, with fish, swans, and flying ships dropping fire onto a burning city. Around 1500, many felt that the end of the world was imminent; it wasn't the end of the world, but it was most definitely the end of the old world-system, and Bosch's imaginative perception of aerial bombardment and burning cities was truly prophetic.

At their best, as in the paintings of Bosch or William Blake, such mystical visions can be prophetic; at their worst they can be manic delusions that substitute historical events for long-term cultural transformations. One can *feel* the implications of a cultural transformation in one's lifetime, but one cannot experience phenomena like the hominization of the primates or the shift from hunting and gathering to agriculture. One could feel the spirit of a new age at the meetings of Ficino's Academy in Florence, but no one there could experience the Italian Renaissance as an event. In the working of the hypnagogic state that turns sensory signals into images and dreams, the imaginative sensitive can fall victim to what A. N. Whitehead called "misplaced concreteness." I was indeed living in a time of the transition from one world-system to another, but the place to experience this newly emerging "planetary culture" was not in a return to nature on a farm in rural Ontario, but in concert with others whose creative lives were the true location of the event.

So Lindisfarne began in New York and Southampton, but as it developed it never fulfilled the needs and longings of Gene Fairly. His fifties and my sixties sensibility were almost a generation apart. Eventually, we went our separate ways, but without him, there never would have been a way to start.

Our postbox, looking up toward the main lodge with its office, meditation room, dining room, lecture hall, and a wing of student rooms.

---

[1] William Wordsworth, The Prelude, Book 11, ll.108-109.

[2] For a philosophical discussion of the aesthetics of improvisation, see Edgar Landgraf's "Improvisation: Form and Event" in *Emergence and Embodiment*, Ed. Bruce Clarke and Mark B. N. Hansen (Durham, NC: Duke University Press, 2009), p. 179.

Chapter 3:
With Gregory Bateson's Mind in Nature

Gregory Bateson

We were six sitting on the porch of Gregory Bateson's cabin at Lindisfarne. The late summer evening's light was shining through the scrub oak trees onto the waters of Fish Cove in Noyack Bay, and all of us were feeling the relaxed atmosphere, not just of the end of the day, but the end of summer, and the end of four years of Lindisfarne in Southampton. Always before we were piously at work, winterizing the 29 cabins, repairing the central Lodge, and transforming a playing field into an organic garden; and, of course, to sustain all the work, fund-raising. For four years the huge mortgage consumed whatever funds I could raise, but, at last, I knew that it was no use, that I would have to give the facility back at summer's end to default on the mortgage and lose everything the community had put into the place in terms of labor and money, so now we were resigned and at peace, and for the first time, simply enjoying the property: enjoying the beach, the walks through the marshes off Swamp

Road near Sag Harbor where Gregory stalked a rare osprey with his costly Nikon zoom lens and his even more precious understanding. We relaxed in the peace of letting go, and I relaxed the community rules and decided to permit the conviviality of wine to touch the hitherto strict severity of our "spiritual" life. Like many of my generation who had made the Journey to the East in the seventies, I was trying very hard to be "spiritual" and not merely intellectual. In that summer of 1977, Gregory was our Scholar-in-Residence and had introduced the very British and civilizing custom of having Dry Sack and Stilton cheese as we met on the porch of his cabin at the end of the workday to philosophize or simply to socialize.

On that particular afternoon, Gregory leaned back and regarded me through the distorting lens of his glass of sherry, and said: "William and Beatrice. Harrumphh!"

Beatrice Madeleine Rudin, Fish Cove 1977 (Photo: Nina Hagen)

William and Beatrice were the names of Gregory's parents. Beatrice is my second wife's name. It was not so much that I was Gregory's father-figure, for I was forty years his junior and a good English foot shorter; it was more that

I was—as the founder— the Big Daddy of Lindisfarne. I was also not one of Gregory's fans, breathless in adoration, who surrounded him at Lindisfarne and Esalen, but was always prodding and pushing him intellectually, as if I knew something that he didn't. Perhaps this was the style of dialogue his father had used with him long before.

Peter Caddy, Co-Founder of Findhorn, Beatrice Rudin, former Findhorn community member, and Gregory Bateson in the Dining Room overlooking Fish Cove 1977.

Gregory was deep into the writing of *Mind and Nature*, and since I had the cabin next to his, I often noticed that his light would be on at four in the morning as he would get up to begin his writing day. As the community rose to attend the morning's seven o'clock sitting of meditation, he would put on his tape of Glenn Gould's *Goldberg Variations*. From the look in his eye when he spoke about "William and Beatrice," I sensed that he felt the book to be his intellectual last will and testament, and in summing up a life's work, he had also summoned up the ghost of his famous father and the shadow of inferiority it had cast across his life. Gregory had resolved to prove himself to the scientific patriarchy; it was not enough for him to rest easy with the hero-worship of such fringe institutions as Lindisfarne, Naropa, Esalen, or Zen Center in San Francisco; no, he wanted both Cambridges to admit that he knew something that they didn't.

And indeed he did. But neither Cambridge has yet owned up to it, and the reviews that were later to come in such voices of the scientific establishment as *Nature* were to be very patronizing indeed. Recently, however, there have been signs of a change, and Gregory seems to be finding his rightful place as a permanent feature of our intellectual landscape as the anthropologist who took the next step after Poincaré in extending the new science of complex dynamical systems into understanding the workings of the family, rituals in culture, and the conscious civilizational process in the larger extended mind of the living environment.

On another one of those afternoons of Sherry and Stilton, I was with Christopher Bamford, Michael Katz, and the eternally silent Dian Woodner and Will Marsh—members of the Lindisfarne community and avid students of Gregory's work. It was Christopher, Dian, and Michael who had first introduced me to *Steps to an Ecology of Mind*. The three of them were making a film on ecology and Gregory's ideas and came to visit me at Lindisfarne "on a dark and stormy night" in the hope that I would fund their project. But it was to be Dian who was later to help with funding for Lindisfarne-in-Manhattan and at the Cathedral. I was open to hearing their pitch about Bateson because I had used Gregory's *Naven* in my undergraduate Honors Thesis at Pomona College in 1962,[1] but I had not caught up with Steps until 1974. That year Gregory, Joyce Carol Oates, and I were members of a panel for a conference in New York that was to help raise funds for Esalen Institute, so I used the occasion to do some catching up on Gregory's more recent work. Michael Katz offered a seminar on *Steps* to the residents of Lindisfarne, and I took the opportunity of meeting Gregory in New York to invite him to visit us out in the Hamptons. In 1975 I invited Gregory to join us in one of our Lindisfarne Conferences on "Conscious Evolution and the Evolution of Consciousness." This conference developed into a hockey face-off between the Confucian mandarinism of Jonas Salk and the ecological Taoism of Gregory Bateson, and the gathering was featured in an article by Ted Morgan in the *New York Times Sunday Magazine*.[2] All of us at Lindisfarne were more sympathetic with Gregory than with Jonas Salk. When I invited Jonas, I specifically asked him not to give the same speech on "Epoch A and Epoch B" that he gave at a conference we were attending in Washington D.C., and that I would have everybody read his book, *The Survival of the Wisest*, before the Lindisfarne conference. But Jonas gave his stump speech, so I was annoyed and frustrated that we could not take it to a higher intellectual level.

Jonas Salk lecturing on Epoch B

I was frustrated because in the Lindisfarne form of conference I had come upon a way to avoid the boring panel discussions in which there were too many speakers for any one person to be able to say anything of lasting value, or the even more boring reading of papers that was the model for most hotel-type conferences that prevailed in the academic world. Our conferences began with a long breakfast, from 8:00 to 10:00, in which lively conversations and debates began over coffee around the tables of the dining room overlooking Fish Cove. At 10:00 we moved into the adjacent lecture room, where one speaker was given a full hour to sing his or her intellectual aria.

Then we would break for coffee, and after the break one of the other speakers would give a ten minute comment to open a period of general discussion that often lasted for an hour and a half. We would then move back to the dining room for lunch, but after lunch there were no afternoon sessions scheduled, so people could break into small groups and take walks along the beach, or go into the village. Those who found the Lindisfarne rule of "no alcohol" too Puritan often went to the Driver's Seat pub in the village to have a drink. We would gather again together for evening meditation, then dinner, and at 8:00 we would gather for a single evening lecture, which was, once again, followed by a ten minute comment and an open discussion.

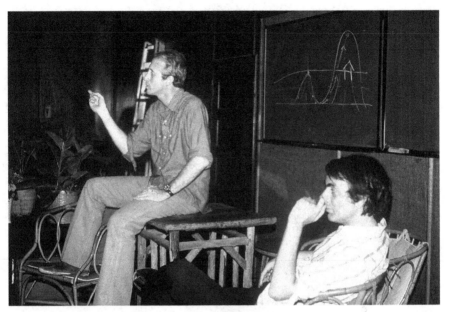

Stewart Brand and Carl Sagan at the 1974 Lindisfarne Conference

Richard Falk from Princeton and John Todd Co-Founder of New Alchemy 1974

Stewart Brand, Harry Hollins from the World Law Fund,
W. I. Thompson, and E. F.Schumacher, 1974

The discussions were exciting, the relaxed atmosphere encouraged the development of friendships, and there often appeared a general sense of participation in a group spirit that was quite extraordinary. Gregory generally preferred small conferences in which a handful of participants could sit around the table, but he warmed to our larger gatherings of seventy or more, and made many new friends which he kept to the end of his days.

To keep the conferences from falling apart, I served as both the host and the director of our intellectual chamber music ensemble. At the opening night of the conference, I would give a welcoming talk that presented an intellectual landscape in which all of those present were important features of the terrain, and at the end of the conference, I would give a wrap-up talk that put all the talks we had heard into a new imaginative landscape that had implications for our future. During the conference, I would introduce the speaker, discuss the importance of his or her work, and show how it related to the work of the previous speaker. The task of being the host at Lindisfarne was no simple toastmaster general's job, but required that I read all the speakers' books beforehand and put these stars into some coherent philosophical constellation.

W. I. Thompson Lecturing at 1975 Lindisfarne Conference

Brother David Steindl-Rast, Saul Mendlowitz, and W. I. Thompson 1974

What emerged in this imaginative landscape of Lindisfarne was a new relationship between epistemology and ecology in Gregory's critique of "conscious purpose" and John Todd's "Living Machines." Baconian science is a strategy of separation, analysis, and control. This is the familiar world I had known at MIT in which "Man" dominated nature. But in John Todd's designs for bioshelters, the bacterial realm was reintroduced in bioplasms that served to break down and digest "pollutants" in a form of environmental remediation that was quite literally cultured.

John Todd's "New Alchemy" was bringing forth a new kind of science based upon pattern recognition, imaginative articulation, and cultural participation. At these Southampton conferences we all could feel that we were in the presence of something new, not simply a new idea or theory, but a new world view. We began to discuss the implications of global warming and climate change, and Ted Morgan in his *New York Times Magazine* article wrote: "What if they are right?"

After attending the first two Lindisfarne conferences, Dean Morton asked me to give an address to an assembly of all the Deans of the cathedrals of the United States and Canada at the Cathedral of St. John the Divine as part of the bicentennial celebrations of 1976. I decided to address the ancient tradition of prophecy and the modern problem of climate change by sharing a morning vision I had had in 1975 of seeing New York under water up to the sixth floor of the buildings.

When Lindisfarne's ecological world view was enhanced by the critique of Computationalism in the "Embodied" cognitive science of Francisco Varela in 1977, and then by the Gaia evolutionary theory of James Lovelock and Lynn Margulis in 1981, it began to be obvious to all of us that a new science was showing its face at Lindisfarne and that just such a science was as critical to the process of planetization as any esoteric philosophy of the past.

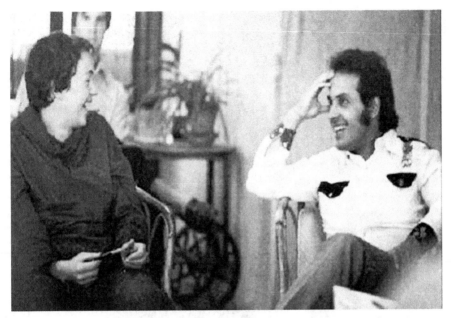

Mary Catherine Bateson and Francisco Varela,
Mind and Nature Conference Fish Cove 1977

In my lectures, both at the beginning and end of these Lindisfarne conferences, I tried to make this imaginary landscape visible to all, for I believed this new world view held out our best hope for effecting the transition from a disintegrating industrial civilization to an emerging planetary culture.

After the intellectual excitement of the summer conference of 1975, Gregory became part of the horizon of Lindisfarne. To recognize that in the presence of people like Gregory and Mary Catherine Bateson, E. F. Schumacher, David Spangler, John and Nancy Todd, and Hazel Henderson, a new kind of group soul was being embodied of those who expressed the spirit of what I called the new planetary culture, I decided to create the Lindisfarne Fellowship within the Association. No longer were teaching fellows simply to be resident faculty or staff, but a special group of those around the world whose works served to help us in articulating and effecting the shift from one world civilization to another.

Michael Katz, Brother David, Carl Sagan, Stewart Brand, Richard Baker-roshi, Yvonne Rand, and W. I. Thompson, and Life as a Bowl of Cherry Tomatoes. 1974

When the Lindisfarne Fellows arrived for their gatherings, the Lindisfarne commune seemed to be lifted up out of the emotional morass of communal living and bathed in the light of a larger world of art and science and global green politics. Later, in a lecture at the Frankfurt Book Fair in 1984, when James Lovelock and Lynn Margulis had already joined the Lindisfarne Fellowship, I would call the political implications of this new culture the Gaia Politique.[3]

James Lovelock at home in Devon

In 1977 I had raised a small amount of money from the Rockefeller Brothers Fund—a grant of $15,000 a year for three years—to support a scholar-in-residence program for our new facility in Manhattan, and Gregory was my first choice to start up this program. We had acquired an abandoned Episcopal Church at the corner of Twentieth Street and Sixth Avenue in Manhattan. The facility included the Church, the Parish Hall, the Rectory, and a small town house called "the Sisters' House"—sisters meaning Episcopal nurses. The rent was only a dollar a year for ninety-nine years, but the White Elephant catch was that the buildings were in very bad shape, and the heating alone would consume $15,000 a year.

Holy Communion Church on Sixth Avenue and 20th St.
became Lindisfarne in Manhattan in from 1976 to 1979.

The condition of Holy Communion Church when we took it over in 1976.
We turned this room into our Meditation Room.
When we left, the disco Limelight turned it into their VIP room.

Gregory accepted my invitation, both to enjoy the last summer of our place by the sea in Southampton, and to flee the steady stream of devotees in California who came to admire but also interrupted. Since Gregory was a slow and painstaking writer, interruptions were often welcome relief, but he knew that it was getting late and that the book had to be finished. Besides, Gregory was not interested in merely being admired; he wanted to be understood, and then respected. So the fact that I liked to argue with him and refused to become a Bateson devotee made him feel more at home at intellectual Lindisfarne than at sensory-awakened Esalen.

When Gregory arrived, we got together to plan a small conference on "Mind and Nature" that would help him gather his thoughts for the final work. His daughter Mary Catherine Bateson was first on our list to invite, because she was absolutely brilliant in helping conferences to focus on the ideas developing among the speakers. Mary Catherine had been indispensable to Gregory in his 1968 Burg Wartenstein Conference in Austria, and she had been equally indispensable to us at our Lindisfarne Conference in 1976. To extend our discussions into physics, technology, and culture, we decided to invite the physicist David Finkelstein and the inventor Arthur Young. And when Gregory and I turned to biology, we both came out with the name "Francisco Varela!" at the same time. Gregory had already met Varela at a conference in California, and I had read Varela's paper from that conference, "Not One, not Two," that Stewart Brand had published in the *Whole Earth Review*. Varela was a destined choice, for in that small *Mind and Nature* conference, he proved so perfect a colleague to us all in the Lindisfarne community that I decided to award the second scholar-in residence position to him so that his period of residency could follow Gregory's return to California. Even with the loss of the Southampton property, those were good days, but on that particular day on the porch I was enjoying a good argument with Gregory.

One of the things about me that frustrated Gregory was that I was a peculiar combination of ignorance and intuition, emotional confusion and intellectual clarity. After my wrap-up lecture in the 1975 conference, in which I tried to show how Gregory's Taoist thinking was more politically benign than the Confucian elitism of Jonas Salk's *Survival of the Wisest*, a few scientists and engineers became angry at me and fumed about the limits of "metaphoric thinking." Lakoff and Johnson had not yet taught the engineers that all thinking is inherently metaphoric—mathematics included—so in those heady days engineers still labored under the illusion that mathematical rigor lived above in a realm of mind uncontaminated by the body.[4] Gregory came nobly to my defense with all his impressive stature and seniority, and paid me a compliment that I still fondly recall: "It takes one to know one," he said with finality, "and Bill's got it!"

But in the next year's first Lindisfarne Fellows Conference on "Art and the Sacred," I went beyond Gregory's limit of tolerance for metaphoric thinking as I began to wax too eloquent about the poetry of structures revealed in Edgerton's famous photograph of the milkdrop corona.[5]

I was picking up where I had left off in my honors thesis on the philosophy of history and riffing on about four-fold patterns in everything from Vico to Carnot cycles to the Archaic-Classic-Baroque-Archaistic/Romantic stylistic sequence in the development of Maya pyramids, and Gregory sprang to the attack as I finished. A milkdrop was a collision of particles; a pyramid was an artifact: one was of the *pleroma*, the other of the *creatura*. One was a mechanical collision, the other "news of a difference" that constituted information. I was not then, nor am I now, convinced that Gregory's strict body/mind dualism of the *pleroma/creatura* is anything other than a cultural framing of perception by a modernist viewer. In my own peculiar combination of Celtic animism and the panpsychism Whitehead discussed in his philosophy of organism, I refused to recant and continued to play Celtic Druid to Gregory's St. Boniface chopping down the idolatrous oak tree.

That summer's afternoon on the porch—a few months after the spring Fellows Conference—Gregory and I continued with the argument, but this time it was my turn to attack, but from two flanks at once: my Celtic animist's monistic rejection of dualism, and Varela's Buddhist position of non-dualism. We both had a good deal of fun with the old mysticism versus science debate, for Gregory was a repressed mystic, and I was a repressed scientist. Both of us had difficulties owning up to our repressions, and both of us chose the same strategy for living with our contradictions: we chose our friends well and then let them carry the repressed side of our natures. And so Gregory surrounded himself, at Lindisfarne and Esalen, with mystics whom he loved to patronize in intellectual superiority, and I surrounded myself with scientists whom I loved to patronize in mystical superiority. Although it was great fun in arguing with Gregory about things like astral projection—prodding him with anomalies in which the subject's out-of-the-body perceptions were not simply dreams but could be externally verified by a third party—he was not willing to change his mind, and at that particular time of his life, the last thing on Earth he wanted to become was a New Age mystic.

So I leaned back in my chair, looked at Gregory over the rim of my sherry glass, and took another tack:

"You know, Gregory, it's interesting: here we are, three students of your work, all men in our thirties, but we are all going further with it than you want. Michael here has moved on into Buddhism and is actually sitting zazen. Christopher is into Christian mysticism and is at work on an anthology of the Western esoteric tradition. And I am carrying on with this Celtic "revitalization movement" called Lindisfarne. The image that I see in my mind's eye is that all four of us have come to the end of the mind of Europe, but now that we are at the edge, we have jumped into the water and are calling back to you to come on in, that the water is warm and fine. But you keep standing there at the edge, refusing to strip yourself of all your European clothing and habits of mind to start swimming."

"Harrummphh!" was all that Gregory said in a deep leonine growl that reverberated in the enormous depths of his 6'6" frame.

At least Gregory did not stroll back and forth along the edge with starched collar and walking stick, making profound speculations on the viscosity of water. He was not like Heidegger, thinking about being, but unwilling to be anything but a Western European thinker. Gregory knew that there were other modes of life out there, and he had been on close and personal terms with dolphins, savages, and schizophrenics; it was just that he had some things he needed to finish. For him, the stripping off of Europe would be the final act in a contemplative death—one that he carried out with courage and honesty when he died three years later at Zen Center in San Francisco.

It is easy to understand why Gregory would refuse to indulge in the New Age thinking of California, and why he would hold on to European science in that last imaginary dialogue with his father, or why he wished to complete a life's work with final recognition from the patriarchate of established science; but it was not always easy to accept Gregory's role as the objective observer who held to the edges of experience, looking for "news of a difference," yet one who remained unwilling to commit himself to either the continent of the past or the ocean of the future. Characteristically, on those times when he chose to join the community in the morning sittings of silent meditation, he would keep his eyes open to study the postures and body language of others, just as once he had filmed the Balinese going into trance. He remained the anthropologist, haunting the edges of civilization and savagery, and loving the shore that allowed him to have the best of sea air that came from the touch of ocean and land. Small wonder he spent so much time at Big Sur. Gregory was not willing to be a brittle, dried-up thinker from Britain, nor a soggy and self-indulgent touchy-feely from California, and he never was.

Later during that summer of 1977 in Southampton, when Francisco Varela came to join us for the small conference on "Mind and Nature" that

Gregory chaired, I asked Cisco about Gregory's intellectual hesitancy, and he answered:

"Gregory has completed one major scientific revolution in his lifetime. You can't expect a man to make a second, especially in his seventies."

Looking back on the cultural period of the seventies in the United States, I think Gregory was right to hold back. We have all seen some trendy scientists leave the community of practicing scientists to launch themselves onto the New Age lecture circuit, where they can only be admired by people who really have no way of knowing whether what they say is true or false. And although Gregory, like the aged Heidegger, was beginning to see that the Buddhist philosophy of mind had something to contribute toward a reconceptualization of epistemology, he knew that the younger generation of people like myself, Francisco Varela, and my son Evan Thompson—who as a fifteen year old was listening in on all our conversations—were in a better position to rethink Europe in the context of the East.[6] For Gregory's generation the shadow of his parents, and the shadows of the cultural grandparents, Darwin, Marx, and Freud, demanded a turning around in California to face toward Europe. But for the people of my generation there could be no simple going back. The giants of modernism, whether Wittgenstein or Joyce, had culturally finished Europe; and although intellectuals like Jurgen Habermas and Jacques Derrida carried on with the old life of the intelligentsia, a xerox of a xerox was not an original.

It is time to swim out or sail on, even though the waters can be dangerous. As one moves away from the shore, that ultimate extension of Europe into California where Gregory spent his last days, one can begin to see how the shore relates to the continental shelf.

For most people, Gregory's last work, *Mind and Nature*, is his ultimate work. For me, *Steps to an Ecology of Mind* is the greater work. The historian of science, Steven Toulmin, characterized Gregory as a scout and the David Levine caricature in the *New York Review of Books* shows Gregory on a horse, learning the territory in advance of the scientific townsfolk who will settle down into their tenured professorships. In *Steps*, Gregory brought together anthropology, cybernetics, epistemology, and psychology together in a freshness of vision that calls to mind the first man to climb out of the Colorado River to look at the entire Grand Canyon and understand the story the strata told. In *Mind and Nature*, Gregory went back to the townsfolk and tried to talk to them in their terms and on their turf. The Batesonian intelligence is there, but it is a routinization of charisma that lacks the visionary power of *Steps*. *Steps* shows Gregory with all his strengths in evidence, but *Mind and Nature* shows his weaknesses in mathematics, biology, and philosophy. Precisely because Gregory was not a professor of mathematics or philosophy, he was free to be original, but constrained also to reinvent the wheel, mainly because he refused to read very much. Gregory came from a privileged class, and at Cambridge he got used to receiving knowledge orally by being present when Russell or Whitehead were presenting their ideas, and that is why he preferred to learn from small conferences, like the Macy Conferences, in which the major players were there in the flesh to embody their ideas.[7] I don't think Gregory ever sat down to read Varela's books, cover to cover. Gregory did not know the basic literature of Western philosophy, and he never rushed about, trying to keep up with all the disciplines that were moving so fast around him. He was a genius, but he was a slow thinker, and his mind moved like a tectonic plate; but when it had moved, the whole landscape was transformed.

Gregory's idea of the "double bind" is no longer thought to be the cause of schizophrenia, but in the way that scholarship is often disguised autobiography, the double bind may have been the cause of Gregory's intellectual genius. Faced with the cognitive dissonance of an intolerable contradiction, his mind had to shift from simple perceptions to creative imagination. For me, Gregory's essay "Form, Substance, and Difference" is a perfect gem of philosophical literature. It has the vernacular freshness of an early Platonic dialogue or Descartes' "Discourse on Method." And just as Descartes' "Discourse" in French was not a tract in Latin intended for Church fathers rooted and rutted in centuries of scholasticism, so Gregory's talks at the end of *Steps* are not merely "papers" read to academic congresses; they are forms of life.

Looking back at the way in which the shore relates to the cliff, and the way the cliff relates to the mountain range, I would say that Gregory Bateson is an important part of the intellectual history of the twentieth century. In the final century of the second millennium *Anno Domini*, there were four major phases to the uncovering of the unconscious. First came the uncovering of the instinctive unconscious, of the basic mammalian life of Eros and Thanatos in the work of Freud. Then came the uncovering of the human psychic life of the collective unconscious in the work of Jung. Then came the uncovering of the intellectual unconscious, of the "positive unconscious" or "episteme" of a preliterate tribe or a literate epoch in the work of Lévi-Strauss and Foucault. And at the end of the century came the uncovering of the civilizational or Spiritual unconscious, that unconscious part of the body-politic or noosphere that we call "the other" of the environment. This Gaian unconscious of contemporary industrial civilization is now the dark, polluted, global ecology in which we all dwell. It is that "organism plus the environment" that is not described by the conscious boundaries and capitalistic goals of our "rational" industrial nation-states, or by our political and technological systems of governance through "conscious purpose." The transition from the uncovering of the intellectual unconscious with Foucault to the uncovering of the civilizational unconscious is expressed in Gregory's essay, "The Effects of Conscious Purpose on Human Adaptation." The conference that Gregory chaired at Burg Wartenstein in Austria in 1968 was a prophetic form of discourse, for what Gregory saw early, all now can see on the evening news about the death of forests and coral reefs, and the melting of glaciers, permafrost, and ice sheets.

To honor Gregory's contribution to the Macy conferences[8] in the forties and fifties, the Burg Wartenstein conference in the sixties, and the Lindisfarne conferences in the seventies, I asked the Lindisfarne Fellows to come together in a memorial conference at San Francisco Zen Center's Green Gulch Farm in 1980 and again in 1981. Heinz von Foerster, one of the founding members of the Macy Conferences, joined with the Santiago School of the Biology of Knowledge represented by Humberto Maturana and Francisco Varela, and the French school of self-organizing systems biology, represented by Henri Atlan. To take these developments in complex dynamical thinking one step further, I also invited James Lovelock and Lynn Margulis, the exponents of what was then called the Gaia Hypothesis. These four groups and had never met before, and I began to see that this bringing together of separate groups so that they could see the larger imaginary landscape in which we all were situated was my truly esoteric mission with Lindisfarne.

Francisco Varela, Heinz Pagels, Heinz von Forster, and Michael Ogden (Builder of the Lindisfarne Fellows House in Crestone, CO.) Green Gulch Conference 1981

Humberto Maturana at Green Gulch conference 1981

Lynn Margulis, W. I. Thompson,
James Lovelock, and Richard Baker-roshi, Green Gulch 1981

Wes Jackson, James Lovelock, Tim O'Shea, Leah Thompson, Francisco Varela,
Green Gulch Farm, San Francisco Zen Center, Fellows Conference 1981

Henri Atlan at Green Gulch Conference 1981

Present also in these gatherings were Mary Catherine Bateson, Hazel Henderson, Gary Snyder, Wendell Berry, Wes Jackson, John and Nancy Todd, Heinz and Elaine Pagels, and for the 1980 gathering the Governor of California, Jerry Brown.[9] As I opened the conference with a moment of silence in memory of Gregory's death at Zen Center the year before, it was evident from the very people in the room that Gregory's work had been at the heart of something new. Gregory stepped, and we are stumbling, but the true Ecology of Mind remains to be realized.

[1] *The Philosophy of World View*, Honors Thesis presented to the faculty in partial fulfillment of the degree of Bachelor of Arts, Pomona College, 1962. In this, my first book-length work, two chapters of which were published in *Main Currents in Modern Thought* in 1962 and 1964, I recognized Bateson's important contribution in modeling a multi-causal process or cyclical chain, but even then I challenged his dualistic schema of ethos and eidos and invoked Whitehead. "This dualistic scheme of ethos and eidos, like all dualistic schemata, is at once convenient and perplexing, for on one hand, the scheme allows us to make distinctions, and on the other, it bifurcates essentially organic experience." p. 89.

[2] See Ted Morgan, "Looking for Epoch B," *New York Times Magazine*, Feb. 29, 1976, p. 32. "I went to Lindisfarne to find out what was new in the 70's...If an avant garde can be found today, it is not in art galleries or book stores. Painting and literature may have lost the capacity to startle, but Lindisfarne was startling."

[3] See *Gaia, a Way of Knowing: Political Implications of the New Biology*, ed. W. I. Thompson (Hudson, NY: Lindisfarne Press, 1987).

[4] See George Lakoff and Mark Johnson, *Metaphors we live by* (Chicago: Univ. of Chicago Press, 1981), and George Lakoff and Rafael Núñez, *Where mathematics come from: how the embodied mind brings mathematics into being* (New York: Basic Books, 2000).

[5] Mary Catherine Bateson also recalls her father's response to this talk and mentions it in her memoir of her parents, *With a Daughter's Eye* (New York: William Morrow, 1984), p. 60.

[6] In the eighties, Varela and I met with Nishitani Keiji in Kyoto. I published Pacific Shift in 1985, and Evan Thompson and Francisco Varela gave lectures together at the Lindisfarne Fellows Conference in Perugia, Italy in 1988 and published their *The Embodied Mind: Cognitive Science and Human Experience* (Cambridge, MA: MIT Press) in 1991.

[7] The talks at this conference were subsequently published in *Gaia, A Way of Knowing*, op.cit.

[8] The Macy Conferences served to articulate the new science of cybernetics by bringing all the major contributors together. For a history of this period, see Jean-Pierre Dupuy, *The Mechanization of the Mind: on the origins of cognitive science*, (Princeton, NJ: Princeton University Press, 2000).

[9] Stewart Brand had introduced Governor Brown to the people and ideas he had encountered at the Lindisfarne Conferences in the seventies, both in Southampton and Manhattan, and the Lindisfarne Fellows Rusty Schweickart and Sim Van der Ryn were given appointments in Brown's administration and Gregory was made a Trustee of the University of California. If Governor Brown rather than Governor Reagan had become President of the United States in 1980 and had implemented the Green politics of the Lindisfarne Fellows, we might not now be facing the American decline and possible global dark age that is in front of us. But Governor Brown was dismissed as "Governor Moonbeam," and Americans voted to ride out the end of industrial civilization in their Hummers and Lincoln Navigators. Character is destiny, and the American character of its "Know Nothing" nativist mentality so perfectly expressed in the world view of Michelle Bachmann and Sarah Palin seems about to bring about our decline.

Chapter 4. Sex and the Commune

Toward the end of the second millennium *anno domini*, the sexual liberation of elite literary modernism was transformed into cable TV populism. The HBO series *Sex and the City* explored the subject of the state of female sexuality in Mayor Giuliani's idealized New York in which a free-lance columnist could afford an apartment in Manhattan, a large wardrobe of designer clothes, and a collection of Manolo Blhanik designer high heel shoes.

The pathbreakers of artistic freedom like James Joyce, D. H. Lawrence, Anais Nin, and Henry Miller had been followed on rollerblades by Erica Jong and the zipless fuck in the seventies, and then by another wave in the nineties when the streets became loud with the crack and stomp of the skateboarders of sex—Bill and Monica—to the wild surmise of older pedestrians who were startled to see the streets and airwaves taken over in such an assertive and public display.

In *Sex and the City* an archetypal quartet of four women—reminding me of my own archetypal four of Hunter, Headman, Shaman, and Fool from my 1971 book *At the Edge of History*—met in restaurants regularly to discuss such delicate subjects as how they felt about cunnilingus when their lover rose to kiss them with the still fresh taste of their own vulvas on his lips, or what they thought of anal intercourse when reminded by the impact of another taxi bumping their taxi from behind.

Although the TV series presented itself as a celebration of women's freedom, it was in its deep structure incredibly sexist. The women are portrayed as shallow airheads who never talk about anything other than shopping and relationships: no serious politics, no science, no philosophy, and no poetry or art except when it presents an occasion for a fashionable opening at a gallery that provides another kind of catwalk for their new designer clothes.

Carries's story is a teenage Harlequin Romance in which Mr. Big rescues her from exile in Paris. Samantha the slut is punished for her sexual excesses— such as giving a gratuitous blowjob to the UPS delivery man in his sexy shorts—by being struck down with cancer of the breast. Miranda the lawyer, whose last name is Hobbes, suggests to me the screenwriters were stoned when they had the naming session in which they came up with the Miranda law requiring the police to read the suspect his rights and the grouchy old man of political theory, Thomas Hobbes. But Miranda, the professional woman, is also brought low, as she falls for a working class bartender, is exiled from

Manhattan to Brooklyn, and is forced to tend her mother-in-law who suffers from dementia. And the WASPY girl, Charlotte of York, is mated to a short, bald, hairy-shouldered Jewish lawyer with the name of Harry Greenblatt. All four women are brought down as reality bites them in the ass and the values of patriarchy are reasserted in a plot that is both sexist and filled with the clichés of anti-Semitism.

From the perspective of literature, the four ladies had it coming, for they celebrated a shallow life of freedom through shopping, so they all end up with their souls enshrouded in the black burqas of fin de siècle Mr. Big American capitalism.

In this Weberian process of the shift from charisma to routine, the persecutions of Joyce and Lawrence in the twenties were followed by the celebration and celebritization of Candace Bushnell/Carrie Bradshaw in the nineties. But the last third of the twentieth century was not limited to television in the cities and wife-swapping in the suburbs, for the Zeitgeist that overlighted the cities also hovered over the alternative rural communes with their *Earth Shoes* and *Birkenstocks* "return to nature."

The palpable feeling of a group soul or angelic mind overlighting our Lindisfarne conferences transported us with the sense of a new *kairos*, but it also introduced a fault line in our commune at Fish Cove, as if tectonic plates were separating into two different continents. The real community was this Lindisfarne Fellowship, this noetic polity; the intentional community did not carry this sense of presence, except at moments in times of silent group meditation when it felt as if an angel had entered the room.

Our intentional community, like many of the others I visited, seemed to become possessed by a matristic neolithic archetype—the shadow of the Great Mother—and was pulled down into a kind of collective neurosis, or psychodrama, in which individuals played out the pain of having been damaged by alcoholic and abusive parents in their childhood. On one side, the young men in the community wanted to assume an alpha male leadership in our primate band and resented my alpha role as founder and fund-raiser; and on the other side, the women in the community resented the pushiness of the alpha and subdominant males in the community meetings and wished to assert a new feminist sisterhood. It would seem that the intentional community, in trying to go forward into the future, was turning on the spiral in a process that McLuhan called cultural retrieval and was retrieving both the primate band of leadership through dominance, and the matristic neolithic village of collective leadership through "the old Ma's."

Snapshots of Communal Life

The Community around the compost heap 1974

Meeting

Cooking

Sacred Dancing

Disco Dancing

Teaching

Composting
Retired Episcopal Bishop Chandler Sterling,
our organic gardener and Contemplative-in-Residence.

Listening: W. I. Thompson and Robin Van Loben Sels, Lindisfarne's First Teaching Fellow, listening to Gregory Bateson at the 1975 Lindisfarne Conference

Making up our own rituals

Hugging: Community members Maribeth Bunn, W. I. Thompson, and Rachel Fletcher, at the 1981 Fellows Conference, San Francisco's Zen Center's Green Gulch Farm in Marin County, CA

Part of what contributed to the emotional confusion of communal living in the seventies was, of course, sex. Sex was a complex dynamical system in which a new strange attractor appeared out of the blue and began to draw people away from the traditional monogamous relationship.

After the period of World War II when so many families had been separated, the upbeat optimism expressed in the advertisements of the fifties portrayed the new world of the suburbs in which the ideal family was a nuclear one of Dad, Mom, one boy, one girl, a dog, a new car for Dad, and a kitchen full of GE labor-saving appliances for Mom. The restlessness of the wife swapping seventies—as portrayed in films like *Bob and Carol and Ted and Alice*, or *The Ice Storm*—was a generation to come.

Over the years since I put down the reductionism of E. O. Wilson's *Sociobiology* in my book, *The Time Falling Bodies Take to Light: Mythology, Sexuality, and the Origins of Culture*, I have come to believe that I was too quickly dismissive of Harvard's Grand Old Man of Science, E. O. Wilson. Scientists like Wilson and Julian Jaynes were trying to look in new ways at human culture, and they needed some time and a lot of research to work things out and outgrow the facile reductionism that energized their start-up enterprises. Forty years later, I have to admit that we in the humanities have learned a great deal from primatology, evolutionary psychology, ethology, and the brain sciences.

For example, we now appreciate that the development of the primate brain owes much to the shift in environments from savannah and lacustrine ecologies. When the primates descended from the trees and had to live in complex groups on the ground, they had to deal with new challenges of the group dynamics expressed in sex and power. In a more vulnerable environment, females and their offspring had to be dependent upon a ring of males to protect them, as well as learn how to navigate around multiplied occasions for copulation. Facial recognition and the ability to read the mood of mate and dominant male became critical for the survival of both female and offspring. A gibbon male is among primates the most monogamous, but he also lives in a dense forest canopy in which the sight lines are highly restricted. No roving eye there.

If one considers the sex life of chimps and bonobos, one can see that there is no such simple thing as "natural" for primates or humans—no matter what fundamentalist Catholic Rick Santorum says about the need to outlaw consensual adult sodomy and police the bedrooms of the nation. Sex has been inseparable from culture for us all for millions of years.

So when a new evolutionary human species descended from the dense canopy of the postwar suburbs, moved from Kansas to California, and started meditating and doing kundalini yoga or Zen, the brain and its embodied hormones also took a quantum step forward into cultural complexity in the planetization of humanity. Suddenly the dyadic simplicity of Mom and Dad, or female and male, no longer was at one with the evolution of consciousness. Gays began to come out of the closet with the Stonewall riots, and the hitherto repressed sexuality confessed to by President Jimmy Carter in his famous *Playboy* interview began to be expressed.

Catholic celibacy and monogamy had always been more honored in the breach than the observance, and even popes had had mistresses, but the White Anglo-Saxon Protestants were more deeply invested in this artificial cultural construct of monogamy — except of course, when even they couldn't take it and experimented with Mormon polygamy. Nevertheless, when TV Evangelical ministers were caught cheating on their wives, it was never an occasion for love or beauty, but for a slumming attraction to truly trashy homely prostitutes on the tacky side of life.

The author and Peter Caddy, Co-Founder of Findhorn, 1974

Usually, the seventies commune had an alpha male as its leader. Think of Baker-roshi at San Francisco Zen Center, Steve Gaskin and the Farm, Peter Caddy at Findhorn, or me at Lindisfarne. In most of these cases, the marriage of the founder did not survive the unfolding development of the community. As was the case with the early utopian *kibbutzim* of Israel, the psychic glue that held the commune together was stolen from the nuclear family. A diffused

Eros began to manifest as part of this sensitivity to an overlighting presence or an experience of a group-soul, and often this diffuse feeling concretized itself in group sex, or at least fantasies and desires for group sex.

Peter Marin wrote a cover article for *Harper's Magazine* in February of 1979 in which he described an incident at Naropa in Boulder in which the poet W. S. Merwin tried to defend himself when the goon/bodyguards of Chogyam Trungpa rinpoche dragged him into a drunken public meeting in which all were to be stripped naked in front of the great lecherous guru.[1]

When Lindisfarne moved into the abandoned Holy Communion Church in Manhattan in 1976, we were picketed on the occasion of a public lecture by David Spangler by a cult from Greenwich Village called *No Secrets* in which all the members were to be open and exposed and to have sex with the cult's leader. The cult members felt that since they were already in the neighborhood, the church should have been given to them and not to Lindisfarne.

What was going on in all these examples of seventies communes is what, following Whitehead's philosophy, could be called a phenomenon of "misplaced concreteness." There was a new Eros of attachment manifesting itself, and in even more conservative communities like Findhorn, San Francisco Zen Center, and Lindisfarne, marriages were dissolving and new partnerships were appearing. These formations of shared Eros were not always couples, but triangles and quadrangles. Consciousness was no longer dyadic, except for the fundamentalists of the Abrahamic religions.

It was all very confusing at the time, but now with the benefit of hindsight and the perspective of old age, I can see that this period was one in which "noise" was drawing us from one basin of attraction to another. Columns now in newspapers like the *Guardian* discuss polyamorous relationships in which men and women maintain their marriages, but also maintain other loving sexual relationships, straight and gay.[2]

A psychic quadrangle might express itself as the four women in *Sex and the City*, or, in Sex and the Commune, as a constellation of Man, Wife, Tantric Shakti, and Mistress. The latter quadrangle is unstable because its emotional stress can distort it into a collapsing parallelogram, or it can collapse entirely into a flattened line in which the three women abandon the man to seek other more stable relations. But if the quadrangle is truly a Tantric process of transformation and not a state of being, each one of the four will have had their lives changed in this process of "stretching" — the root meaning of the Sanscrit word *tantra* — and will enter into their new relationships as new beings.

The quadrangle is also highly unstable because it is the "right structure, but the wrong content." An initiatic quadrangle, or what I have described elsewhere as an evolutionary *Entelechy*,[3] is one in which the practioner of *yoga nidra* becomes a "Fantastic Four" of the yogi, the spiritual guide or post-incarnate graduated human being, the angel, and the elemental, or chthonic spirit. As the Eros of connection shifts from being projected into karmic relations in the physical world, it becomes more settled and stable in the psychic and spiritual worlds.

Another version of this esoteric quaternity can be seen in the esoteric parable masquerading as a children's book, Frank Baum's *The Wizard of Oz*. Dorothy's companions on the road to the Emerald City are the subtle bodies. As the great Sufi scholar Henri Corbin explained this intermediate realm of *Hurqalya*:

> So, to become aware of it is to see the world of Soul, to see all things as they are in the Earth of Hurqalya, the Earth of emerald cities, it is the *visio smaragdina*, which is the surrection and the resurrection of the world of the soul.[4]

And still another version of this esoteric quaternity can be seen in Japanese *Bunraku*—the puppetry theatre in which the puppet (the ego in time) is manipulated by three figures clothed in black, suggesting their invisibility.

In the seventies, women—against their better rational judgment— were attracted to the alpha male figure at the head of one of these communes, because he stood figured against this larger horizon of the evolution of consciousness, but then they became furious at the man and themselves for allowing their unconscious evolutionary biology to swamp their conscious wills. Feminism began to assert itself both to balance and challenge this atavistic *Übermensch* horizon of dominance. (Recall that *Superman* as a movie came out in 1978; the antidote, Terry Gilliam's *Brazil* did not appear until 1985.) This new Feminism—as opposed to the Suffragette movement of Britain and America from 1910 to 1920—first appeared in the revolutionary sixties with Betty Friedan's bestseller *The Feminine Mystique* in 1963 and then with the radical Black Panthers. Revolutionary as the Black Power movement claimed to be, the leaders were male and tended to look at black women as servants who could work as secretaries and handmaidens. "Stepandfetchit" shifted from racism to sexism.

Leaders like Joan Baez and Angela Davis helped to break this mold, but the leaders of the alternative movement were still overwhelmingly male. Think of Stewart Brand, Gary Snyder, Baker-roshi, and Michael Murphy on the West Coast, and Allen Ginsberg, Baba Ram Das, Eido-roshi, and Pir Villayat Khan on the East Coast, and Chogyam Trungpa rinpoche in the middle in Boulder. As the *aresteias* of the males began to display themselves at the Lindisfarne conferences, the women were attracted to these males, and at the same time furious that there were so many men speaking and so few women.

The elderly feminist sociologist and Quaker Elise Boulding was not comfortable with this new alternative counterculture of the seventies and with Lindisfarne, so she resigned as a Fellow, and Michaela Walsh, who came from the alpha male world of Wall Street and the Rockefeller Brothers Fund, took me in hand and tried to re-educate me. Michaela introduced me to Hazel Henderson, and I invited both of them to become Lindisfarne Fellows and began to work toward achieving a better balance by inviting Alice Tepper Marlin and Elaine Pagels to lecture at Lindisfarne-in-Manhattan.

Michaela Walsh challenging Baker-roshi

Saul Mendlovitz, Hazel Henderson,
Steven Rockefeller Fellows Conference, Manhattan 1978

Claire Schweickart, Rusty Schweickart, astronaut, Elise Boulding,
sociologist, fiilmaker Andre Gregory, and community members
June Cobb and Leon Leeds, 1977

But my efforts towards gender balance were not considered sufficient
to staunch the wound of centuries and millennia, and my deconstruction
of the myth of patriarchy in my 1977 lectures at Lindisfarne-in-Manhattan
that became my 1981 book *The Time Falling Bodies Take to Light* also did not
still the collective rage. Charlene Spretnak reviewed the book for a West

Coast journal and claimed I did not take women's scholarship into account. I felt that such a knee-jerk ideological reaction was absurd, since the whole book was constructed on the science and scholarship of Jane Goodall, Sarah Blaffer Hrdy, Marija Gimbutas, Elaine Pagels, Martha McClintock, and Elise Boulding.

As Feminism really began to pick up steam in the eighties, the anger directed at me continued to vent itself at our Lindisfarne Fellows meetings in Crestone. I remember one particularly explosive occasion at the 1992 meeting when Michaela Walsh and Joan Halifax—both Lindisfarne Fellows—joined in a heated attack. I was deeply hurt, repressed my feelings so as not to derail the meeting, but felt that after all I had done to listen to their criticisms and correct the gender balance at Lindisfarne, they were being unfair and acting like ideological zealots.

But gender cannot be balanced, because sexuality is an evolutionary force and not simply a static weight of cultural baggage. Women were enraged, I think, because they were both attracted to and repelled by charismatic males like Baker-roshi and Francisco Varela. Baker-roshi was expelled from the abbotship of San Francisco Zen Center for buying an expensive white BMW for his personal use and for having sexual relations with his students, and Francisco Varela was a classic example of the Don Juan archetype. I saw women line up outside his apartment in Boulder to have their time with him, and at Lindisfarne-in-Manhattan there was a continuing procession of different women admirers who came to visit him. Varela was both charismatically attractive, and aloof and detached, and his friend and teacher in Boulder, Chogyam Trungpa rinpoche, was turning Buddhist detachment into a rationale for a "Crazy Wisdom" in which sex without commitment was a path to Enlightenment.

When the women came forth in the eighties to denounce the fallen leader in his disgrace, I always wondered why they had had sex with the man in the first place. I can't help thinking that this rage at men was also a rage at themselves for letting their biology dictate their behavior. "Anatomy is destiny," as Freud said.

I was not the Don Juan archetype, for I am much more the Romantic and generally fall in love and project my soul onto the woman. In my seventy odd years, there have only been less than a dozen women in my life, and that would simply be a quiet summer for a New Age Don Juan. But even as a more old-fashioned Romantic, I did notice that when I was giving public lectures around the country that women were attracted to power, whether it was economic, political, or psychic. In New York at cocktail parties no woman took notice of me, or if they were stuck with me, their eyes would look over my shoulder to see if some celebrity had just arrived at the party so that they could move on and up. But after my lecture when I would speak without notes to a very large audience in a large hall and constellate a psychic sense of the presence of an invisible back-up band, I suddenly had the offer of a girlfriend for the night.

Once when I was describing some pop New Age figure as a charismatic mind-fucker, the woman with whom I was talking—a very pretty brunette—stopped me and said: "Listen, I was at your lecture at the Jung Foundation in New York. You had every woman in the audience wet, including me, so you're no one to talk." The remark was memorable, but I still behaved with decorum and my relations with the pretty young woman in question remained limited to words, not because of any scruples, but because I realized she was not really interested in me. She was looking at me as an object in a power game of the witch vs. the wizard—Morgan le Fay vs. Merlin.

The reason I am going into these matters so frankly now as a paunchy and infirm old man is to provide some explanation for the contradictory behavior of sex and spirituality in the seventies in which numerous gurus were exposed and expelled for their sexual relations with their students. The seventies were about sexual and spiritual exploration, and even for the unspiritual life of the suburbs, it was an era of wife-swapping and newspaper scandals about adulterous politicians. Recall that Nelson Rockefeller died in the arms of his mistress.

But Zeitgeists are temporary attractors that excite and destabilize the old adaptive landscape of peaks and valleys. Now we are in a different era, women have gained much more power, and so the attention to liberation has shifted to issues like gay marriage and transgender acceptance. And now within the Lindisfarne Fellowship, the alpha male seems an old evolutionary dinosaur, as a creative sisterhood has come forth to replace the Freudian Bruderbund of *Totem and Taboo*. The New Left movements like *Occupy Wall Street* are no longer led by the Jerry Rubins and Tom Haydens of the sixties, but by a horizontal democracy in which the sound bites, slogans, and fast food for thought take-out of the media are replaced by slow thought and consensus.

[1] Peter Marin, "Spiritual Obedience: the Transcendental Game of Follow the Leader", *Harper's Magazine*, February, 1979.

[2] http://www.guardian.co.uk/commentisfree/2012/jan/20/newt-gingrich-open-marriage-polyamory?INTCMP=SRCH

[3] See *Seven Pillars, http://www.sevenpillarshouse.org/ "The End of the Age of Religion and the Birth of Symbiotic Consciousness,"* December 17, 2008.

[4] Henri Corbin, *Spiritual Body and Celestial Earth: from Mazdean Iran to Shi'ite Iran* (Princeton University Press: Princeton, NJ, 1977), p.81

Chapter 5: Taking Time for Evan and Hilary: Reflections of a Homeschooling Parent

What is a parent to do with kids who want to learn, are smart—and maybe even smarter than their teachers—and are getting persecuted by their fellow students for not fitting into the dumb-it-down culture of modern America?

Millions of parents have now decided that what you do is take your kids out of school and organize an alternative approach through homeschooling. National Public Radio has estimated that there are now over four million families who have chosen to take the time to homeschool their children. The Associated Press more conservatively estimates that two million kids are now in homeschooling.[1] Admittedly, many of these parents are Christian fundamentalists in flight from evolutionary science, but some are intellectuals who are not comfortable with the mass culture of school bullying, sports triumphalism, and the kind of patriotically distorted history that I experienced as a child in the McCarthy era of the 1950s. Since I was a homeschooling parent way back in the seventies, I now like to think of myself as a trendsetter who discovered that homeschooling is a daytime extension—and equally enjoyable form—of bedtime story-telling, as well as a new electronically assisted form of shamanic, mind-to-mind transmission from parent to child, and, surprisingly, back again, from child to parent in a learning process in which the child becomes the teacher.

Lacking the resources of a private income, or the salary of a university professor, I could not afford to send my kids to expensive private schools. I had to lay down a path by walking on the fog-obscured path of the writer that manifested one step at a time from public lectures or modest advances for books, but did provide opportunities for travel in which my expenses were paid by the hosting organization for a conference. On every occasion that it was possible, I tried to bring my kids along with me. This form of economic *bricolage* is very much the life of the artist, and became my way of life when I decided to walk out on the university to seek another way of life for the mind, heart, and spirit.

Hilary and Evan at Disney World 1972, the year the Lindisfarne Association was incorporated and before we moved to Lindisfarne in Southampton, NY

Evan in Grindelwald, Switzerland, 1979

There are many reasons to opt for homeschooling: drug use in schools, teenage gangs, school violence and cruel hazing, and a mass culture in which art and science are not valued as much as sports, money, and celebrity idolatry. Sports have so parasitized schools—both public and private—that cultural and intellectual values have a hard time making their way through the halls without harassment. Sports have always been considered useful in building the team spirit necessary for soldiers and good team players in corporations that it is most unlikely that their dominance will disappear any time soon. Indeed, the popularity of televised sports and their merger with the presentation of the Super Bowl of American Presidential politics means that they are as tightly coupled as the Church and the land-owning aristocracy were in the Middle Ages.

The emotional turning point came for me when my eleven year old son Evan was abjectly sobbing over his misery in public school, and then turned to me and said: "If you love me, how can you do this to me?" Looking into his eyes, I could see that this was not the theatrics of a kid trying to play hooky, but the cry of an old soul and brilliant mind trapped in a kid's body and in an institution that hadn't a clue about what to do with intelligent children who truly wanted to learn.

It was then that I proposed to Evan and Hilary's mother Gail that we take the kids out of school and that I would set up a little school as part of Lindisfarne's cultural experiment in exploring new directions for education. We did take Evan out of the sixth grade, and he never went back—to junior or senior high. However, when Gail and I split up in 1975, she and Hilary moved back to California, and Hilary, with much pain on her part, returned to the awful world of the American Junior High. All I could offer to Hilary was a "radical sabbatical" in which she quit school for a semester and went traveling with me in Europe. After the death of her parents in California, Gail and Hilary decided to move back East to return to Toronto where we had lived before we set up Lindisfarne in Southampton. Hilary did attend and graduate from High School in Toronto, but Evan because he lived with me in Manhattan, and because I was a stay-at-home writer who could be with him all day and take the time to supervise his tutorial program, never attended Junior or Senior High School. At sixteen, he went off to Amherst College, loved it, and graduated with honors four years later. He went on to get his Ph.D. in philosophy at the University of Toronto and is now a Professor of Philosophy at the University of British Columbia.

As a first effort in escaping the Southampton public schools, I secured the permission from the local school board to set up a Lindisfarne School. We had six teachers for four kids, and Linda Leeds agreed to direct and co-ordinate the efforts of the teachers. Those of us with experience in education took our turn by offering a course in one of the cabins converted into a little brown schoolhouse.

When Lindisfarne had to default on our mortgage for lack of funds, two of the families broke up—mine included—and most of the kids moved to northern California. My wife and daughter were among them, but my fourteen-year old son Evan stayed with me and moved to Lindisfarne-in-Manhattan.

From sitting at the table in the dining hall and listening in on the morning conversations with Gregory Bateson in 1975-76, and then Francisco Varela in 1977-78, Evan decided at the beginning of adolescence that adulthood was more interesting and free than childhood and so he decided to become an adult immediately. Lindisfarne's program in philosophy, ecology, Asian thought, and the practice of Tai Chi interested him more than school and play, so he had no desire to leave Lindisfarne to return to public education. In effect, Evan apprenticed himself to Francisco Varela and sat in on all his lectures and seminars, and I tutored him in expository writing.

Francisco Varela, Linda Leeds, Gordon Leeds, and Evan Thompson in the Parish Hall of Lindisfarne in Manhattan, Chistmas, 1978. The painting in the background is by Haydn Stubbing and is now, along with two other Stubbings, in the permanent collection of the Cathedral of St. John the Divine in New York.

I could not offer my daughter the same advantages that came from living at Lindisfarne-in-Manhattan, but when at sixteen she was depressed and dissatisfied with public high school, her mother and I agreed to let Hilary spend the spring semester traveling with me around Western Europe and visiting many museums to pursue Hilary's interest in art. She would later call it her "Radical Sabbatical."

Hilary in Paris, 1981

Hilary met philosophers like Henri Atlan in cafes in Paris, and traveled with me and the poet Kathleen Raine through England and Scotland on our way to spend a week on Iona. As we drove through the Lakes Country around Windermere, Kathleen pointed out the window and said: "Oh, look, Hilary! There is where Wordsworth stole the rowboat." I thought to myself, "Now that is the way to learn English literature!—not in a classroom but in the inspiring landscape with a living English poet." On Iona, each afternoon, Hilary and I would walk down from Traigh Bhan to Kathleen's cottage in the fishing village to hear Kathleen read the poem she had written that day. Then Kathleen and I would have what she calls in her poems "whiskey at six," and Hilary realized that what she had just heard would someday be in a book.

W. I. Thompson and Kathleen Raine in her Home in London 2001

When Hilary was big enough to push open the door of the Ladies Room, we began having Father and Daughter Days in which I would take her to children's theatre or museums, first in Toronto, then in New York. On one of these expeditions, when Hilary was nine, we drove in from Southampton to Manhattan to go to MoMA. I thought Hilary would like Van Gogh's "Starry Night," but to my amazement, she fell in love with Jackson Pollack and said, "Oh, I could look at this all day!" When we returned home, she took the book of the paintings of Jackson Pollack off my shelf and went to bed with it, as if it were a cuddly Teddy Bear.

Traigh Bhan on Iona, Retreat House of the Findhorn Foundation

Hilary giving a talk at the 1988 Lindisfarne Fellows Conference at Esalen, Big Sur. From left to right: Nena and Bob Thurman, Hilary, W. I. Thompson, Sandy and James Lovelock

When Hilary returned to Toronto from her Radical Sabbatical, she decided to take the direction of her education into her own hands. The high school she had been attending in her neighborhood had a very upper middle class smug and materialistic culture, so she decided to look at the alternatives. She found the formless and free countercultural schools too silly and settled on a large, impersonal, but multicultural school that was more to her liking. Large impersonal institutions, paradoxically, Hilary felt, offered her the freedom to go her own way, and since she knew her own way, their size and impersonal focus was just fine with her. She graduated from Northern Secondary High School, went to Trent University in Peterborough, Ontario for a year, found it too small and intellectually confining, and then transferred to the University of Toronto. She took an Honours Degree in English literature and won a Mellon Fellowship to the University of Michigan where she completed its Ph.D. program in English. After teaching for a few years at Michigan, she moved to Bowdoin College, where she is now an Assistant Professor.

The recoil of the parent and child from mass culture and mass education can bounce in opposite directions: on the one hand, we can have an intellectual's longing to withdraw from a debased consumer culture to raise children in a more philosophically and scientifically advanced supraculture, and on the other, a fundamentalist's religious withdrawal from a secular-humanist, multicultural society into a rigidly controlled rural White subculture. Both of these conditions can cause a parent or a student to be unhappy with mass society and mass education. Whether for the scientist wanting to escape the Creationism of a school board taken over by Christian fundamentalists, or for the artist wanting to escape a school faculty taken over by a postmodernist nihilism in which all works of genius are seen as nothing but discourses of patriarchal dominance and oppression, or for the religious fundamentalist wanting to escape the eroticized mass media of capitalist consumption, there are many impulses energizing the search for educational alternatives. All these diversely caused social impulses are going on simultaneously and contributing to the emergence of a new complex ecology of education in which public, private, and charter schools, internet schooling, co-housing collaborative efforts of residents and neighbors, and homeschooling by parents are all developing at the same time.

As for the social containers of public schools, I don't foresee them disappearing from the face of the land in a "rapture" in which we are taken up into some completely new post-historical state of being. Great waves of immigration to the United States will continue to lift and support our collective societal need for good public schools. Such a need is essential for an open and just democratic society. But at the other end of our pluralistic society, there is another wave of emigration going on in which an electronic American culture is emigrating from the New World to an even Newer World.

Given the size of public school systems and the "America First!" social pressure brought to bear on them, I believe it is unrealistic to think that public schools will be the source of educational innovation and cultural transformation to this Newer World. Public schools will have all they can handle merely to deal with the new waves of immigration and to stabilize safe and modestly academic environments for their students. It is far more realistic to expect innovation and transformative learning to come from new private schools, charter schools, co-housing efforts, Internet and homeschooling alternatives.

Lest I be accused of being antidemocratic, let me present a sketch of my own educational and socio-economic background to show "where I am coming from."

I was part of the vast postwar movement from the Midwest into Southern California. In 1945 the suburban tracts had not yet been built, there was not sufficient housing for families, and most landlords with apartments did not wish to take in noisy children, so at the age of seven I was packed off to St. Catherine's Catholic military boarding school in Anaheim, a school that was more like an orphanage or prison than your usual upper class boarding school. I stayed there for two years, summers included, before my parents found a one-bedroom apartment for our family of five, and I was able to live at home and go to a Catholic parochial school.

Neither my mother nor my father was educated beyond the eighth grade, so my socioeconomic background can be described as Irish-American working class. My mother had been "lace curtain Irish," but she fell from grace and was disowned when she married a divorced Protestant, so the life of my parents in the Depression was anything but middle class. As an Irish Catholic born in Chicago—but whose own mother had been born in Ireland— my mother was raised in what E. R. Dodds has called "a guilt culture."[2] Traditional Ireland was "the land of saints and scholars," and in the revolutionary tradition of "the hedge schools" that defied the Penal Laws of the English, learning was respected, even by the poor. But in moving from the Irish subculture of Chicago to the Latino culture of Los Angeles, my mother did not realize that she was also moving from a "guilt culture" to a "shame culture." In a shame culture, to excel is to threaten the integrity of the group, to cause others to lose honor or self-respect. To appear smart, to identify with the teacher rather than the class of one's peers, is a violation of group integrity. Excellence is only tolerated in sports, for this form of macho demonstration serves to enhance the pride and self-respect of the group. This cultural predicament is also experienced by bright African-American students, for whom doing well in school is considered "acting white."

My mother had tried to do her best to help me by once again trying to send me to a private military boarding school in the eighth grade, because just when my older brothers had gone off into the army and navy during the time of the Korean War, my father had collapsed from the incurable disease of sclerderma and had gone off to be cared for in a veterans hospital. She was also worried about me because two years earlier, I had been diagnosed with leukemia and the doctors told her that I would probably die within a year. The osteopathic doctors she consulted for a second opinion took out my tumor in two operations, told her it was a goiter in the wrong place, and hoped for the best. But a goiter it was not, and the primary tumor in the thyroid was left to produce and distribute its malignant metastases.

The 1940s and 50s was not a healthy time to grow up. There was, as there is today, an idolatrous belief in the invincibility and utopian perfection of technology. I remember waking early to watch the sky light up as Man beat Nature to the punch with the pre-emptive strike of an early dawn in an open air nuclear explosion. When the Santa Anna wind blew the dust into the San Gabriel Valley where the cattle grazed, the milk was never destroyed, and Iodine 131 made its merry way through the food chain and into the children's thyroids, much as it did in the Ukraine after Chernobyl. To make matters worse, there were also X-ray machines in all the shoe stores. I remember twinkling my boney toes in the eerie green light. And to make matters even worse for me, I was given X-ray therapy for my tumor, which only made the cancer more malignant.

And then there was smoking. Everyone smoked everywhere. In my family of five, the other four members all smoked in the confining space of our one bedroom demi-bungalow. Not surprisingly, I developed asthma and had difficulty breathing. So with a sick husband and son, and two children off to war, my mother had a lot to contend with. Since she had to work in an office, and did not want me to be home alone, she sought out yet another military boarding school, Urban Military Academy in Brentwood. For a year I went to this private school, where world history was taught by the Headmaster, a Ph.D. who had taught European history at U.S.C. He insisted on running his eighth grade class as he had in university, and I loved it. It was wonderful to be treated as an adult, and I was fascinated with his more human approach to European history. The nuns in parochial school had certainly never told me that Popes had mistresses and children, or nephews that they would make cardinals at thirteen, my own age at the time. I excelled in the class and became an honor student. But the school was not in central L.A. where I lived, but in wealthy Brentwood. My school friend was the only other bookish student in the class, one who delighted in history and happened to live in a mansion overlooking the Pacific Palisades and had a weekend horse ranch in Santa Barbara.

The author at age thirteen, at Urban Military Academy, Brentwood, California

Invited to be his house guest, I was stunned by the luxury of having a room of my own, by the strangeness of a bathroom with a bidet, by the unreality of being driven to the movies by a chauffeur in a Cadillac limousine, of being driven to a birthday party at Douglas Fairbanks's house, where the Firestone children threw ice cream at the others in a spoiled rich kids' food fight— creating a mess they expected the servants to clean up. At dinner in his home, I was disoriented by being served exotic dishes, such as barracuda, on silver platters offered by a butler and a maid. I had never even experienced a middle class life of having a home, a dining room, or a bedroom of my own, and I certainly knew nothing about the protocol of dressing for dinner, so I showed up in the formal dining room in my playclothes of school T-shirt and chinos—much to the disapproval of my colleague's mother. I continued to annoy her as I developed a fierce attack of hay fever at their horse ranch in Santa Barbara and spent an entire weekend sneezing violently— and feeling mortally ashamed, as only thirteen-year-olds can.

My mother had meant well, and had simply not wanted me to be a latch-key kid when she was away at work, but she could not keep up with the costs of the school, even though the headmaster tried to encourage her to pay by informing my classmates, in front of me, that she had not yet paid for my uniforms or the semester's tuition. Her social experiment lasted only one year, and for the ninth grade I returned to a Catholic high school in south central L.A.

At St. Agnes High School that year, when I was fourteen, there was a pretty girl in my history class who I liked, and she responded to me flirtatiously, but also liked to compete with me in class. One day, we were given some national machine-scored test in world history. She smiled at me, offering to race me through the course. Stupidly, I responded, and finished the whole test at half-time. When the marks were returned a week or two later, the nun made the mistake of letting the class know that I had gone off the charts, receiving an impossible score higher than the hundredth percentile. I had only missed one question out of 100. The girl was livid, as she saw she could not compete with me and even come close.

Although she had flirted with me, she could not afford the loss of face by associating with the likes of me, and she had already chosen as her boyfriend a Mexican who was head of the Latino teenage gang that ran the school. So in her state of rage, it was a simple matter to aim her boyfriend in my direction in revenge for her loss of face. It became impossible for me to go out to the schoolyard at recess and lunch, and impossible even to continue at that high school. Fourteen-year olds did not pack Uzis in those days, but they did carry switchblade knives. At St. Agnes High I was risking eternal damnation by reading *Candide* in the ninth grade, and risking death by daring to go out into the playground, so I transferred to Los Angeles High, and although I was terrified to attend a large public high school of 2400 students, it was at that time a fairly safe if un-intellectual school. In the McCarthy era, intellectuals were held in contempt and ridiculed, but not attacked on the playground; it was as if we were untouchable perverts against the natural order of things— teenage popularity, sports, cars, and money. I was often accused of being un-American and communist simply, and rather ironically, because I had read Emerson, Thoreau, and Melville on my own and quoted them in class. "Whoso would be a man, must be a non-conformist" and "To be great is to be misunderstood" were among my favorite quotes.

Pomona College, Claremont, CA

After the hell of St. Agnes High, the purgatory of L.A. High and two more operations for cancer of the thyroid, I went on to the intellectual paradise of Pomona College, where I was admitted as a maverick who did not fit into their usual SAT formulaic profile. In my senior year, I received a Woodrow Wilson Fellowship for graduate study at Cornell. Pomona College was both emotionally and intellectually fulfilling, but grad school was a grind—more a form of hyper-professional training than education, but, in truth, Cornell did everything for me that a grad school is supposed to do. The English Department was small and personal, and the professors pretty much knew every graduate student by name. Nevertheless, the first year was depressing, and after one more operation in the summer break—my fifth for cancer of the thyroid—I thought about dropping out, but decided that the best way out was to get out as fast as I could by finishing. When I passed my oral defense of my thesis, I was told by the Registrar that I had set a record by finishing the requirements for the M.A. and Ph.D. in three years.

Cornell University and Lake Cayuga. Ithaca, NY

My dissertation was accepted for publication by Oxford University Press and is still in print forty-six years later. In the "publish or perish" culture of academe, the fact that I had five articles and a book from my graduate school work empowered me to receive job offers from Cornell, Stanford, MIT, and Pomona College. I chose MIT for my first academic position because I wanted to live in Cambridge and preferred to teach in an interdisciplinary Humanities program rather than in the more narrow confines of an English department.

MIT, Cambridge, MA

I am offering these personal anecdotal remarks simply to indicate to other parents that I have experienced the cultural extremes of education in America, and to indicate as well that my commitment to an intellectual elitism comes from an economically deprived person's desire to escape poverty and violence for a world of culture and commitment to excellence.

For a specific program of homeschooling, one should consult my book *Transforming History* in which I outline an evolution of consciousness curriculum. This curriculum can be easily adapted by the parent for homeschooling. Public and private schools go from kindergarten to grade twelve, but I would suggest that homeschooling and "high school" should stop at age sixteen. This is an idea that I proposed in 1974, but that more recently Dr. Leon Botstein, the President of Bard College in New York, has put forward in the aftermath of the shootings at Columbine High School. Dr. Botstein feels that collectivizing teenagers in large groups during the years from sixteen to eighteen is asking for precisely the kind of trouble we have seen, and "that high school is a failure not worth reforming."[3] Sixteen year olds, Dr. Botstein argues, belong in the company of adults where they can be socialized to an adult life through training on the job as apprentices, or, if they are naturally inclined intellectuals, as students in colleges and universities. In my 1974 work, *Passages about Earth: an Exploration of the New Planetary Culture,*

I argued that there was a naturally oscillating cycle of periods of *Homo Faber* and *Homo Ludens*, and that the years from 14 to 21 were definitely under the spell of *Homo Ludens*.

Homeschooling should stop at age sixteen and at that point the student should go away to a good liberal arts college, or engage in some experiential program of work and apprenticeship under a mentor other than his parents or former tutors. After receiving my program of homeschooling, my son went to Amherst at age 16 and graduated with honors four years later. I was able to homeschool my son because I worked at home and could be with him throughout the day. Thanks to personal computers, many parents, and not simply writers, now work at home, so the possibilities for homeschooling have increased. However, even if one is in the privileged position of working at home and can take on the responsibility of homeschooling as a parent, it is still wise to try to work in association with others, either through co-housing or collaborative efforts with friends and colleagues. If suburban parents can get together for Little League, soccer, Campfire Girls and Boy Scouts, then they can also do the same for philosophy and science. But if one is a parent who must leave home to go work at an office or factory, then homeschooling is not a realistic option. Under these circumstances, it would be better to choose a private or charter school if one wishes to have an alternative to the public school system.

Culture is a shared system of values, and no child can be healthily raised in a parentally-controlled isolation tank, so play groups, and clubs for activities will need to be arranged to supplement any homeschooling program. If one wishes to escape the competitive and aggressive subculture of sports, then one can substitute group classes in Tai Chi or Aikido, music and dance school, or the wonderful classes that many art museums now offer for children. In our particular case, since we were living in New York, Evan and I took advantage of the city, even though in the seventies, New York was at a low point in terms of grime and crime. My son studied Tai Chi in Chinatown, took intermediate recorder lessons in Greenwich Village, studied classical Greek at the Greek Language Center on 57th Street, and sat in on the lectures on science and philosophy given at Lindisfarne by Gregory Bateson and Francisco Varela. If he felt that he needed a more intense course in science or math, then he took an adult night school course at N.Y.U., where high school level courses were offered for adults who did not want the embarrassment of having to go back to an actual high school and sit in class with teenagers.

With a resident staff of twenty-four living communally, Lindisfarne functioned as a co-housing experiment, so there were many adults around for my son to interact with as he participated in the house-cleaning chores of keeping the communal institute going. For my part, I gave him formal instruction in the research and writing of term papers, took him on research trips, and brought him with me on any public lecture or conference talk that I was asked to give. I reasoned that if a blacksmith's son learned a trade by watching his father, then my son could learn my trade by watching me.

To complete his homeschooling experience, I asked Evan to do an Honors Thesis to bring his studies into some sort of personal synthetic vision. Because he had been studying New Testament Greek, Evan chose to write on the philosopher Heidegger and the idea of the logos. When I showed the finished thesis to our Scholar-in-Residence Francisco Varela, I remember the look of astonishment in Cisco's eyes as he looked up at me from the couch where he was sitting.

"Shit!" Cisco exclaimed, "Evan shouldn't be able to write like this at fifteen!"

Cisco was one to talk, since he had studied Heidegger with the Jesuits in Santiago, Chile, and gone off to graduate school at Harvard at 19. The two had a lot in common besides being scholars in residence at Lindisfarne-in-Manhattan. And this commonality would continue to grow over the years as Evan became first Varela's student, then his research assistant, and finally his colleague and co-author of *The Embodied Mind*.

When, years later in 2002, I was recuperating from open heart surgery and too weak to be able to be the proud papa to attend Evan's keynote address at the Mind and Life Conference with the Dalai Lama at MIT, I thought, as I watched the videotape, of how after Evan's graduation from Amherst I told him that my graduation present to him for his B.A. in Asian Studies was that I would take him with me to meet the Dalai Lama at conference on science and religion at Alpbach in Austria. Clearly, the homeschooling of Evan at Lindisfarne had been what he knew he needed when he cried out so tearfully to me to get him out of the hell realm of public school.

Evan presenting research findings in Cognitive Science to the Dalai Lama
at his home in Dharmasala for the Mind and Life Conferences. 2007.

But the most important thing to keep in mind about homeschooling is that the parent must take much more time to be with the child than a normal working parent does. The parent must not only take the time to tutor the child, but also provide occasions for group play and association with neighbors or neighborhood institutions. If one is raising a child in rural circumstances, then nature itself provides other sorts of opportunities, and on-line courses with museums can help if one is not in a position to take the subway to the Metropolitan Museum. With the resources of the World Wide Web, homeschooling is now much more of a practical alternative than it was a decade ago. Nevertheless, the most important element is still the home, and if the parent cannot take the time to be with the child, then the Internet certainly cannot make up for the loss.

Many spiritual philosophies, in differing religious traditions, claim that we take on a body to experience a world of love and compassion. If we lose the body in collective systems and networks of data-processing, we can lose compassion and become intellectually cruel and economically insensitive. We forget that it was through the body that our child was brought forth, and we forget how to be with another in a sense of presence that enhances our feeling for the meaning of life. Like "the hungry ghosts" of Buddhist philosophy, we become wraiths—grey shades whose lives have been parasitized by computer and cell phone—and do not realize that they are dead and are only haunting the places of life. Homeschooling is one way for a parent to move from a career to a way of life in which the child also becomes the teacher and opens up for the parent a new path to compassionate understanding.

Father and Son Opening Talk for the Lindisfarne Fellows Conference at the Sufi Seven Pillars Academy New Lebanon, NY, 2011.

---

[1] Steve Giegrich, "Colleges Noticing Home Schooled Kids," Associated Press/Yahoo, Monday, January 26, 2004.

[2] See E. R. Dodd's "From Shame-Culture to Guilt-Culture" in *The Greeks and the Irrational* (Berkeley: University of California Press, 1951), 28-63

[3] Leon Botstein, "Let Teen-Agers Try Adulthood," Op-Ed page essay, *The New York Times*, May 17, 1999, p. A21.

Chapter 6: Lindisfarne-in-Manhattan, 1977-1979

Beatrice Rudin Thompson and son Andrew

When my second wife Beatrice looked back on Lindisfarne in Manhattan from the distance of thirty years later in Zürich, one incident stood out for her and seemed to sum up the whole spirit of the place. She was upstairs in the kitchen of the rectory of the old church, feeding our infant son Andrew his morning porridge and talking to him, as she always did, in the mother tongue of the Bernese dialect of Swiss German. Off to the corner of the kitchen at the breakfast table over their morning coffee, Humberto Maturana and Francisco Varela were going at it full throttle in Chilean Spanish. They were scribbling diagrams with intensity, and anyone could see, no matter how weak her Spanish, that the young student and the older master were experiencing divergent evolution.

Varela was about to publish his own book, *Principles of Biological Autonomy*, and you could sense that the book itself was expressing his own autonomy from Maturana. Heinz von Foerster, one of the founding fathers of cybernetics and the philosophy of self-organization, liked to call this couple "Maturella," in recognition of their important contributions that culminated in their book *Autopoiesis and Cognition*.[1] To this day, Maturana insists that autopoiesis was his idea and that Varela was merely his student. Personally, I don't believe him, as Maturana was the kind of scientist who could lecture about pure categories of the understanding—thinking that he had discovered something really big—and not be aware that Immanuel Kant had been there before him. Varela had studied philosophy and phenomenology with the Jesuits in high school in Chile, so he came to university-level science with a good background in philosophy. Of course, the two scientists had been so closely ribbed for years in Santiago, that it would be difficult for anyone to say with certainty who had the idea first over morning coffee in Santiago. Over this particular morning coffee in a corner of Lindisfarne-in-Manhattan, one thing was certain to Beatrice, something important was going on.

Humberto Maturana

Francisco Varela (Lindisfarne Fellow Luigi Luisi in Background)

Beatrice looked at them as she spooned out the porridge over Andrew's baby lips, and felt her own sense of satisfaction and deep nourishment. As a Swiss, she told me, she had always felt that culture was something that always was going on somewhere other than Switzerland. Whether it was the Summer of Love in 1967 in the Haight-Ashbury of San Francisco, or the student revolts in the Paris of 1968, culture was always happening somewhere else. But now for the first time she felt that she was finally "where it was at," and that whatever these two guys were up to, it was an important part of what the work of her generation was all about. In one room, Maturana and Varela were formulating autopoiesis as a model for the origins of life; and downstairs in the old Parish Hall, Gregory Bateson was lecturing about "the pattern that connects" mind and nature, and David Finkelstein was conducting a seminar with the stage and film director Andre Gregory on the philosophical implications of quantum physics, and I was giving the lectures that became my two books, *Darkness and Scattered Light* and *The Time Falling Bodies Take to Light*.

New paradigm science played a large part in our lives, but the public events that really packed the old church were the artistic events. André Gregory taught a workshop on the material that became his film, *My Dinner with André*, and I laughed when I heard several of my dialogues with André put into the mouth of Wally Shawn. André had first appeared at Lindisfarne in Southampton one afternoon in 1975, and as we went for a walk along the shore of Fish Cove and Peconic Bay he discussed his feelings of frustration and limitation with conventional theatre and recounted his experiences with his production of *Alice in Wonderland*. I told him that the present moment was more about playing with consciousness than working with mimetic re-presentations of a consensual reality in conventional genres of art, that theatre had gone back to the rituals and ritual community that had preceded Greek comedy and tragedy, and that in places like Findhorn, where animism was being retrieved in the context of an electronic, postindustrial society, people were playing in a new Imaginary that included elves, nature spirits, and extraterrestrials, and were receiving transmissions from angelic Celestial Intelligences. Castaneda had opted for the solitary path of the Yaqui shaman, but at places like Findhorn in Scotland and Auroville in India, the theatre of group consciousness was the new shared Imaginary.

André dutifully went off to Findhorn, and then in his film with Louis Malle he mythologized this New Age community even more with his riff on the roof of the Universal Hall. When he returned to New York, he wanted me to sponsor a Lindisfarne workshop in which our New York students and resident members of the community would go off with him to the Morrocan dessert to look for the Little Prince. André was nothing if not a classic *puer eternus*, so his fascination with the Little Prince made sense for him, but not to me, as I felt Antoine de Saint Exupery's novel was sentimental kitsch, so I declined the offer, and said that we at Lindisfarne did not have to go traipsing around the world on expensive workshops, that all we had to do was take a few steps into our meditation room to take our own cosmic voyage. My words ended up in Wally Shawn's mouth, but this time not as the mystic, patronizing the rich *puer* and self-indulgent artist, but the unimaginative skeptic who lacked André's risk-taking yet playful imagination.

It was good fun to argue with André Gregory, because he was always charming and polite, and only gently manipulative in his desire to seek dominance in any one-to-one relationship. My response to his need for dominance was to go along with the game, but play Dean to his professor and establish limits to what he could get away with at Lindisfarne. André didn't seem to mind and made many contributions to our communal life: bringing actors from the Polish Lab Theatre in Warsaw to live with us for several weeks to teach a workshop, and on one memorable evening, manifesting an epiphany of the great Jerzy Grotowski himself. And for this shaman of theatre as the new Eleusinian Mystery religion, the old church was packed and we had standing room only.

Andre Gregory talking to Beatrice outside the
Parish Hall of Lindisfarne in Manhattan 1977

Exploring the relationship between art and spirituality was much more our focus in Manhattan than it had been in Southampton. I asked Paul Winter to give a spring equinox concert for St. Cuthbert's Day (March 20) in the church, and Dean Morton was so transported by the evening that he transported the whole program uptown to the Cathedral of St. John the Divine, where these concerts evolved into the famous St. Francis Day Mass with the Animals and the annual celebration of the winter solstice.

Our Vice President Maribeth Bunn and Paul Winter, hanging up our sign on the Corner of Sixth Avenue and Twentieth St., 1976

Gary Snyder, 1978

Robert Bly gave a reading of his Rumi translations, Gary Snyder and Paul Winter presented a poetry and jazz evening on the theme of *Turtle Island*, and Wendell Berry and Allen Ginsberg gave poetry readings. Wendell's reading was inspiring and filled with that quiet dignity that emanates from Wendell when his rambunctious Huck Finn sense of humor isn't up and running, but Allen filled the church with the scruffiest audience we ever had. I became annoyed with Allen because he began to get off on the naughtiness of standing in the pulpit of the old church and reading a poem on licking assholes. The poem was quite literally a crappy work of art, more an expression of gay politics than poetics, but then, I have to confess that I never really liked Allen's poetry and found it to be merely declamatory rhetoric. As the host of the evening, I was standing next to Allen at the end of the reading, after he had descended from the pulpit to the altar. An unctuous hippie fan came up to him and asked Allen to give him his autograph on a roll of toilet paper. Although I thought the request was appropriate to Allen's subject, Allen himself was incensed and said the request was insulting. The absurdity of Allen's reaction was not apparent to him, but I decided to avoid such future conflicts of taste by not asking Allen to give a reading at Lindisfarne again. Allen belonged in the Naropa Institute in Boulder where his aesthetic could fit in quite comfortably with Trüngpa's dissolute style and the ethos of the Kerouac School of Disembodied Poetics.

Samuel Menashe

Much more appealing to me were the small, hard, tectonicly compressed carbon of Samuel Menashe's short poems, which Samuel read to a much smaller audience, but one that included the English poet Kathleen Raine, in the Parish Hall. On the walls of this Parish Hall—which was our second largest building—was an exhibition of the abstract landscapes of Haydn Stubbing. (Later Yvonne Hagen Stubbing and I donated three of these large canvases to the Cathedral of St John the Divine, where they now should be found in the St. James Chapel on the south side of the High Altar.)

Yvonne Hagen and Haydn Stubbing with Wendell and Tanya Berry 1977

Haydn Stubbing's exhibition was part of our Fellows Conference on the theme of Art and the Sacred that we held both in Manhattan and Southampton in the spring of 1977. When I set up Lindisfarne in 1973 there was great pressure from the young generation to make Lindisfarne a clone of the Esalen of the sixties, and equal pressure from the older generation who had had their glorious moment in the fifties to make it a Hamptonite salon for artists. Dorothy Norman presided over a brilliant salon in East Hampton, where I saw such notables as Willem de Kooning, Lee Krasner, Alfonso Osorio, Clement Greenberg, Isamu Noguchi, Lewis Thomas, and Ivan Illich. Dorothy had heard of Lindisfarne from friends in East Hampton and began to show up at Fish Cove quite often, even though our countercultural aesthetic was clearly not to her taste. I made it clear to her and everyone else I met in the Hamptons' artisic scene that I regarded artists as fallen angels who had lost their cultural authority and prophetic leadership. When I met the English painter Haydn Stubbing—who lived nearby in Sagaponack—I tried to explain to him why I needed to keep the local artistic scene at arm's length in order to find the space, in Emerson's words, to do my own thing.

Haydn decided to challenge my prejudices. One day I was busy in the kitchen of the main Lodge at Fish Cove, and as I came out hurriedly through the swinging doors to the kitchen to the buffet counter where we set out the food, I noticed that someone had put up a whole exhibition of small paintings. I was about to hurry on into the office, but was stopped by the presence of these works that hovered in clouds of colors between landscape and thoughtscape. I stopped and then began to study them more closely. To my surprise and delight, I found them to be truly contemplative works that gently forced you to stop whatever you were doing or thinking and just stay with them. I also noticed out of the corner of my eye, that Haydn was off in the corner of the dining room, studying me as intently as I was studying the canvases.

"Did you do these?," I asked, for Haydn looked more like a British eccentric or bearded general from a Monty Python skit than a New York artist.

"Yes," he answered with a clipped finality.

"But these are good!" I said, expressing a disbelief that anything around there really could be.

"Yes, I think so too," Haydn said and smiled. He had given me a test to see if I was just an opinionated jerk, or was open to having my prejudices challenged.

Having lost the argument, I began to take Haydn very seriously, and visited his studio in Sagaponack, and then, in the fall of 1976, his studio in London. Together we began to work on an exhibition of his paintings for Lindisfarne-in-Manhattan for the spring of 1977.

To have Varela as our scientist in residence and Stubbing as our artist in residence brought forth an ecology of mind in which Varela's studies of color perception and Haydn's contemplative "spots of time" were dependant co-orginations of a shared culture. Ted Morgan's essay on Lindisfarne in the *New York Times Magazine* was right. Lindisfarne was serving the function that had hitherto been characteristic of the Parisian café or salon. In *Le Lapin Agile*, Picasso would listen to discussions about the fourth dimension, the philosophy of Poincaré, the time-space of Einstein, and then go home to work on *Les Demoiselles d'Avignon.*[2] At Lindisfarne, Varela would describe in his lectures how color was not an impression made by frequencies of light on a passive subject, but a performance of the nervous system that used the entire body, and that color vision was a concert in which all the elements we might wish to single out as "red" did not come in as signals at the same time; they had to be orchestrated by the brain in order to perform the embodied experience we called "red." Listening to Varela, Stubbing was confirmed in his artistic experiments in his own studio and worked even harder to cross the diachronic and the synchronic in which object and subject became participations of color, space, and time rather than representations of objects within a single linear source of light.

Haydn Stubbing stopped time to turn space into a process of color in his exhibition of paintings in the Parish Hall, and in this same Parish Hall, the cinematographer Hilary Harris showed his films that sped up time to reveal the city as a giant organism that only became visible if we saw space and time in a different relationship. Harris's footage became more widely known later when it showed up in Godfrey Reggio's film *Koyaanisqatsi*, accompanied by the music of Phillip Glass.

When I was in London visiting Haydn in his studio in the fall of 1976, I also met with the Research into Lost Knowledge Group, and from this contact I invited Keith Critchlow, Warren Kenton, John Michell, and Kathleen Raine to come to spend a period of residency as scholars at Lindisfarne-in-Manhattan. This London quartet proved to be outstanding contributors to Lindisfarne's program, and they delighted so much in being in New York that they taught me how to appreciate the city more deeply and not get caught by the negativity of our neighborhood's crime and attempted and break-ins. Warren Kenton had a wonderful sense of humor and was a companionable housemate, and he loved ranging all over the city on the days he was not teaching. He went to Brooklyn to meet with "the Rebbi" of the Lubuvitcher community, and on all the subways he bravely went where no Lindisfarner had gone before. Charming and charmed he was, and with his economy return ticket to London in hand, he was unexplainedly bumped up by British Airways to business class and given his flight home on the Concorde. John Michell chose to walk all over the city, and for a farewell gift to the community, he hired his favorite street musician—a Country Western steel guitarist from the Village—to give a command performance for us all in the Parish Hall. Keith Critchlow and his beautiful daughters who accompanied him during his residency were especially popular and his course of lectures on sacred architecture inspired a whole group of followers. Keith shared with us the material from his new book, *Time Stands Still*. John Michell gave the material from his book *The View over Atlantis* and shared with us the material from what was to become his next book, *Megalolithomania*., Warren Kenton (a.k.a. Zev ben Shimon Halevi) taught a course on the Cabbalah that was a preview of his popular Thames and Hudson books on the Cabbalah, and Kathleen Raine gave a series of lectures on Blake's *Book of Job* that also became her next book with Thames and Hudson. Lindisfarne, it seemed was indeed expressing a civilized riverine culture of both the Thames and the Hudson.

John Michell

Warren Kenton, a.k.a. Zev Ben Shimon Halevi
and Kathleen Raine

I was a little anxious in inviting the very proper Kathleen Raine to come to live in a commune, for Kathleen looked and talked like Agatha Christie's Miss Marples. I bought flowers and a bottle of sherry for her guest room, and hoped what was really the rector's converted dining room without an outside window would be acceptable to her. Upon her arrival, Kathleen surveryed the room, and said, "This will do nicely, but please get rid of that bottle of sherry and get me a bottle of Scotch. " I relaxed and knew that we would get along nicely. I had introduced our Chilean scientist in residence to the esoteric mysteries of *Laphroaig*—the kind of Islay single malt Scotch you drink with a knife and fork—so Kathleen's request was easier to accommodate than John Michel's insistence on smoking his odiferous herbs so close to the entry.

In fact, Kathleen became the most enthusiastic Lindisfarne communard of the London Gang of Four. Kathleen ends her three volume autobiography on an elegiac note in contemplation of Gavin Maxwell's death and her own readiness for death, but she took on a new life when she left Lindisfarne and she told me later, when we were traveling in the Lakes Country and Scotland with my daughter Hilary, that she was so impressed with my going ahead with Lindisfarne in spite of all the financial difficulties, that she decided that one should just go ahead and do whatever cultural project one felt was right for the time, and not worry about its economic feasibility; so, upon returning to London after her scholar-in-residency, she established the elegant literary journal *Temenos*, kept it going for a decade, and then passed on her leadership to an expanded board, as she founded the even more ambitious Temenos Academy. In spite of her angina—or perhaps because of the Scotch she said she took for it—Kathleen kept at it into her nineties, when she received a C.B.E from the Queen. With the patronage of the Prince of Wales, the Temenos Academy and the Prince's School of Sacred Architecture continued what Keith had started at Lindisfarne's School of Sacred Architecture in New York and Crestone.

A new green and sacred architecture being envisioned by Sim Van der Ryn, John Todd, and Keith Critchlow at the 1978 Fellows Conference at Lindisfarne in Manhattan

Amplifying this work of an anti-modernist recovery of the sacred was the work of another British scholar, Lindisfarne's own community member, Christopher Bamford, who offered a seminar on the Western Hermetic tradition. The Jungian analysts Robin van Löben Sels and Julie Bresciani taught seminars on analytic psychology, Jungian astrology, or conducted dream workshops. David Spangler lectured on esoteric Christianity, and was picketed by members of a Greenwich Village cult whose rituals involved keeping no secrets among themselves and sleeping in lay equality with the leader. (They seemed particularly vexed that the church had been given to Lindisfarne and not to them.) And continuing with our theme of the planetization of the esoteric, Elaine Pagels from Princeton lectured on Christian Gnosticism, Pir Villayat Khan gave a program on Sufism, two Tibetan rinpoches lived with us as contemplatives in residence, and we developed a working partnership with Baker-roshi and the San Francisco Zen Center. Culturally, we were becoming bicoastal.

Christopher Bamford in Crestone, 1982

And to insure that we were not simply arty and other-worldly, we also had a colloquium on world order with Saul Mendlovitz's Institute for World Order, and various global thinkers such as Richard Falk, Elise Boulding, Ali Mazrui, John Mbuti, Alasdair Taylor, Seyed Hosein Nasr, and Nechung Rinpoche—who had been Tibet's ambassador to China when he was imprisoned by Mao—gave public lectures. And I, for my contribution to the curriculum, gave the lectures that became my two books—one on contemporary affairs, the other on the re-visioning of patriarchal prehistory—

Darkness and Scattered Light: Four Talks on the Future and *The Time Falling Bodies Take to Light: Mythology, Sexuality, and the Origins of Culture.*

Paradoxically, this high time of the seventies that was Lindisfarne's bright moment of cultural relevance was, economically, the worst possible time to try to fund-raise to restore our historical landmark church. The Carter years of stagflation was a time of grime and crime for New York and the city was going bankrupt. Every cultural and social institution was hard-pressed and calling down on the limited economic resources of the city. In spite of all our activity for three years, every single foundation, individual, or group turned us down for the funds needed to restore the four buildings of the church, which at that time was only $250,000. The only funds I was able to raise were one general operating grant from the Lilly Endowment and two grants for our scholars in residence program from the Rockefeller Brothers Fund and the Humanities Division of the larger Rockefeller Foundation, as well as an anonymous donation from one of our resident students.

The Community of Lindisfarne-in-Manhattan

For the twenty-five years of building three different centers for Lindisfarne—in Southampton, Manhattan, and Crestone—my life was fundamentally shaped by the all too real cultural process of fund-raising. And if I have anything like grandfatherly advice to pass on to the generation of my grandchildren about founding new cultural projects and institutions, it is not to look to foundations, wealthy individuals, and the general process of fund-raising to support the work. The institution should be a wealth-producing collective from the start and its Fellows should not only be poets and painters, but scientists whose discoveries and inventions can produce the royalties to support the whole endeavor on its own activities. No doubt, this strategy will generate conflict between the scientists with patents and fat checks versus the poets with slim volumes, but if all donate a percentage of their royalties, a poet with a bestseller—like Robert Bly with his *Iron John*—may be able to match a scientist with a new drug, technology, or software. Lindisfarne was too dependent on fund-raising, and in this process, it could not possibly compete with Columbia and Princeton, or with social services desperately in need of funds for people in extreme situations.

The most important supporter of Lindisfarne throughout its history was Laurance Rockefeller. I had met "Mr. Laurance"—after the plantation fashion of distinguishing among the Rockefeller brothers in Room 5600 at Rockefeller Center—for the first time when he came to one of my public lectures, in March of 1974, at Synod House in the Close of the Cathedral of St. John the Divine in New York. He liked my lecture and invited me to lunch with him and Jean Lanier the following week at a small restaurant on the Upper East Side, and there he invited me to serve on his brother Nelson's "Critical Choices Commission" for Nelson's run for the presidency. When I declined, and explained that basic to my philosophy with Lindisfarne was the necessity for the separation of cultural authority from political power, he was pleasantly surprised. He seemed to be taking it for granted that those who rise in the career open to talents—men such as Harvard's Henry Kissinger or Columbia's Zbigniew Brzezinski—reach a point where they are invited to switch from the academic to the governing class, and usually jump for it. When we had lunch together again in 1978—this time by ourselves atop Rockefeller Center—I was afraid to ask outright for the hundreds of thousands of dollars it would have taken to sustain Lindisfarne-in-Manhattan. I found it difficult to be direct with Laurance because he spoke about various people and projects in an indirect and eliptical manner that always baffled me. Over the years, and in no small measure because of Laurance's firm corrections, I began to understand that I was too brusque and candid in intellectually criticizing others, and just too blunt for the social norms of his class. Since I never really had a father present during my adolescence to teach me how the social world worked, I thought I could just study, work hard, and get ahead. But in Laurance's class, there is a whole set of unspoken rules and inbred manners that one learns from one's parents and that become reinforced in prep school and Ivy League universities. In this social world, I was completely lost. But, unfortunately for Lindisfarne, this world is the world of fund-raising for schools, institutes, museums, universities, and charities.

Laurance Rockefeller at the construction site of
the Lindisfarne Chapel in Crestone, Colorado

Gregory Bateson also came from a privileged class, but he spent most of his life trying to escape that world, and for Gregory, unlike many of his British compatriots, intelligence always trumped class, so I could relax in his presence and enjoy the philosophical banter. In fact, Gregory's arrival to live at the Lindisfarne Association as its scholar-in-residence in 1977 marked a turning point in my own development. At the beginning of Lindisfarne in Southampton in 1973, I was very much under the influence of the spiritual communities of Findhorn in Scotland and Auroville in India. Auroville was full of youthful energy, redolent of the French utopian socialism of the nineteenth century, and full of a twentieth century's concern for ecological thinking, so I tried to set up a network of cultural exchange in which people from Arcosanti, San Francisco Zen Center, Auroville, the Research Foundation for Eastern Wisdom and Western Science in Starnberg, Germany, and Findhorn in Scotland could come to Lindisfarne. But the only connections that really took hold were with Zen Center and Findhorn. Because I did not wish to turn Lindisfarne into a spiritual ashram with me as its guru or central personality, I made myself emotionally unavailable to followers, and this frustrated the majority of the people living in the community precisely because they had dropped out of school in search of more personally sustaining forms of knowledge. Consequently our community members often tried to make David Spangler into their guru; indeed at that time, David became my own councilor and confessor, but he steadfastly resisted becoming a guru for the community. Frustrated, some turned to the charismatic Richard Baker-roshi as the abbot people were looking for and missing in me, and Baker-roshi sent his senior monks from the San Francisco Zen Center, Dan Welch and Reb Anderson, to serve as our first contemplatives in residence and teaching fellows. But along with this process of positive projection onto David Spangler or Baker-roshi also came a negative oedipal psychodynamic, and I served as the screen for the comnunity's resentments. Intentional communities tend to attract people from failed or broken families who come to community in pain and in search of a second chance with another kind of family. Since they were all entirely dependent upon my fund-raising abilities to sustain our household, I became the shadow parental figure. Because I was not comfortable being admired, or lovingly caring for a garden of followers, I tended to give an unconscious energy to the community members' psychological attacks, as these were useful in proving that Lindisfarne was democratic and not hierarchical like Paolo Soleri's Arcosanti or Steve Gaskin's The Farm. So when Gregory Bateson came to live with us, this articulator of the double-bind was the perfect anthropologist to begin the process of my shifting Lindisfarne away from the emotional swamp of utopian community to the brighter air of a scientific circle working to articulate a new planetary culture.

I had discovered Gregory's *Naven* in the stacks of Honnold Library at Pomona College when I was doing my research for my senior honors thesis. My teachers at Pomona were still working on the difference between Wittgenstein and the Vienna circle, and no one there knew enough to point me in the direction of cybernetics, the Macy Conferences, and the birth of what we would now call complex dynamical systems. Furthermore, no one on the faculty at Pomona knew enough to point me in the direction of Vico when I rediscovered the wheel of the Viconian cycle. As I articulated the isomorphic processes in the cultural progression of archaic Greek statuary, Mayan architecture, and English poetry, no one there was familiar with Jean Gebser's first articulation of cultural phenomenology in the nineteen-forties. But at least Pomona, in the spirit of a good liberal arts college, did allow me to write a thesis on my own philosophy of history instead of insisting that I do a study of a single author or a single text.

When I read Varela's paper on non-dualism, "Not One, Not Two," in *The Whole Earth Quarterly*, I knew that I wanted Varela to succeed Bateson as our second scholar-in-residence for our new facility of Lindisfarne-in-Manhattan. Varela's non-dualism seemed to get at the heart of my discomfort with Gregory's dualism of object and information, *pleroma* and *creatura*, mind and nature. And where I looked to Whitehead for help in thinking my way out of what Whitehead called "the bifurcation of nature," Varela looked to Nagarjuna and Indian Buddhist Madhyamika philosophy, and appeared to be working on a synthesis of philosophies East and West that was highly appropriate for Lindisfarne's mission to articulate a new planetary culture. At the time Varela published, "Not One, Not Two," he was finishing the work on his book *Principles of Biological Autonomy*, so with his residency at Lindisfarne we were taking a big step forward in the emergence of the new mentality, or what I would now call the shift from the linear causal systems of the Galilean Dynamical Mentality to the Complex Dynamical Mentality—a mentality ushered in by Poincaré in Paris in 1889.[3]

In the universities at this time modernism—like a comet breaking up into a shower of smaller meteorites—was breaking up into postmodernism. The "Big Narratives," as Francois Lyotard had argued—of Darwin, Marx, and Freud—were breaking up into *les pétits récits* of Richard Dawkins, Michel Foucault, and Jacques Lacan. The reductionism of linear causality was being replaced by a decentered system of Jacques Derrida's *différance* and Paul De Man's deconstructionism. In Gebser's terms, I would classify this as the

107

deficient mode of the dying Mental structure and not the efficient mode of the emerging Integral structure. While my former graduate school classmate from Cornell, Gayatri Spivak, was leading the charge for deconstructionism uptown at Columbia, I was downtown at Lindisfarne in Chelsea working to articulate the new Integral mentality.

Because I came to Lindisfarne out of a university background at Cornell, MIT, and York University, I kept looking back to the academic community for recognition, but its entering into the era of postmodernism and deconstructionism insured that it would never accept anything I was trying to do. I suppose because universities are owned and operated by big business and big sports, the faculty in the humanities are alienated from this success culture of Winners and locked into a mood of anger and resentment in their unending cold war of Marxism versus capitalism. Stalinism can be discredited, the Berlin Wall can fall, and the Soviet Union can disintegrate, but academics in the humanities—like Jehovah Witnesses waiting for the End of the World—simply cannot let go of their Marxist materialist world view; they simply move from Marxism to postmarxism and just keep on trucking from postmodernism to the New Historicism. It was a complete waste of time for me to look to academe for the constituency of Lindisfarne.

Ironically, it was Hollywood and the business community that appropriated the whole New Age movement and found out how to make millions out of it. I simply entered the market too early with Lindisfarne in the Hamptons. Like Kaiser's *Henry J* small car, introduced in the late forties, that failed, and then was succeeded by the Volkswagen beetle, my meta-academic center with lectures on holistic health, meditation, yoga, Tai Chi, Sufi drumming, and new paradigm science was too soon and too cheap. Had we ignored students and academic drop-outs and addressed ourselves to professionals in search of an interesting weekend in the Hamptons, and charged five times as much as we did, we would not have lost Fish Cove but would have been the Next New Thing for the seventies and on into the eighties, but I simply didn't have the heart, or the stomach, for that kind of market-driven popular cultural activity.

As modernism was disintegrating into numerous postmodernisms in the university, a small intellectual elite was at work on articulating the new Integral mentality, but a greater number of people in the counterculture were at work trying to culturally retrieve the premodernist world-view that had been obsolesced by modernism at the beginning of our era. As Marshall McLuhan pointed out in his *Laws of Media*[4], when a new medium comes in, it obsolesces the dominant medium and culturally retrieves the previously obsolesced medium. At Lindisfarne-in-Manhattan, we worked to effect the shift from the Mental to the Integral, and, at the same time, we worked to retrieve the premodern in a fanciful "return to nature." In one part of the program, we had Bateson and Varela, and the shift to complex dynamical systems, but at the other pole we had courses on the Western Esoteric tradition, the Cabbalah, medieval sacred geometry and architecture.

To sustain our program of classes and public lectures, to man the doors, take tickets, and clean the streets of all the litter of a single downtown day, our resident urban commune of 24 people had to work as our support staff in exchange for their room in the facility and a small stipend. In the spirit of democracy, I took the same stipend and shared in the communal labor.

The non-resident members and students of Lindisfarne who lived in Manhattan had jobs and independent lives, were interested in Lindisfarne's program and responded enthusiastically, but their tuition for courses only made up 13% of our budget. They, for the most part, disliked the resident commune. The commune returned the favor, as many of them hated living in the city and wanted to be living a crunchy granola way of life in the country. Lindisfarne was psychically split down the middle and was simply unsustainable, both psychologically and economically. When I received the 28th rejection for funds to restore the buildings, I knew I would have to give up. Ironically, after we left, a Canadian millionaire acquired the four buildings and spent millions to turn the church into the hot disco, *Limelight*. By then the seven year cycle of the seventies' idealistic counterculture was over and the Reagan anti-environmental eighties were on their way, fifties' materialism was back in, and the hippie became a yuppie as the new pattern of drug abuse became, not looking for God with LSD, but searching for pleasurable contacts with cocaine and ecstasy. It was definitely not a time to hang on, waiting for Lindisfarne to be appreciated.

When Lindisfarne-in-Manhattan did disband in 1979, it dispersed in three groups. Beatrice and I accepted Maurice and Hanne Strong's invitation to establish Lindisfarne as a retreat and conference center in Crestone, Colorado. Christopher Bamford, Dian Woodner Bamford, Will Marsh, and Dana Cummings moved to the Berkshires to expand the series of Lindisfarne Books I had established with Harper and Row into an independent small publishing venture, The Lindisfarne Press. And Michael Katz and Nina Hagen, and the O'Shea family moved to the San Francisco Zen Center to continue studying with Baker-roshi and Reb Anderson. To help develop our relation with Zen Center, we also made a donation to the San Francisco Zen Center from funds Lindisfarne had received amounting to $32,000 to buy a facility outside the city to serve as our conference center. I had looked at the Bob Dylan House in Woodstock, as well as other houses upstate in Cooperstown, but these funds were not sufficient for a down payment and mortgage payments, so we donated the funds to Zen Center toward building a guest house for their Green Gulch conference center, where we hoped to hold our future Fellows meetings. Baker-roshi was able to raise other matching funds and the Lindisfarne Guest House is still there as part of Zen Center's Green Gulch farm.

Lindisfarne Guest House, Green Gulch Farm, San Francisco Zen Center

From 1976 to 1979, Lindisfarne in Manhattan sustained a non-stop concert of ideas, artistic expressions, and a political vision that was neither red nor blue, but green a good seven years before the Greens in Germany tried to articulate the third way between socialism and capitalism. In designing our 1978 Lindisfarne Fellows Conference on "The Cultural Contradictions of Power," which took place in Manhattan and not Southampton, I tried to challenge Stewart Brand's eager desire to serve as a countercultural Brzezinski in Jerry Brown's campaign for the presidency by casting all our shadows into the light. To me, it seemed as if the counterculture was becoming the over-the-counter culture. In this outrightly political conference, Hazel Henderson, Wendell Berry, and Francisco Varela challenged Howard T. Odum's engineering approach to the environment and biological systems, Robert Thurman gave a talk on "The Politics of Enlightenment," and Sim Van der Ryn spoke of the difficulties of being a green State Architect for California. But I need not have worried about our gang becoming corrupted in the move from *mystique* to *politique*, for the Governor of California who was going to become President was Ronald Reagan and not Jerry Brown.

Robert Thurman after his talk in the Parish Hall, Fellows Meeting 1978

But to initiate an energy in a culture is not the same thing as institutionalizing it. Ralph White came from Findhorn in Scotland to visit Lindisfarne-in-Manhattan, and he always credited us with being the precursors for what he set up after us as The Open Center in Soho. The metaphor I often used was that Lindisfarne was the crocus announcing a change of season, but not the tree that would bear fruit for the autumn of another season.

Sim Van der Ryn, Lindisfarne Fellows Conference 1978

My Andy Warhol fifteen minutes of fame that had enabled me to establish Lindisfarne actually lasted for seven years—from the interview with me in *Time* magazine in 1972 to the *Bill Moyers' Journal* television program in 1979. This PBS program aired in March, but by then it was too late to do Lindisfarne any good, and the public response only confirmed me in my distaste for a celebrity life in America. The program was repeated about five times around the country, I got hundreds of letters, some of them absolutely crazy, and some full of hate or a desire to convert me to their sect. To be a public figure in America—be it politician, rock star, or famous writer—you obviously had to be rich enough not just to have personal assistants but your own personal Secret Service.

There was simply no such thing as an authentic intellectual in the new Technetronic America. You were either a figure of power like Kissinger or Brzezinski, or an egomaniac and TV celebrity hungry for media canonization. The era of my childhood in which cultural figures such as Thomas Mann or William Faulkner could be writers and concentrate on their work was gone. Two experiences at that time confirmed my contact dermatitis to fame and my disgust at the vulgarity it took to survive in book tour America.

The first was on a lecture in Ohio. I had finished my talk and was walking out when a young woman came up to me, jammed a microphone into my face and said:

"I didn't hear your lecture, and I haven't read any of your books, but give me the gist of your message for our radio station." She assumed, as did many working in the media, that she was doing me a favor to take notice of me, and that like any salesman on the road, I should have a pitch ready that could be compressed into a soundbite or two.

I refused to give her the interview, but I thought of her again when a man from Stockholm interviewed me a few months later in Greenwich Village for Swedish radio. He had read several of my books and actually asked me questions that had to do with ideas and philosophy, and not with my favorite flavor of ice cream or the kind of pop music I liked.

The second experience came when I was packing up at Lindisfarne-in-Manhattan and preparing to move out. When the doorbell rang, I thought it was one of our shippers, but I was met by a middle aged woman with what looked to be her teenage daughter. When she saw me, the mother screamed in delight like an aging Beatles fan: "Oh! It's you! I brought my daughter to meet you! I saw you on the *Bill Moyer's Journal*."

I tried to be polite, as this woman was not rude and insulting, even if she was overenthusiastic. She went on in a torrent of questions that had nothing to do with books, ideas, or anything else I had discussed with Bill Moyers. Finally, after going on at length, even she realized it was time to go, so she thanked me for taking the time with her, and as she turned, she looked back at me and said:

"Oh, by the way, what was your name again?"

As I closed the door, I smiled to myself as I realized that the interview must have lasted sixteen minutes because my Warholian fifteen minutes of fame had obviously expired while we were talking.

Now when I visit the old neighborhood in Chelsea, I do find myself fantasizing what it would have been like if I had been able to raise the funds to restore the church and effect a shift for Lindisfarne from what Joan Halifax calls "the volunteerany" of a commune to a professionally hired and competent staff. In the gritty and dark culture of New York in the seventies, the neighborhood was filthy with garbage and litter, we had several break-ins, and one student was raped going home after a lecture. Now the neighborhood has been completely transformed. Cambridge University Press is directly across the street, along with several other academic publishers, a block-long Barnes and Noble bookstore is on Sixth Avenue, Armani is around the corner on Fifth Avenue, and scores of art galleries are scattered throughout Chelsea. In keeping with the hypercapitalism of the new century, the old church has been transformed into a minimall of boutiques.

Once again, as with a New Age intellectual spa in the Hamptons in 1973, I was too early in articulating cultural trends and too unskilled and uninterested in the business of generating wealth to be a real American. I was just too full of a working class kid's naïve fantasies of wanting to grow up to be an authentic European intellectual to know how to survive as an intellectual in Baudrillard's simulacrum of *Amérique*.[5]

---

[1] Humberto Maturana and Francisco J. Varela, Autopoiesis and Cognition: the realization of the living (Dordrecht, Holland ; Boston : D. Reidel Pub. Co., 1980.).

[2] See Arthur I. Miller, *"How Picasso Discovered Les Demoiselles d'Avignon"* in *Einstein, Picasso: Space, Time, and the Beauty That Creates Havoc* (New York: Basic Books, 2001), 85-127.

[3] See W. I. Thompson, "Literary and Archetypal Mathematical Mentalities in the Evolution of Culture" in *Self and Society: Studies in the Evolution of Culture* (Exeter, UK: Academic Imprint, 2004).

[4] Marshall and Eric McLuhan, *The Laws of Media* (Toronto; University of Toronto Press, 1988), p. 7.

[5] See Jean Baudrillard, *Amérique* (Paris: Grasset, 1986).
For Tapes and on-line audio recordings of the Lindisfarne Conferences in Southampton and Manhattan, New York, consult the website:
http://centerforneweconomics.org/content/lindisfarne-tapes?utm_source=Schuma cher+Center+eNewsletter&utm_campaign=961219d1f1-Lindisfarne7_5_2013&utm_ medium=email&utm_term=0_aefb5a81d7-961219d1f1-70175241

Chapter 7: Lindisfarne
in Crestone, Colorado, 1979-2007

Maurice Strong and I in his backyard of the Baca Ranch at the
1979 Lindisfarne Fellows Conference on the Solar Village for Crestone

Two very strong experiences at Lindisfarne in Southampton determined my goals for the establishment of a new retreat and conference center for Lindisfarne in the Sangre de Cristo Mountains of southern Colorado. Both occurred at our bicentennial conference of 1976, "A Light Governance for America." The first experience occurred in the small meditation room in the Lodge during the conference, the second occurred in our conference meeting room.

The "planetization of the esoteric" had been one of my founding goals in establishing the Lindisfarne Association. I wished to bring the esoteric knowledge and meditational practices of Yoga, Sufi'sm, Cabbalah, and Buddhism together as seeds with which to back-propagate a new kind of post-religious Christianity in association with a new and more participatory kind of Pythagorean science.

Maribeth Bunn, Evan Thompson, Christopher Bamford,
Thomas Banyaca of the Hopi, and Janet McCloud of the Seattle Indians 1976

My inspiring philosopher for this Integral Science had been my teenage hero, A. N. Whitehead, whom I had read intently in the year I was recuperating from extensive surgery for cancer of the thyroid. Along my way in life I had also picked up new insights as I encountered the Hindu-Christian syncretism of Paramhansa Yogananda, the Integral Yoga of Sri Aurobindo, and the esoteric Christianity of Rudolf Steiner, and, finally, my own contemporary

David Spangler. As the guest speakers of our 1976 conference gathered in a meditation room that was too small for our numbers, I knew I would have to design an architectural form that would be appropriate both for our numbers and our new intention.

As we sat on the zafus and zabutons we had purchased from our colleagues at the San Francisco Zen Center, I looked around the room and felt a deep sense of satisfaction that we were coming closer to what I really wanted for Lindisfarne: not an intentional community collectively working out the neuroses we had acquired in the sad family histories of our personal lives, but a cultural vessel, a grail, if you will, for a new world manifestation. In this small room there was Nechung Rinpoche and Gomeyn Keyn Rinpoche from Tibet, Eido-roshi from Japan, Baker-roshi from California, Thomas Banyaca from the Hopi Nation, Janet McCloud from the Seattle Indians, the Episcopal Bishop Chandler Sterling, Rabbi Herb Weiner, and the Catholic Cistercian priest, Father Basil Pennington.

W. I. Thompson, Nechung Rinpoche, Robert Thurman, and Michael Katz 1976

But as we sat down to settle into the thick silence that often descended on us like a bell jar that served to take out all the pressure and pollution so that we could create a perfect vacuum in which to feel the presence of the infinitesimal as well as the infinite, I was startled as Eido roshi stood up in his robes, moved to the low plank that served as a simple altar, lit a stick of incense, picked up a small Japanese hand bell, and began to chant in Japanese.

Eido-roshi simply could not resist the temptation of priestcraft to try to own the experience for his tradition. I found this to be completely inappropriate. Why Eido-roshi and not Nechung-Rinpoche, or Rabbi Weiner, or Janet McCloud? Would we have to go around the room in some absurd democratic gesture to allow every tradition present to play with its bells and whistles to say, in effect, that my tradition is bigger than yours. Besides, all that ritual theatre would simply postpone the real experience of the thickening of the silence. Instead of creating a post-religious epiphany, I was creating the space for a religious Donnybrook—which, in case you are not Irish, is the place the tinkers get together, get drunk, and brawl.

As Eido-roshi finished his little theatre piece of religious appropriation, I looked around the room again and realized it was my fault as creator of the space. I had brought into the room religious artifacts that I had acquired as I had traveled around the world. So there was a copper flask of Ganges water I purchased in Varanasi, a Buddha from Thailand, a Japanese handbell from Kyoto, a page from the Koran from Turkey that I had bought in London, and a large Eye of God from Toluca, Mexico. Instead of the fullness of a radical Emptiness, I had filled the space with the noise of sixties religious kitsch. Clearly, I would have to design a new form, a Lindisfarne Chapel, that could serve as the vessel for this new post-religious epiphany of the sacred.

When we finally did get on with the silent meditation, the ineffable did manifest, palpably. In the Christian tradition, there is the phrase that served as the foundational idea for the Church: "Where two or three are gathered together in my name, there am I in the midst of them." In our daily group meditations, this sense of the thickening of the silence in which a presence filled the room became evident to us all, and it actually made it easier for us to live together and tended to tone down the noise of personality conflicts —although these never went away entirely. Even my son Evan, who was about twelve encountered this presence, though he did not describe the experience in Christian terms, as I had not raised him in the Catholic Church of my own childhood. He sat with us for the usual forty minute sitting, and then when the bell was rung at the end of the session, we all filed out, but Evan remained sitting, and he stayed there for almost another hour. When I talked to him about why he had remained in the room, he said: "Oh, I heard the bell at the end of the sitting, but it was like it was at the end of the horizon and was the least interesting thing going on."

Evan preparing the fertilizer in early spring for the organic garden

Evan has always been more interested in Taoism and Buddhism, both in its Tibetan and Sri Lankan Vipassana traditions, and this childhood experience of the absorptive state of *samadhi* was how he experienced this kind of group meditation. Each person experienced it in his or her own way, and I tried not to put forth any religious language that would over-determine it. In some cases, I could tell with certain individuals—from their body language—that meditation was for them an impossibly foreign experience and that they simply could not settle down and in, but that their minds seemed to race with inner dialogue and a fidgeting impatience for the period to end. For this sort of person, the exoteric physical activity of ritual—like the language of prayer and the up and down movements of the Catholic Mass or the Protestant singing of hymns—is their preferred approach to the presence of the sacred that connects the part to the Whole.

The second experience that came out of this 1976 Lindisfarne Conference was an exchange of their traditional prophecies for the end of our world-cycle between the two Tibetan rinpoches, Nechung and Gomeyn Keyn, and the Hopi spokesperson, Thomas Banyaca. These two Gelupa lamas, with Professor Robert Thurman present as their translator, were basically passing on the shamanic transmissions of the Gelpua Oracle of Tibet, and Thomas Banyaca was passing on the Kachina transmissions of his tribal Elders. The "planetization of the esoteric" that I had hoped for in setting up Lindisfarne as an "Association" had indeed taken place.

Thomas Banyaca, Spokesman for the Hopi Elders, W. I. Thompson,
Bob Thurman, Nechung-rinpoche, Philip Henley.

A similar goal had always been at the heart of Hanne Marstrand Strong's attraction to Tibetan Buddhism and native American traditions. Hanne first met with the Hopi and their Spokesman Thomas Banyaca in 1972. I met with White Bear Fredericks, the co-author with Frank Waters of *The Book of the Hopi,* on the Hopi lands in 1971, so we both were being drawn to the sacred mountains of the Southwest in the same period of cultural transformation. When her husband Maurice Strong acquired the Luis Maria Baca Grant Ranch in the San Luis Valley in southern, Colorado, she knew as she felt the spirit of Mount Blanca, one of the four sacred mountains of the West for the Hopi that she wanted to create there a place of refuge where all the sacred traditions of the world could come together at a time of their prophesied earth changes.

Hanne and Maurice Strong at the Baca Grant Ranch

W. I. Thompson, John Todd, Jack Dempsey, Crestone Mountain Guide, and
Maurice Strong at the Baca Grant Ranch when I chose the land for Lindisfarne
1979

Hanne Strong and W. I. Thompsonon land to the south in sight of the Sand Dunes and Mount Blanca, closer to Deadman Creek. The land I finally chose for Lindisfarne was on Spanish Creek, but still within sight of Mount Blanca and the Great National Sand Dunes. 1979

My path crossed with the Strongs even before we met. After Maurice acquired the controlling interest in the AZL Corporation in Phoenix, he toured the Southwest to take inventory of its real estate holdings, among which were the Angel Fire ski resort in Taos and the Baca Grande subdivision in Crestone, Colorado. On this tour, Hanne attended a meeting of the Hopi Elders in Arizona. The traditionalists of "the Hopi Nation" were seeking more autonomy from the U.S. Government, which was always willing to sell out Hopi cultural interests to the Peabody Coal Company in the hopes of "economically developing" and modernizing the world-view of the Hopi community. The traditionalist Elders knew that Maurice Strong, through his position as an Under-Secretary responsible for founding the United Nations Environmental Program (UNEP) had also been instrumental in securing recognition of the Kingdom of Bhutan as a nation by the U.N. so as to protect it from being taken over by communist China after the manner of their violent conquest of Tibet. The Elders felt that if Maurice could help the Hopi with their presentations to the U.N., then their culture too could be saved. As Hanne entered the room where the Elders were seated around a table, she saw that each participant was given a xerox of a three page interview with me in *Time* magazine from August 21, 1972. In this interview, I had mentioned the Hopi and their cosmology. Then, when Hanne and Maurice returned to New York, they had lunch with Professor Saul Mendlovitz of the Institute for World Order, and as they discussed both Buddhism and ecology, Maurice asked Saul how he had come upon this mix of the two subjects, and Saul answered, "at the Lindisfarne meetings." When the word "Lindisfarne" kept popping up as Hanne and Maurice moved around New York—from the interview with me on the *Bill Moyers Journal*, to meetings at the Rockefeller Brothers Fund or with Curtiss Roosevelt at the U.N.—they decided that I might be the right person to help them transform Crestone, Colorado from a failed and tacky suburban real estate development to a cultural center. If I were to hold my Lindisfarne meetings in Crestone, then Lindisfarne could be the string in the liquid salt solution that could serve to crystallize something more substantial for Crestone than the failed Baca Grande Phoenix-style subdivision. And, in fact, Lindisfarne did just that.

Our paths finally came together personally when Maurice and I were invited to speak at a solar village conference organized by John and Nancy Todd of the New Alchemy Institute and funded by a grant from the U.S. Department of Energy. I was asked to give the opening address for this conference and spoke on the need for meta-industrial villages in which we could miniaturize technology in order to scale nature up and scale down our physical impact on the environment.[1] After my talk, Maurice and Hanne took me aside, and Maurice said: "Lindisfarne is looking for land, well, I have a 150,000 acre ranch in Colorado. Come and choose the land you need for Lindisfarne." Thus began a new and more cultural future in Crestone that still continues to this day.

Mary Catherine Bateson and W. I. Thompson
looking over the land in 1979

John Todd, Mary Catherine Bateson, and I flew out to Colorado with Maurice, and Maurice and Hanne drove us from one end of their ranch to the other. John and Mary Catherine were Lindisfarne Fellows and also served on our board of directors, but they very graciously allowed me to choose the land in my own way using what I jokingly referred to as "my Druid Radar." I chose 80 acres on a shelf overlooking the valley at an altitude of 8000 feet that bordered on the all-year flowing stream of Spanish Creek. Behind us was a magnificent Chinese-looking peak with a dragon face that appeared when the angle of the sun and the shadows of the rock were just right. And behind this peak, the spectacular escarpment of the Needles and Kit Karson carried on up to an altitude of 14, 300 feet. To the south, one had the horizon of Mt. Blanca and the Great National Sand Dunes, to the west a view of the entire San Luis Valley and the Continental Divide of the San Juan Mountains, and to the north, a clear view of the next valley with its fourteeners of Mt. Princeton and the Ivy League range. One could see for 100 miles in three directions, and the backyard just went on up into the sky.

Choosing the site for the Lindisfarne Chapel

View to the South showing Mount Blanca, Sand Dunes, and New Mexico

View to the West across the San Luis Valley
to the San Juan Mountains and the Continental Divide

View to the North and Poncha Springs Pass

Sangre de Cristo Mountain Range turning red at sunset

To build in the wilderness was, of course, another matter. On the human level, there was nothing there, so roads, water, energy, and materials would all have to be brought in before we could set to work. I chose the land in May and Beatrice and I moved to the Ranch at the beginning of July of 1979 in time for our son Andrew's first birthday. Through the generosity of Maurice, Beatrice, Andrew, and I were moved from New York and were given an attractive little ranch house that had been the home of the previous assistant manager of the Luis Maria Baca Grant Ranch. It shared the backyard with the house that had been the home of the ranch's Manager and now served as the Crestone home and headquarters for Hanne and Maurice.

The house was in the flatlands of the valley and looked up at the entire range of the Sangre. To make sure that Lindisfarne would not simply sell the property and head back to Manhattan, the terms of our donation from Maurice's AZL corporation required that we had to carry on with an educational program for three years before the land was owned outright by Lindisfarne. So Beatrice and I set to work together in a partnership in which I organized the programs for the conferences and summer schools, and she managed the office, kept the books, and served as innkeeper to arrange the accommodations for the students and the often demanding Diva-like teachers. And to secure a senior water right on Spanish Creek—which in the Southwest is often as valuable as the land itself—I haggled with AZL's lawyers for the whole three-year probationary period of the foundation of the Lindisfarne Mountain Retreat.

Beatrice and Andrew in the yard of the ranch house
with the Sangre de Cristo Mountains in background, 1979

The next step in the development of the Batesonian "pattern that connects" Mind to Nature was to extend Lindisfarne's interest in biology to architecture and ecology in a conference on solar architecture to decide upon the design for Lindisfarne in Crestone. I set to work on the project by organizing a conference with the leading architects of the alternative movement to choose among them who was to build the Lindisfarne Fellows House. I invited a whole leonine pride of solar energy architects to come to Crestone to offer their designs for ways in which Lindisfarne could dwell appropriately in that place.

1979 Crestone Fellows Conference Nancy Todd, John Todd, Stewart Brand, Franicsco Varela, Paul Winter, Hazel Henderson.

1979 Brother David, Sara Raine, Evelyn Ames, Paul Winter, Michael Murphy

Dean James Morton officiating with Red Ute and Al Wong at the very syncretic marriage rite of Hunter Sheldon and Amory Lovins in an aspen grove, Lindisfarne Fellows Conference, 1979,

1979 Fellows Conference, Hunter Lovins, Amory Lovins,
John Todd, and Hanne Strong

It was in a series of lectures at Lindisfarne-in-Manhattan that became my 1978 book, *Darkness and Scattered Light: Four Talks on the Future*, that I first outlined the concept of "the meta-industrial village," so Crestone in 1979 became an opportunity to embody this philosophy of using electronics to miniaturize industrial technology so that nature could be scaled up at the same time that industrial hardware was scaled down or completely made invisible. (This was, of course, before personal computers and the Internet and their enormous energy consumption for climate-controlling the servers.) In my opening talk to the architects I proposed that every structure—as well as every social organization—casts a shadow; so instead of waiting for the process of time to reveal that shadow in space, —the *enantiodromia* that turned an institution into the opposite of its founding vision that I had discussed in *Evil and World Order*—good design should accelerate the cultural process by making the shadow an integral part of the structure from the very beginning. In essence, I was responding to John Todd's concept of "Living Machines" by seeking to extend it into a realm of cultural phenomenology and not just bacteriology. Whatever the structure produced in terms of pollution should be made part of its metabolic structure from the start. A truly "green architecture" should be a symbiotic architecture of energy-production and pollution-consumption. Obviously, we are still decades away from being able to achieve such a goal, but in places like Cape Cod, Crestone, and Biosphere II in Oracle, Arizona, people were beginning to take the first steps in this direction. At the end of the conference, I chose Sim Van der Ryn, professor of architecture at U.C. Berkeley, because he was willing to work with the land and me as the client to come up with a design that worked for all three of us.[2]

I insisted that the building be earth-bermed into the land and built of rocks from the site, and Sim chose a passive solar design with sod roof, and the builder Michael Ogden from Findhorn chose large spruce beams from local trees that had been killed by a recent beetle infestation. My wife Beatrice and I designed the kitchen, because we both had experience in cooking for large groups of people. And I designed the large living room so that it could serve for intimate living room conferences that yet could accommodate up to eighty or ninety people.

Sim Van der Ryn, now Dean of Green Architecture in the USA
(photos: Nina Hagen at the 2011 Lindisfarne Fellows Conference)

As I talked to Sim Van der Ryn about the kind of design I wanted for Lindisfarne there, we sat on a beautiful large flat rock with colorful striations that one can still see there today between the garden and the green house. As I explained to Sim why I wanted the elemental force of the stones from the site as the muscular tissue of the house itself, he took out his watercolor set and began to do a painting of the site that he could take back with him to his office in California. Doing a watercolor was Sim's artistic way of attuning to the site before making his first sketch of the building. Watching Sim paint, I felt confirmed in my choice of him as the architect for the project. I contrasted the imagined Lindisfarne Fellows House with the Earth Sciences Building by I. M. Pei that I used to look at out of the window of my office at MIT. This building is a container that is imposed monumentally on the site as a kind of colossus that expresses technology's domination over nature. Strangely for a Chinese architect, Pei forgot about the wind. *Feng-sui* in Chinese means wind and water. But this building by the waters of the Charles River forgot the wind as it arose on its two legs through which the wind funneled with such force that the secretaries had not the strength to open the doors to go to work. I guess in revenge for the architect's locking nature out, the wind locked the people out. As Pei went from this commission to do the John Hancock building on the Boston's side of the Charles, the wind did not let up on him, and for months the wind was popping out the windows of this glass tower and hurtling them to the streets below. For Crestone, I wanted the mirror-opposite of this approach: not a transcendental celebration of technology, but an immanental form that participated with the landscape.

As a thought-experiment, let us consider what Lindisfarne would have looked like had it achieved all its goals. If one took the evolution of consciousness curriculum that I later designed for the Ross School in East Hampton, New York and put it together with a traditional American liberal arts college—only this college would have symbiotic architecture rather than educational Gothic—you would have the kind of educational community I had in mind in 1979. If one adds to the educational economy, a vision of spin-off products and services that could generate income to sustain the educational investments, then you would come up with a more romantic vision of a meta-industrial economy that was appearing right at the time the mega-industrial economy was about to take over America with its Silicon Valleys and dot.com start-ups, or its MIT East Cambridge explosion of Genentech industries.

FROM THE MENTAL TO THE INTEGRAL:
Retrieval of Samadhi, Mythic Correspondent States, & Gnosis in Symbiotic Consciousness in Shift from *Wissenschaft* to *Wissenskunst*

- **MIT, Earth Sciences**
- **Valued State: Domination**

- Lindisfarne Fellows House: Enlightened Participation

I. M. Pei's Earth Sciences Building at MIT with the Calder Stabile

But there was a shadow to our social group itself. Looking at Lindisfarne, Arcosanti, the Rocky Mountain Institute with Amory and Hunter Lovins, or the Meadowcreek project with the Orr brothers, our shadow was intellectual feudalism. We had turned on the spiral in McLuhan's process of cultural retrieval and reanimated the Manor of the Laird and the crofters. But America, under Reagan, was going in the opposite direction of neomedievalism and was about to play a game of industrial chicken with the Soviet Union. Through tax cuts, massive defense spending, and huge deficits, America was going to go mega and prove to the Russians that their economy would collapse before ours would.

Think back on the time of Queen Elizabeth when she used Francis Drake's piracy to negate the power of the land barons and through a combination of world trade, crime, war, and a secret government with its secret police, she created the centralized state. Both the English and the Dutch were forging the iron and carbon of capitalism and war to create the hard steel of the modern nation-state.

As FDR proved again in World War II, a modern economy needs an enemy to inspire and sustain it. The triple circulation of capitalism, war, and organized crime as the "Deep State" of secret government was the heart, lungs, and brain of the new American body-politic.[3] And until we have a scientific economy that does not require an enemy to sustain it, we will not be able to move forward. James Lovelock has suggested that the "Greening of Mars"–in which we build up slowly the planet's cyanobacterial foundation for life–could be such a project. A meta-industrial village of symbiotic cultural-ecologies of life was not possible in the pickup truck and parking lot culture of drive-in religious centers of Crestone during my life-time, but as the contradictions of global capitalism continue to play themselves out, there is no way of telling how climate collapse will affect the little and the large of the biomes and the biosphere.

If I had called for the shadow to be part of the design structure from the very beginning, I was absolutely trumped by Reagan, Bush Sr., Cheney, Rumsfeld and Company whose shadow cartels and "Deep State" invisible government formed a kind of capitalist al Qaeda. The Republicans had mastered the Italian Renaissance art of turning government into organized crime, and then recycling it for public consumption as an evangelizing civic religion. That Cheney Rumsfeld Bush and Company and al Qaeda—as mirror-images of one another—should now divide the world between them spoke volumes about how the world of the modern middle class democratic nation-state had come to an end.

The essence of the Republican strategy was to energize the shadow-structure of the unconscious through a fierce denial of its existence. Bush always spoke of the exact opposite of his intentions, so clear-cutting was called forest management, the destruction of social welfare was called the implementation of faith-based charities, the elimination of Social Security was called insurance privatization, and the hostile take-over of an uncooperative Halliburton business partner like Saddam Hussein was called the freeing of Iraq. Journalists, afraid to lose their White House Press Cards, became palace eunuchs to the Emperor and were easily co-opted into this system of governance by consensual delusion and chose never to disturb this arrangement by asking a real question. Since the media were owned by Bush's business partners, the co-operation of the journalistic eunuchs was guaranteed, if they wished to continue to work in the palace of the White House.

In 1972, I had talked about "planetary culture" in a more positive sense, and in this intuitive feeling I was coeval with other expressions such as James Lovelock's first paper on Gaia or Tarkovsky's film, *Solaris*; but we Americans missed our chance in the seventies, and succumbing to the propagandistic manipulations of Reagan and the Bushes, we failed imaginatively to create our destiny, and so now we are having our fate more literally inflicted upon us.

It is fair to say that in the seventies I was a hopeless romantic, as long as one also realizes that the Romantic poets can teach us more about the complete phenomenology of the Industrial Revolution than could the elected members of Parliament at the time.

The 1979 Lindisfarne conference expressed the movement outward from the Batesonian ecologies of mind to ecological design. Once we had finished the Lindisfarne Fellows House in 1982, we invited the Fellows inside for a large conference—around 100 people—concerned with the theme of the land and the politics of ecology.

Maurice Strong and Hazel Henderson, Fellows Conference, 1982

Paolo Soleri, Hanne Strong, Maria Mondragon and daughter

Maurice Strong took part in this meeting, so this conference for him was ten years after the 1972 conference in Stockholm that served in the founding of the UN's Ecological Program, and ten years before the Rio Summit of world leaders on the global environment. In the presentations of Paul Sears, David Ehrenfeld, Gary Nabhan, and such Lindisfarne Fellows as Hazel Henderson, Wes and Dana Jackson from the Land Institute in Salina, Kansas, Wendell Berry from Port Royal, Kentucky, Amory and Hunter Lovins from the Rocky Mountain Institute in Snowmass, John and Nancy Todd from New Alchemy on Cape Cod, David Orr from the Meadowcreek Project in Fox, Arkansas, Jim Lovelock from Cornwall, and Sim Van der Ryn from the Farallones Institute in northern California, Maurice Strong was treated to the visions of the alternative movement, undiluted by bureaucratic NGO's and government agencies. Maurice was impressed with our gang and told me so. One of the construction crew also told me that he was stunned as he saw all the people he had been reading for the last ten years gathered into a single living room.

Paul Sears, Founding Father of Ecology, 1982 Fellows Conference

David Orr, Hazel Henderson, John Todd,
and Rusty Schweickart, 1982 Conference

Wendell Berry, Paul Hawken. Wes Jackson, and Baker-roshi, 1982

1978 Gary Snyder in the Parish Hall at the 1978 Fellows Conference

But the image of that meeting that remains with me many years later is the image of Gary Snyder and Jim Lovelock hiking up to Willow Lake in the next ridge above our 8000 feet location and discussing nature and science together. Like Wordsworth on top Mount Snowden in *The Prelude,* or Petrarch on top Mount Ventoux in Provence, here was the poet on top the mountain, not alone in contemplation but in conversation with the atmospheric chemist who had articulated the Gaia Theory. For me the alchemical bringing together of the opposites of poetry and science was what Lindisfarne was all about. The 1982 Lindisfarne Conference in Crestone on "The Land" was a hearty mix, but like a great single malt scotch whisky that was about to go on the mass market, it would be blended with tamer grain liquors and served on ice by the time it caught up with the world leaders in Rio ten years later.

The initial 1979 Lindisfarne conference on solar architecture did immediately what Maurice Strong wanted Lindisfarne to do, and the local Alamosa newspaper had an article that read: "Lindisfarne brings outstanding thinkers to Valley." We had taken the first step in what would be a decades-long journey.

Rachel Fletcher, Faculty Member of the Summer School of Sacred Architecture, at the site of her design for a Greek Theatre marked out in stones in front of a very ancient Juniper Tree with Bobby Mann, founder of the Juliard String Quarter, and Haydn Stubbing, our Artist-in-Residence, and Robert Lawlor, another member of our faculty along with Keith Critchlow and John Michel. Bobby played Bach's Chaconne and Kathleen Raine read her poetry. 1981

Kathleen Raine reads her poetry as John Michel listens and protects himself from the Southwestern sun. 1981

W. I. Thompson, David Spangler, Owen Barfield, and Christopher Bamford
for the 1982 Seminar on the "Evolution of Consciousness"

The next to join us in Crestone were the Carmelites from Sedona, Arizona.
Father William MacNamara and Mother Tessa Bielecki told me that they
agreed to come to Crestone because Lindisfarne was there. Then came the
Aspen Institute, but they left after a few years, and the Center was given over
to Colorado College in Colorado Springs to serve as its ancillary campus. Then
through the work of Hanne Strong came four Tibetan Buddhist centers, both

Nyingma and Kagyu, a Sri Aurobindo House, a Jain Center, and a Harikan Baba Hindu ashram.

The presence of the Haidakhan Babaji Ashram for me embodies some of the mysteries of Crestone that had first attracted Hanne Strong there. When I met my wife Beatrice at Findhorn in Scotland in 1976 she told me as we walked together on Cluny Hill that after her stay at Findhorn she was going to go to the Haidakhan Babaji Ashram in India, and although this was our first date I gave into an intuitive prompting and said: "No you're not. You are going to come to New York to live with me." She, quite correctly, thought I was some kind of crazy American New Age nut, and dismissed the thought. But, of course, she did indeed come to New York in 1977 and we were married on March 1, 1979—St. David's Day, the national feast day for the Welsh.

And it was also in 1979 that another strange intuitive prompting took hold of me. It was after the Fellows conference and before we had begun even to turn a stone on the land I had chosen for Lindisfarne. I was sitting in my study and reading, when a Daimonic voice began to speak to me silently in my head. It was the same voice that had said to me as we crossed Spanish Creek on our search for land: "This is the land we wish you to choose for Lindisfarne." I told Maurice to stop the SUV and I went out on to the land by the road, looked up at a tall Ponderosa pine tree framed against the notch on the summit of Kit Carson Peak—now called Challenger Peak—heard the silent voice and went back to the Chevy Suburban and told Maurice: "This is it. I have found the place." Maurice laughed and said: "But we just started, there is still 100,000 acres to look over!" I replied: "We can look at the rest, but this is it."

This Daimonic voice first appeared when I was 13 and threatened at gunpoint by a child molester in Brentwood, California. I was about to try to wrest the gun from his hand and fight him, when this voice broke into my consciousness and said: "Do absolutely nothing and we will get you out of this." Since then the voice has become a regular part of my life. My cognitive scientist son Evan thinks this spiritual guide is just an aspect of my self that I experience as a traditional shamanic guide, so you may take your pick of whatever explanation you prefer for experiences like this that happen to people like me, David Spangler, or Eileen Caddy of Findhorn.

Eileen Caddy, the Co-Founder of Findhorn, at the
construction site of the Lindisfarne chapel in 1981.

When I was sitting and reading in my study in the ranch house, this voice appeared again and said: "We want you to go up into the mountains on the site we chose now." I have learned never to ignore this voice, so I set down my book, got into the SUV that Maurice had leased for Lindisfarne, and went up to the site, parked and climbed up a hill overlooking Spanish Creek. The experience began to take on an Old Testament atmosphere for an afternoon lightning storm had gathered and lightning was flashing to the north and south of me. I made a circle of large stones for fire protection and lit a small *puja* fire and began to chant the mantra *Om Nama Shivaya*. As I was chanting, I turned and looked down the slope to a clearing on the other side of Spanish Creek. It is at this exact spot that the buildings of the Harikan Baba ashram now are located, and, of course, the mantram this Kashmiri Shaivite ashram habitually uses is *Om Nama Shivaya*.

But stay with me, for the story gets even spookier. As I was chanting and looking at the fire, a large king snake of about five feet in length came and joined me in the ceremony. I greeted him and said "Hail, Grandfather," and continued to chant. The lightning struck more closely on the other side of Spanish Creek, and the voice of the spiritual guide returned and said: "None of this is going to be for you personally. It is all for others, but you must go ahead and build it anyway."

I exploded in tears as all the emotional excitement of finally finding a home for Lindisfarne and me was struck down as in a lightning bolt. I had lost everything even before I had begun. Carefully, I put out the fire and covered the ashes with a thick layer of dirt. The snake slithered away, and I returned to the SUV and drove back in sadness to the ranch house. When I was back in my study and reading a life of Pythagoras in preparation for Lindisfarne's coming conference on Pythagoreanism, I read that if a snake appears during a ritual that it was a considered to be a theriomorphic epiphany of the god. When we actually started to build on the site in 1980 and 1981, I put the prophecy of the spiritual guide out of my mind and carried on as if the place were to be a permanent home for me and for Lindisfarne.

Unfortunately, the fundamentalist Christians and theocratic Dominionists in the Valley were outraged at this invasion of New Age syncretism, and they looked upon Maurice and Hanne as agents of Satan, and Jack Dempsey, our original guide in looking over the land in May of 1979, became hostile to our presence in Crestone and told me that I was a dupe of the Rockefellers' scheme for "A New World Order." Thus began a campaign of demonization and vilification that still goes on. Two of the rumors that they circulated on the other side of the Valley in Del Norte and Monte Vista were that the Rockefellers and their were planning on instigating a global nuclear war and shifting their world headquarters from Manhattan to Crestone—which considering all the beautiful pieces of real estate the Rockefeller family had in Hawaii, Jackson Hole, Wyoming, or Caneel Bay in the Virgin Islands, was truly ignorant gossip; but one needs to remember that these are the sort of God-fearing country folk who believe that Satan created the dinosaurs to make people doubt the six thousand year chronology of the Bible—Bishop Usher's and not the Almighty to be more historically accurate. The other gossip they spread was that Lindisfarne was practicing human sacrifice of young virgins in its Lindisfarne Chapel. I guess because the Lindisfarne Chapel, instead of being a Bible box with a pulpit for sermons, was round and had an oil lamp on top of a 300 year old millstone from the Hispanic village of San Luis in the Valley at its center in place of an altar, the fundamentalists felt we had to be up to no good, and the only no-good they could imagine for the millstone was, not a reference to *Hamlet's Mill* and the 25,920 year cycle of the precession of the equinox,[4] but human sacrifice. We received all kinds of crazy hate mail and death threats, so the San Luis Valley made Manhattan look like a warm and loving community.

Keith Critchlow and the indigenous Native American leader Red Ute and his grandson at the site I had chosen for the construction for the Lindisfarne Chapel

Our 1979 Lindisfarne conference in Crestone had such high energy that I decided to continue the program on sacred architecture that I had begun in Lindisfarne-in-Manhattan by establishing a regular summer school for architects who were bored with building suburban houses and strip mall shopping centers. Keith Critchlow, Robert Lawlor, John Michel, and Rachel Fletcher served as our founding faculty, and professional architects and students came from all around the country.

Rachel Fletcher, a Faculty Member willing to do
hands-on work on the glue laminations for the Chapel, 1981

Keith Critchlow was an inspiring lecturer and he soon attracted a devoted following. To supplement this program, I organized more conferences on ecology, Pythagorean philosophy, and—to show the locals we were not heathen—a conference on Christianity to which I invited Dean Morton from the Cathedral of St. John the Divine in New York, Mother Tessa Bielecki, and our local Baptist minister. And, in a spirit of neighborly co-operation, I also agreed to attend the local Evangelical Christian men's breakfast and prepare my own recipe for blue corn crêpes for the entire assembly.

The split down the middle of Lindisfarne-in-Manhattan that had pulled the anti-modernists to one side and the new scientists of complex dynamical systems to the other became a large fault line in Crestone. Keith Critchlow and I had very different visions for the Lindisfarne Chapel, as Keith was more inclined toward creating a Christian Mosque in which the entry could be consecrated to ablutions and ritual and was so awash with esoteric symbolism that a simple chapel soon became New Age rococo cathedral. Keith wanted a large structure that would seat 360 people and have twelve windows. I wanted a space of radical emptiness in which there were no rituals and no cultural iconography, only silence and geometry. When I saw that the tiered system of petals I had originally designed for the floor was looking too much like a neo-Hindu lotus temple of syncretic religious kitsch, I rejected Keith's design and personally redesigned the Chapel to make it more of a simple Southwest

147

kiva rather than a New Age temple. I eliminated the entry room that Keith wanted for rituals of ablution and substituted a simple adobe wall to begin the definition of the space, leveled the tiered floor, and put in simple terra cotta bricks, but still keeping a logarithmic sunflower spiral pattern that was so loved by Keith and emphasized in his lectures.

Red Ute and grandson and Ivan Hess, construction manager for the Chapel

To this day, the Lindisfarne Chapel is not finished. The glue lams at the top of the dome and the copper roofing all need to be completed to finish this project that began thirty-six years ago. But the beautiful interwoven lattice of beams that Keith Critchlow created for my circular design and that Tony Hunt engineered is still there and the Chapel is constantly in use for Crestone Mountain Zen Center's summer guest program.

Tony Hunt from England, the structural engineer for the Lindisfarne Chapel

Interior of the Chapel 2010, with dome designed by Keith Critchlow,
floor by W. I. Thompson, and skylight by Marie Louise Baker

Architecture, unlike poetry, is an expensive art, and sacred architecture is an even more costly expression of striving for an ideal in a real world. I had no idea of what I was getting into when I decided to begin Lindisfarne's cultural program with the School of Sacred Architecture. Maurice Strong tried to warn me, and insisted that his donations be restricted to the more practical construction of the Lindisfarne Fellows House that was to serve as the conference center for the meetings that were Lindisfarne's strength. I felt that the Chapel would actually draw a new energy to the area and serve to express what Lindisfarne's post-religious spirituality was all about, so I insisted on continuing with the project. I had no idea that the Chapel would actually cost a half a million dollars, as the architects and builders kept insisting we could do it by building it ourselves for one hundred thousand, so I went ahead. But even unsacred architecture can be costly and go five or ten times over budget—famous examples of which are the Brooklyn Bridge and the Sydney Opera House. (Of course, like many people who have lived in New York, from Hart Crane on, I might wish to include the Brooklyn Bridge under the category of sacred architecture.)

Visitor, Karin Marstrand, Sylvie Nathanson, a major patron, and W. I. Thompson at the construction site of the Lindisfarne Fellows House 1980

Beginning of the Lindisfarne Chapel 1981.
Hilary on top, Beatrice with Andrew, and me.

So my commitment to the School of Sacred Architecture and the Lindisfarne Chapel meant that I would have to divert all our funds to support this program. Ironically, as it turned out, that meant there would be no money to sustain me at Lindisfarne as a scholar-in-residence whose books and lectures could serve to give expression to what Lindisfarne was all about. After three years the enthusiasm of beginnings began to wear thin for Maurice as he fell on hard times with a global downturn of the oil business and his holdings in general, so he needed to cut back on his sustenance, and since other religious groups had arrived in Crestone, Hanne Strong needed to help them get established. In the American culture of venture capital and philanthropy, there is a widely shared philosophy that one should serve to aid a start-up, but if after three years or so, it is not self-sustaining, then one should cut one's losses, and seek other projects that can be more attractive to capital formation. Lindisfarne in Crestone went into a period of contraction, with just one or two people living there in the winter, and my wife Beatrice led me to follow her to Bern, Switzerland where, with her Swiss degrees she was able to get a teaching position to support us and educate our young son in the public school where she worked.

Swiss Beatrice at home on the range for her first time on a horse

To contribute to our support and put my son Evan through Amherst College, and my daughter through Trent University and the University of Toronto, I traveled and gave lectures around the country, and in Toronto, Halifax, Paris, Munich, Frankfurt, Hanover, Oslo, Kyoto, and Hyraklion, Crete; and, as well, served two twelve week terms as a Visiting Professor at the University of Toronto and the University of Hawaii at Manoa. And throughout the eighties and up to 1996, I continued to organize Lindisfarne Fellows Conferences and conduct a Lindisfarne Symposium at the Cathedral of St. John the Divine in New York.[5] These Fellows Conferences included a public symposium on Gaia with Lynn Margulis, and a conference on the proposed Bioshelter for the Cathedral with the architect Santiago Calatrava.

Lecturing at the Lindisfarne Symposium at the
Cathedral of St. John the Divine in New York, 1996

The architectural project of a Bioshelter of trees atop the Cathedral of St. John the Divine—a project that brought the talents of Santiago Calatrava, John Todd, and Paul Mankiewicz together—never materialized. It remained a work of conceptual art of the "the Green Dean's," James Parks Morton. The scheme was just too expensive, and when Calatrava realized that the project would never rise aloft, he lost interest in the Cathedral and the visionary projects of Lindisfarne and only attended one of the meetings of the Lindisfarne Fellows. As a world-class star architect, Calatrva did not need to waste his time on hippie fantasies and shifted to more fundable projects like the train station for Lyon, the Art Museum for Milwaukee, and the Path train station for southern Manhattan.

But while the Lindisfarne Fellows were still at work on the project and riffing together across disciplinary lines, I proposed a project of "Electronic Stained Glass" for the Bioshelter and organized in 1992 a concert performance of Ralph Abraham's Visual Math Institute from Santa Cruz in which three mathematicians played algorithmic music on computers that looked more like stringed instruments and harpsichords than HAL. With visual transforms of invisible micro-structures of time projected onto a large screen set up on the high altar, it was not your ordinary concert, and we had a large and very interested audience of artists, designers, media experimenters, and a generally hip scene of the sort of people you would expect to see at a La Monte Young piano concert in Soho. But I must confess that after a while, the cellular automata began to look more like a child's kaleidoscope to me than an electronic cosmic rose window—especially if one was not stoned.

My idea for "Electronic Stained Glass" for the Bioshelter was that we would use James Lovelock's electron capture device to read the changing atmosphere of the visitors' breaths in communion with the trees and plants, and then transform these through the use of computers into musical and visual analogues on large panels set into the walls. As well as presenting this completely interactive art, I proposed that the Cathedral or Lindisfarne should commission various musicians and artists to compose works for this array of panels of electronic Stained Glass. With John Todd's miniaturization of the Creation in his "Living Machines," and Paul Mankiewicz's waterfalls of liverwort moss to cool the walls, we would add Baudelaire's "forest of symbols" to the trees atop the largest cathedral in the world.

One of the characteristics of the shift from matter to electronics and virtual cultures is that some ideas remain as quantum potential states and do not collapse into the actualized causal sequence of events we call reality. Permanent institutions become "things" of the past and are replaced by concerts of ideas.

Lindisfarne-in-Manhattan, and Lindisfarne-at-the-Cathedral, and even James Morton's whole twenty-four year tenure as Dean from 1972 to 1996 were just such concerts of ideas. From this perspective of looking back, I think that the Lindisfarne Association was my generation's anticipation of the temporality of the present Burning Man gatherings in the Nevada desert.

Architects are used to having their hearts broken by love affairs with buildings that are never granted the kiss of life, and I as a writer am happy that I need only pen and paper to write poetry and essays, but I do sigh and feel a sense of loss for all the projects I attempted but failed to realize—from the educational community in Southampton to Lindisfarne-in-Manhattan or the meta-industrial village for Crestone, Colorado. These physical incarnations of the Lindisfarne Association proved to be, not permanent institutions, but time-bound concerts.

One concert of ideas that had a little more lasting impact than my other projects was the 1981 Lindisfarne Fellows Conference at the San Francisco Zen Center's Green Gulch Farm. For this gathering—and for which I had to sell my Jeep to get the money for the airfares—I chose to bring three groups that had never met to see if a larger moiré pattern would emerge from their overlapping. The first group was the theoretical biologists of self-organizing systems, Heinz von Forster from the San Francisco Bay Area and Henri Atlan from Paris, the second was the School of biologists in Santiago, Chile of Humberto Maturana and Francisco Varela, and the third was the proponents of the Gaia Hypothesis James Lovelock and Lynn Margulis from England and New England respectively. We came together as a group of about forty people in Green Gulch's Wheelwright Center in the living room space I prefer for intellectual discussions. Present in the room to listen and participate were Heinz and Elaine Pagels, Wendell Berry and Wes Jackson, and the musician Paul Winter. From the inspirational impact of this meeting, Paul composed his *Missa Gaia,* and Lynn Margulis made Maturana and Varela's theory of "autopoiesis" part of her theory of symbiosis and acquired genomes. And I, for my part, was inspired to write my poetic cycle of "Gaian Cosmologies" and my 1989 book, *Imaginary Landscape: Making Worlds of Myth and Science.* Looking back over his life's work in Franz Reichle's feature film, *Monte Grande,* Francisco Varela credits Lindisfarne with having had an enormous impact on his scientific work. And in considering my own writings, I tend to think that this particular conference was one of our very best.

When I arrived at the small apartment that Beatrice found for us in Bern in 1982, I set down my briefcase, looked at the table and said: "I have to write a novel." I had never thought of writing a novel before, and this announcement was as much of a surprise to me as to her. This was the time before Macs, and Beatrice's wedding present to me had been one of those tough, durable, steel Olivetti foreign correspondent-style portable typewriters. Throughout that winter of 1982-83, I became possessed with the novel. I wrote 600 pages on this small Olivetti, but the writing felt more as if I were channeling the akashic record than creating fiction. I would break down, sobbing in pain, as I wrote about the rescue of the children, and all my suppressed rejections of the authoritarian side of the anti-modernists came exploding out. At the time, I had not known that the guru of sacred architecture, Schwaller de Lubicz, so beloved of Robert Lawlor, was an anti-Semitic member of a French fascist group, or that the Islamic side of Keith Critchlow was closer to René Guenon's rejection of modernization than it was to me and my working class democratic sympathies for William Blake and Walt Whitman. Naively, in Crestone I had felt that if it was sacred, it had to be good. And though I loved Kathleen Raine dearly as a friend, Kathleen was a monarchist and felt there should be a caste system in which poets were supported by a laboring class that could enable the more sublime poets to work in peace and quiet on great estates devoted to the arts. When Kathleen returned to England, inspired as she said she was by Lindisfarne, she founded her *Temenos Review* and its subsequent Temenos Academy, and it would be the Prince of Wales who became her patron and who continues to support Keith Critchlow and the Temenos Academy. But as an Irish-American born into the working class in the Depression, I was two revolutions—American and Irish—away from any sympathy for monarchy, religious hierarchy, or right wing cryptofascist cabals.

Evelyn Ames, Kathleen, Raine, and Dulce Murphy
at the 1979 Fellows Conference

All of this came out through my novel *Islands out of Time* as soon as I got distance from Crestone. Dial Press in New York published the work in 1985, and like an exiled Jazz musician in Europe I began to be appreciated more over there than in the States. For this work I was awarded the Oslo International Poetry Festival Award in 1986, and there appeared an English paperback edition in 1987 and a German paperback translation in 1989.

Islands out of Time expressed a kind of organ transplant rejection of the hierarchical and Platonic sacred geometry I had sought to transplant from London to Crestone. And the book I wrote alongside it in the eighties in Bern, *Pacific Shift,* expressed my shift from rigid medieval geometries to the contemporary geometrical phase portraits of behavior in chaos dynamics.. In the mind jazz manner in which I like to riff with other intellectuals in small ensembles, I now began to play accompaniment to the U. C. Santa Cruz chaos dynamics mathematician Ralph Abraham, whom I met in Los Angeles in 1985. Through *Pacific Shift,* I became known to Andra Akers and her Los Angeles-based group International Synergy, and she invited me to lecture there, and at her home, she introduced me to the chaos mathematician Ralph Abraham. As I began to read Ralph's essays, I finally understood what I and Lindisfarne had really been all about—all the way back to my undergraduate honors thesis in 1962 with its toddling steps to articulate the shift to Gregory Bateson's circular causality and complex dynamical systems. Out of this collaboration with Ralph was to come our designs for the cultural history "Evolution of Consciousness" curriculum for the Ross School.

So in the middle eighties I began to drop my emphasis on the planetization of the esoteric, and let the Buddhist/Christian dialogue carry on by itself, as Chögyam Trungpa Rinpoche was conducting annual conferences on this theme at the Naropa Institute in Boulder, Colorado. Instead, I shifted my focus to science and through Lindisfarne Fellows Conferences at Perugia, Italy, Esalen Institute in Big Sur, the Cathedral of St. John the Divine in New York in the late eighties, and two large conferences in Crestone in the early nineties, I worked to articulate the scientific side of Lindisfarne through meetings with Ralph Abraham, Mary Catherine Bateson, David Finklestein, Stuart Kauffman, Tim Kennedy, Jim Lovelock, Lynn Margulis, Susan Oyama, Evan Thompson, John Todd, Francisco Varela, and Arthur Zajonc. In the eighties, Laurance Rockefeller had given grants for the Lindisfarne Chapel, but in the nineties he began to be more of a spiritual godfather and personal helper. When I had tried to interest Laurance in Crestone in the early eighties, he had been focusing on his larger donations in the order of twenty-five millions dollars for the Center for the Study of Human Values at Princeton and the Sloan Memorial Cancer Center in New York. But around 1992, he began to take a stronger interest in Crestone and the California Institute for Integral Studies in San Francisco. Laurance never visited Lindisfarne in Southampton and Manhattan, but he came out every year to Crestone, on his way to the JR Ranch in Jackson Hole, Wyoming. He gave donations to Mother Tessa and the Carmelites, to Hanne Strong and her Manitou Foundation, to Lindisfarne in Crestone, and in our new symbiotic association, to the Crestone Mountain Zen Center. Laurance also donated funds to Joan Halifax-roshi and her Santa Fe Upaya Zen Center, and helped work out an exchange of properties in which Baker-roshi transfered his Dharma Sangha facility in Santa Fe to Joan Halifax-roshi, I transferred our land and Lindisfarne Fellows House to Baker-roshi, and Laurance built a new log cabin home for me on five acres around the Lindisfarne Chapel that Lindisfarne was to retain as a kind of organelle within the organism of the Crestone Mountain Zen Center.

Joan Halifax, Laurance Rockefeller, Richard Baker-roshi, and I
during the construction of the floor for the Lindisfarne Chapel.

Redesigned Entrance to the Chapel

The symbiosis, however, did not work out, and Lindisfarne could not
continue as a mitochondrion within the larger eukaryotic cell of Crestone
Mountain Zen Center. I became violently allergic to pinyon sap and pollen
and had to leave.

In my absence caused by this illness, Baker-roshi took over my cabin without consulting me and made it into his personal family home. The artworks Baker-roshi didn't like—such as inexpensive reproductions from the Book of Kells—-were thrown out, and my furniture was scattered among the student and guest rooms. When finally I did come back in 2005, I remember seeing a poster I had brought back from the Rietberg Museum in Zurich tossed on a woodpile in the workshed. The large frame and the glass had cost more than the poster, but now the glass was cracked and the brass frame broken. Baker-roshi didn't like cheap art posters or reproductions, and one of the points of contention with his sangha in San Francisco arose over his purchase of expensive original works of art that ended up in the three personal homes he maintained in the city, in Tassajara, and Green Gulch Farm in Marin County.

Poster of Shiva/Avalokitisvara from
Rietberg Museum in my bedroom in the log house

In Crestone, Baker-roshi also built a costly traditionally carpentered Japanese Tea House for his study, but he continued to use my old study in the "tower" of the stone house as a place to store his books and take naps. In essence, Baker-roshi was living again in three houses on the property Lindisfarne had transferred to him in 1988, but his students were living in single rooms or adaptations of waterless garden Tough Sheds. And even these three houses were not enough to hold all the stuff Baker-roshi owned, for he had to buy two storage sheds to hold all the paintings, tea bowls, statues, and designer furniture had had accumulated over the years in his compulsive acquisition of objects and things in his pursuit of Emptiness.

When I came back to try again to live there in 2005, I was assigned one of these waterless huts, and when I asked if I could use the bathroom in his Japanese Dokusan House next door while he was away in Germany, he explained that the abbot's space was sacred and that only his servant could be allowed to enter when he cleaned it or brought him tea. In exasperation at this form of psychic inflation and mystification of hierarchy, I exclaimed: "I have given you five bathrooms and you are telling me you can't share one! I didn't donate this place to you so you could carry on like the Lord of the Manor with the peasants living in shacks." Baker-roshi was incensed that I would dare challenge his supreme rule, or seek to undermine his authority in front of his students.

Baker-roshi's two studies: Tower and Dokusan House

In this expression of one of the Seven Deadly Sins, *Superbia*, Baker-roshi was very much like Chogyam Trungpa rinpoche in Boulder and Eido-roshi in New York. But the problem of my living within a cult run by a psychically inflated guru eventually sorted itself out. Due to dehydration within my waterless cabin and living at high altitude, my kidneys collapsed and I had to be hospitalized, first in Alamosa, then in Santa Fe. Although I had fought and won a battle with Maurice Strong to secure the senior water rights for the Lindisfarne land, Baker-roshi won this battle over water closets, and my challenge to his autocratic mode of ruling the community was successfully eliminated. Cults cannot hold together without the mystifications of supposedly enlightened guru. In his form of psychic inflation and narcissism, Baker-roshi was no different from Yogi Bhajan, Eido-roshi, or Chögyam Trungpa Rinpoche.

Ironically, when I was in the near-death state of kidney-collapse while sitting in my chair and practicing *yoga nidra*—the yoga of sleep and dreams—I had the experience of entering a hypersphere of light and cognitive bliss that Christians would call God and Buddhists would call Buddha Mind. As I came out of this state, I realized that enlightenment was the default setting of the human mind. If one subtracted perception and discursive thinking from the mind, one experienced this foundational Mind of Light that Baker-roshi had mythologized into his "I have got a secret" presentation of Enlightenment.

Enlightenment isn't a secret that will be opened to you in mind-to-mind transmission after thirty years of obedience to a Zen Master, it is the natural, essential, and foundational condition of the human mind. The ordinary human being is simply distracted by the perception of objects, habitual patterns of thinking, and the grasping feelings of desire. The much less mythologized and less pretentious approach of *Vipassana* Buddhism and Joseph Goldstein's Insight Meditation groups seem to me to be a more healthy and democratic approach to Buddhism for Americans than Baker'roshi or Trungpa's foregrounding of Japanese and Tibetan medieval cultures and their elevation of the Absolutism of the teacher. *"Zen? mais c'est moi!"* was certainly Baker-roshi's self-serving non-self philosophy.

I had no one to blame but myself for my failure to understand the nature of Baker-roshi's approach to *sangha*. At Lindisfarne at Fish Cove in the seventies, Reb Anderson now one of the abbots of the San Francisco Zen Center had confided in me that Baker-roshi had spent hundreds of thousands of dollars on his High Priest silk robes because he insisted on having only those robes that were made by National Treasure artisans. Only what was good enough for the Emperor of Japan was good enough for Zentatsu Baker-roshi.

Zentatsu Baker-roshi

At Lindisfarne-in-Manhattan in 1978, I organized a dinner to bring the San Francisco Zen Center and the New York Cathedral of St. John the Divine together to celebrate Lindisfarne's bicoastal activities. I personally cooked the meal of Greek food for fifty people and set the places to make Baker-roshi, Dean James Morton, and Nancy Wilson Ross the guests of honor. Baker-roshi never showed up, because on the spur of the moment Mick Jagger had invited him to go to his rock concert in the Meadowlands in his Rolls Royce. This so-called enlightened man with no ego was so thrilled that like an ecstatic teenager jumping up and down in excitement, he jumped at the opportunity. And I was left to wonder, staring at the empty chair, what had happened to him. My wife Beatrice told me that should have been sign enough for me and I should have dropped him from the Lindisfarne Fellowship then. But I was dumb and overly impressed with the theatrics and robes of Zen. Years later when Baker-roshi married Her Royal Highness the Princess Marie Louise von Baden and was invited to have tea with the Queen in Buckingham Palace, I listened to Baker-roshi's bragging report and remembered the occasion with Mick Jagger and the Rolls, and began to wonder about why he always talked about no-self but had the biggest ego of anyone I knew.

The con-man, like the Wizard of Oz, needs a stage-set and a costume, and Baker-roshi certainly was the best con-man I ever met and he did indeed con me into thinking he was some sort of Enlightened Being who could read minds in Dokusan. But if Zen is simply a technique for staring at nothing until you can you suspend thinking and sensory-motor activity to achieve the default setting of the mind as "the Mind of Light," then even I could claim to be "enlightened" and could have set up Lindisfarne as a cult with me as its leader, but to prove that Lindisfarne was a We and not a Me I had established the Lindisfarne Fellowship.

The experience of Enlightenment may be simply a natural, brain-based phenomenon, or not, as the Dalai Lama claims. I have no way of getting out of myself to prove the question one way or another. A cognitive scientist would say that because I was in a near-death state from dehydration and kidney failure, I naturally experienced deliriums and felt I was out of my body, entering a hypersphere of Divine Light, for this was the nature of my personal imagination. Joe Six-Pack in the same situation might have visions of driving a Ferrari or making love to Christina Hendricks.

Cognitive scientists can reasonably claim that the Asian religions have simply mythologized this experience of Light into Enlightenment to advance their agenda in a medieval lust for hierarchical power. The proof for this scientific contention can be seen when the so-called enlightened being gets up from the cushion and returns to being the same old selfish and egocentric jerk he was when he sat down—only now he was a much more pretentious and psychically inflated jerk—a narcissist in the case of Baker-roshi, a lecher in the case of Eido-roshi, and a drunk in the case of Trungpa rinpoche. Trungpa was able to con his followers into thinking his lechery, drunkenness, and delusions about establishing a Buddhist theocracy in Nova Scotia—and printing its own currency in advance—was a Buddhist and shamanic Bonn manifestation of "Crazy Wisdom." In religion, you get the guru you deserve.[6]

When I moved back to Crestone, it was a move of desperation, for I was broke from a whole Lindisfarne career of living without an adequate professional salary to support myself and my family, and I needed to find a place to retire in my old age where I would not have to pay the expensive rents of Cambridge and Manhattan, but could live simply on my Social Security in a contemplative center. I had hoped that the contemplative center I had built might be an appropriate place for me, but these conditions of dire necessity were not the right reasons to live in the *sangha* of the Crestone Mountain Zen Center. There are homeless people everywhere, but filling monasteries with the homeless and unemployed is not the right use of these centers devoted to a demanding and traditionally based esoteric practice.

Countless people besides Reb Anderson, mostly women, had tried to warn me about Baker-roshi, but I did not pay sufficient attention to them, and thought that he had reformed after his scandalous exit from San Francisco Zen Center. But it is characteristic of the narcissistic personality that it cannot admit error and always blames others. As I listened to and believed Baker-roshi's endless narratives of innocence and complete self-vindication for his actions in San Francisco, I was taken in. When I was recovering in Santa Fe from kidney collapse and dehydration exacerbated by high altitude—thanks to the compassionate ministrations of Joan Halifax-roshi and her more humane sangha at the Upaya Zen Center, one that is devoted to the care of the dying—and was trying to determine what I should do about Baker-roshi's outrageously selfish behavior, the Daimonic voice of my spiritual guide again came forth and said: "Do nothing. Do not engage with or seek to chastise Richard. He will be dealt with by the holders of his lineage." I had visions of a Buddhist court martial trial in *Bardo* in which Dogen Zenji and Susuki-roshi interrogated Richard over each reported case of his abuse of power during his career as an abbot and roshi.

Perhaps it was for the best in the long run for me to do nothing and allow Richard's sangha to grow beyond him and without him after his death, and twenty-five years from now the Crestone Mountain Zen Center will still be there, but under a more balanced and benign leadership. Perhaps this is the reason the Daimonic voice of my spiritual guide had said to choose the land where the Crestone Mountain Zen Center now sits. And perhaps after Richard Baker-roshi's sad and misguided career has come to its end, the much more congenial Christian Dillo will prove a more modest and compassionate leader than Zentatsu. I like to think that both Baker-roshi's grasping and collecting of objects, and my continual loss of them were being used by the Guardians of the Dharma for a higher purpose that will not become visible in either of our lifetimes.

The beautiful transformation of Lindisfarne's conference meeting room by Dan Welch and Christian Dillo into a contemplative dinning room for seshins and study periods.

Under Laurance Rockefeller's plan for co-operation between the Lindisfarne Association, the Crestone Mountain Zen Center, the Santa Fe Upaya Zen Center, and the California Institute of Integral Studies, Lindisfarne was to conduct an annual conference of the Fellows in the original stone Lindisfarne Fellows House that Sim Van der Ryn had designed. To stabilize the whole project, Laurance paid for re-engineering the water and utilities for the campus and provided the funds for carrying on with the construction of the Lindisfarne Chapel, and built the log house for me in my retirement. As Laurance and I sat in the completed house, he said: "Well, Bill, you've got your cabin the sky."

Dean James Morton, Lindisfarne's Chairman and I as Lindisfarne's
President meeting in the Lindisfarne Mountain Retreat Log House 1992

In the gatherings inside the Lindisfarne Fellows House at the new Crestone Mountain Zen Center, it became clear to all that Lindisfarne was embodying a noetic polity in much the same way that the artists and scientists of Paris had embodied one as they gathered in their cafés like *Le lapin agile*. Michael Murphy, the founder of Esalen, approached me at one of these gatherings, his eyes aglow with that extraterrestrial Walk-in radiance he has, and expressed how uplifted he felt. I remembered back to our first conversation about counterfoil institutions at the wine bar of his Esalen Institute in the summer of 1967, a quarter century before. All had not been in vain.

The troika of Baker-roshi, Joan Halifax-roshi, and me ran very well at the start, and Joan contributed greatly to several of the Lindisfarne Fellows Gatherings. I divided my time from 1992-1995 between my new log cabin home in Crestone and serving in the winter to spring as Rockefeller Scholar at the California Institute for Integral Studies in San Francisco. During that time I gave 42 public lectures for the Institute — lectures that became my book, *Coming into Being: Texts and Artifacts in the Evolution of Consciousness*.

At long last, after twenty years of work, the efforts were beginning to pull together and make sense. In the 1994 Lindisfarne Fellows Conference, I surveyed the group and felt grateful that I had been able to conduct these gatherings for an entire generation, from 1974 to 1994. With the lectures of Tim Kennedy and Evan Thompson, I had actually been able to pass the torch from one generation to another. I had homeschooled Evan at Lindisfarne-in-Manhattan, and Tim had taken part in my Lindisfarne Symposium at the Cathedral of St. John the Divine while he was still a graduate student at Columbia. With Stuart Kauffman from the Santa Fe Institute for the Study of Complex Systems, Ralph Abraham from U.C. Santa Cruz, and Francisco Varela from CREA at the Ecole Polytechnique in Paris all present in the 1994 meeting, I felt that Lindisfarne had lived up to its founding goals. The program for Biology, Cognition, and Ethics that Francisco Varela and I had initiated in Kyoto in 1985 — thanks to a grant from Billy Wood Prince and the Prince Trust in Chicago — was now inspiring a whole new generation of young post-docs through Evan and Cisco's work in Paris and Toronto. The waters of the rivulet of Lindisfarne had hit and moved aside a rock of reductionist scientific materialism and now other streams were joining together in a much larger watershed.

The growth of the California Institute of Integral Studies in San Francisco in the mid-nineties seemed to signal a general shift in the countercultural movement in the United States. C.I.I.S., which had been established by Haridas Chadhuri, a disciple of Sri Aurobindo, had originally been an Institute of Asian Studies founded on Sri Aurobindo's vision of Integral Yoga. It was always hard pressed for funds, and was in danger of going under completely when Laurance Rockefeller came to its rescue with a donation of several millions. Robert McDermott, who was a student of the philosophy of Aurobindo and had a given a course of lectures on him at Lindisfarne-in-Manhattan in 1976, became the president of the new institute — renamed the California Institute of Integral Studies — and helped it become an accredited graduate school with a strong faculty giving graduate degrees in psychology and philosophy.

Along with Robert McDermott's shift to C.I.I.S. came a general shift from independent institutes back to the university and the degree-granting academic world. The New Alchemy Institute and its spin-off Ocean Arks were no longer the central focus of John Todd's work in biological design as he began to work for the Institute of Natural Resources at the University of Vermont in Burlington. David Orr gave up on his Meadowcreek Project in Fox, Arkansas, and became the Dean of Environmental Studies at Oberlin College, and Sim Van der Ryn shifted his energies away from the alternative Farallones Institute back to his architectural practice and his professorship at the School of Architecture at the University of California at Berkeley. And Arthur Zajonc and David Scott began to work on the design of a Center for Integrative Learning and Action for the Five Colleges at Amherst, Massachusetts. So my serving as Rockefeller Scholar at C.I.I.S. for three years and working on the design of a new evolution of consciousness curriculum for the children of the Ross School in East Hampton, New York seemed to indicate that as the year 2000 approached a generation of experimentation was ending and that the university as an institution was going to absorb whatever changes or innovations it felt were appropriate to its traditional mission. Concurrent with this educational shift was also a shift in the popular religious sensibility, as fundamentalism in all the major religions began to express the spirit of a new time. Clearly, my efforts to articulate a post-religious spirituality for a new planetary culture would have to wait until fundamentalism and neoconservative capitalism had failed to deliver the Good and the goods.

Lindisfarne, New Alchemy, Farallones, and the Meadowcreek Project all subsided after a generation of work because these "alternative" institutions were exhausted from the unending work of fund-raising. Lindisfarne died for lack of funds every year of the twenty-five years I kept it alive by an act of will. Enough funds would trickle in slowly from philanthropists and foundations to keep the Gaian visionaries at their work, but the real money still went to the major leagues of Harvard, MIT, and Princeton. By contrast to the small funds given to Lindisfarne or Meadowcreek at that time, from the seventies to the nineties, enormous funds went into the Neocon think tanks—the Hoover Institute, the Project for a New American Century, the Heritage Foundation, the Cato Institute—and the academics who co-operated with this rising wave found themselves well rewarded and swept up into influence and power. The handful of powerful men—billionaires like Rupert Murdoch—who controlled the media not only owned the tabloids and cable networks, but also the major publishing houses like Harper Collins; so intellectuals and cultural philosophers who did not go along with the system often found that their books were either not reviewed or accepted for publication in the first place. And as for the state universities, investment in sports replaced investment in the humanities, and cultural figures became celebrities who were spotlighted to distract the country and keep us thinking about personalities and not ideas. Traditional literary figures moved onto the reservation of Creative Writing, collected their subsidy, and clung to the dying rituals of their increasingly artificial pseudo-literary cultures to vend their tribal wares in boutiques for tourists like *American Poetry Review, Prairie Schooner* and *Poetry*. In the new dumbed-down America, if you couldn't pitch your idea and flog your book with a joke and a slogan on Oprah or John Stewart in a two-minute slot, you did not exist.

In founding Lindisfarne, I had reached back into a historical Imaginary and invoked a mythic landscape of the decentralized Celtic Church, with its roots in an esoteric past that went back to megalithic stone circles and Hyperborean visions. The Synod of Whitby, with its mythical battle of the Celtic Church of John versus the imperial Church of Peter in Rome, was a symbolic displacement for the battle of the alternative, environmentalist culture versus the globalist culture of the multinational corporation—the Gaia Politique vs. the Neocon agenda.[7] But in becoming, as the Jungians phrase it, "possessed by an archetype," I had also brought forth that archetype's shadow, as well as its light. There were no cities in Ireland, and knowledge was stored in monasteries. But the single shamanistic abbot could not equal the societal power of a new civilization in which expanding populations and growing cities would become dioceses ruled over by a bishop, responsible to the bishop of bishops in Rome. The alternative movement of the seventies and eighties was similarly decentralized, and though various institutions like New Alchemy on Cape Cod, the Meadowcreek Project in Fox, Arkansas, and the Farallones Institute in Marin County, California could become sources of imaginative innovation, they could never become economically self-sustaining and always were dependent upon the fund-raising abilities of their leaders. Just as the Church of Rome swallowed up the Celtic Church of John at the end of the dark ages and the rise of medieval civilization, so within a single generation did the university reabsorb the works of people like John Todd, Sim Van der Ryn, David Orr, and me. It was in recognition of my shortcomings and those of Lindisfarne that I decided to honor the monastic impulse I had invoked and donated the land and facilities of the Lindisfarne Mountain Retreat to a monastery—the Crestone Mountain Zen Center.

With the needs of his new second family of wife and daughter in mind, Baker-roshi and his princess wife eyed my cabin above the Zendo and thought it was a shame to let it sit there empty, awaiting my return, a return that might never happen, and so they decided to take it over without consulting me. Laurance Rockefeller was upset at the wreckage of his plans for the cultural network of Lindisfarne, Crestone Mountain Zen Center, Upaya Zen Center in Santa Fe, and the California Institute for Integral Studies in San Francisco and said to me in a mood of both anger and frustration: "Richard ends up with it all!"

My loss was indeed Zen Center's gain. Dan Welch, the assistant Abbot, who had served as Lindisfarne's first contemplative in residence in Southampton in 1974, told me on the phone in 2005 as we discussed my return and retirement that the apple trees Beatrice and I had planted in front of the Lindisfarne Fellows House twenty four years before were now giving fruit, and that the community was having applesauce for breakfast and apple cobbler for dinner. So, to take the longer view than one of personal possession, mine or Baker-roshi's, I can now in old age sit back in my rocker—far away from Lindisfarne in Southampton, Manhattan, or Crestone—and finally enjoy being as American as apple pie and Johnny Appleseed.

Flowering apple tree in front of the former Lindisfarne Fellows House

---

[1] See also W. I. Thompson, "The Meta-industrial Village" in Darkness and Scattered Light (New York; Doubleday Anchor Books, 1978).

[2] See Sim Van der Ryn, *Design for Life* (Gibbs Smith: Salt Lake City, UT, 2005).

[3] See the writings of Peter Dale Scott for a discussion of the idea of the *Deep State, such as American War Machine: Deep Politics, the CIA Global Drug Connection and the Road to Afghanistan* (Rowan and Littlefield: London and Boulder, 2010).

[4] See Giorgio de Santillana and Hertha von Dechend's *Hamlet's Mill: An essay on myth and the frame of time* (Gambit: Boston, 1969); see also W. I. Thompson, *The Time Falling Bodies Take to Light; Mythology, Sexuality, and the Origins of Culture* (New York: St. Martin's Press, 1981), p. 217.

[5] These unscripted talks were the first oral form of what became my book *Coming into Being: Artifacts and Texts in the Evolution of Consciousness* (New York: St. Martin's Press, 1996 and an expanded paperback edition in 1998).

[6] See Geoffrey D. Falk, *Stripping the Gurus: Sex, Violence, and Enlightenment* (Toronto: Million Monkeys Press, 2009), and Michael Downing, *Shoes outside the Door: Desire, Devotion, and Excess at San Francisco Zen Center* (Counterpoint: Washington D.C., 2001).

[7] See W. I. Thompson, "Gaia and the Politics of Life: a Program for the Nineties?" in *Gaia, A Way of Knowing* (Hudson, NY: Lindisfarne Press, 1987). For a discussion of the multinational corporation's Disaster Capitalism, see Naomi Klein's brilliant book, *The Shock Doctrine* (New York: Henry Holts & Co., 2007).

Chapter 8: Science and Spirituality:

Farewell Address at the Lindisfarne Fellows
Conference, Fetzer Institute, Kalamazoo, Michigan, 1997

The alternative communities of the seventies were a new genre of ontic rather than mimetic art in which a new Eros of sexual exploration, organic gardening, slow food "natural cooking," home-schooling, arts and crafts, democratic community meetings, Tai Chi and Hatha Yoga, sacred dance, and meditation created a new cultural Imaginary in the new electronic environment. Eros brought forth a new polyamorous body politic that differed from the traditional rural community or the new suburbs. Religion on Sunday was replaced with spirituality in a daily way of life, as was prefigured in the early American utopian communities like the Shakers.

Although I founded Lindisfarne greatly under the influence of intentional communities like Findhorn in Scotland and Auroville in India, what actually developed through the Fellowship was an institute and think tank for a new planetary civilization of green architecture, Gaian science, and a more contemplative neurophenomenolgy in which meditation became part of a new expanded liberal arts education. And now through the innovative work of our Fellows David Orr and John Todd, much of our way of thinking has been accepted by liberal arts colleges like Oberlin and even state universities like the University of Vermont. And outside Lindisfarne, environmental thinkers like Bill McKibben have influenced Middlebury in Vermont and the College of the Atlantic in Maine. A stand alone Lindisfarne Association that was called for in 1972 is no longer necessary. My own kids who grew up at Lindisfarne are proof of that, because my daughter Hilary teaches at Bowdoin College and my son Evan at the University of British Columbia in Vancouver.

My work in founding and directing the Lindisfarne Association went on for the twenty-five years from 1972 to 1997. After resigning from the presidency with its frustrating and draining work of continual fund-raising in 1997, various Lindisfarne Fellows such as Arthur Zajonc, Mary Catherine Bateson, and Vivienne Hull came forward to organize Fellows conferences in Crestone, Colorado and Whidbey Island in Washington in the years in between 1997 and 2001, but slowly the energy and kairos of the meetings began to age with the aging of our group.

Santa Fe Fellows Conference, 2009

In the seventies, in my essay on "The Meta-Industrial Village" in my book, *Darkness and Scattered Light: Four Talks on the Future,* I had hoped that electronics would allow a miniaturization of technology in which nature would be scaled up and industrial technology would be scaled down or made invisible through the "Living Machines" that John Todd was then just beginning to design. Unfortunately, this transformation simply did not happen as industrial society shifted to a global financial society of investment banking transactions and mass shopping built upon the network of the Internet and World Wide Web—a network that required not factories but vast warehouses of servers in climate-controlled conditions that consumed even more energy than twentieth-century industrial society. It was not technology that had become miniaturized, but nature itself in preparation for stuffing it into space stations and space colonies.

In 2009, Dr. Joan Halifax-roshi asked me to come out of retirement and organize and conduct a new cycle of Lindisfarne Fellows Conferences at her Upaya Zen Center in Santa Fe, New Mexico. I organized and directed three conferences from 2007 to 2010, but at the last moment I could not attend the 2010 meeting, because I had to have a second open-heart surgery for a decayed bovine mitral valve and a blood clot. I recovered and was able to organize two more Lindisfarne Fellows meetings for the years 2011 and 2012. At the request of our Lindisfarne Fellow Pir Zia Inayat-Khan, these meetings took place at his Seven Pillars Academy in New Lebanon, New York. The 2012 meeting ended on a very high and celebrative note with a dinner for my 74th birthday, but when I returned home and began to think about the theme and organization for another Lindisfarne Conference for 2013, I realized that the years from 1972 to 2012 expressed its own Zeitgeist, and that two full generations of work on my perspective of Teilhard de Chardin's idea of planetization had expressed itself. Forty years was enough. The kairos was no longer with us. The times had changed and it was now time for the Lindisfarne Association to regroup, or metamorphose into some new form of cultural institution under the creative direction of a younger generation—or, failing that, then to disband, if there were no longer hearts and minds for "the study and realization of a new planetary culture."

These conferences and gatherings of creative people in what Margaret Mead called "sapiental circles" are performances in and of time. In his time, C. G. Jung organized the Eranos Conferences. For me, when I read the papers presented at these illustrious gatherings—when they were published by the Bollingen Foundation and Princeton University Press at the time I was an undergraduate at Pomona College at the beginning of the sixties—this prestigious group of, for the most part, male scholars, was awe inspiring. For a college kid in Southern California, the ethos of this high culture gathering of the European mind was precisely what I was looking for in my effort to get away from the shallow media culture of the Hollywood, Disneyland, and the movie and television studios that had dominated the Los Angeles in which I had grown up and come of age.

Birthday Celebration at the Seven Pillars Academy,
New Lebanon, New York, 2012

But when it came time to organize the first Lindisfarne Conference in the summer of 1974 in the Hamptons of New York, the Eranos Conferences became the model of precisely what I did not want. I did not want to be the great man sucking on his pipe at the father's head of a table set outside in the sunlit Ticino of Switzerland. I did not want to play the intellectual alpha male to whom all the conversation was directed and flowed out again through the reducing valve of his singular world-view. I wanted to play a different role, to bring people together who had never met but needed to, to be something more like the first chair violinist-director of an intellectual chamber music ensemble than a grand Von Karajan directing the Berlin Philharmonic.

Both the Eranos and the Macy Conferences that had embodied the Zeitgeist of their times had been small, so in order to achieve diversity and complexity, I wanted my first Lindisfarne Conference to be larger, so I had closer to twenty presenters and an audience of around eighty. To avoid panel discussions in which celebrities simply performed their celebrityhood, I wanted to give the presenter a whole lecture hour for a talk—and not an academic reading of a paper—in which the speakers could sing out an aria and display why they had become celebrities in the first place. But in spite of my design, celebrities like Jonas Salk and Carl Sagan carried on in the manner to which they had become accustomed to be admired. Jonas Salk gave his single stump speech that I had explicitly asked him not to give again, and Carl Sagan acted as if he were on a late night TV talk show—more Johnny Carson than Dick Cavett—to name the stars of that time.

What was required of me was not the role of Master of Ceremonies or Ring Master of the Circus, but the more challenging one of choosing the people to invite, reading their books, and weaving all the disparate ideas into a momentary tapestry of rapidly flowing words that gave voice to the Zeitgeist as I introduced each speaker, explained why he or she was there and how his or her ideas related to the talk of the previous speaker. And to insure that the conference with such diversity did not spin apart like wet clay upon a potter's wheel, I gave an introductory lecture to energize the gathering with a sense of excitement of what was to come, and then a wrap-up lecture to show how what we had heard during the week had moved the new planetary culture forward.

The talk I am presenting below is not necessarily the best one I ever gave in my forty years of doing that sort of thing, but it does show how I tried to weave all the ideas of the Fellows and Guest Speakers into an oral presentation that tried to be not just Wissenschaft but Wissenskunst.

****

Our twenty-fifth anniversary conference takes its theme from Stuart Kauffman's new book, *At Home in the Universe*.[1] In the conclusion to this work, Stuart speaks of re-inventing the sacred for an emerging global civilization, and this has certainly been the mission of Lindisfarne since I founded the Association in New York a quarter-century ago to serve as a vehicle for the exploration and realization of what I then called "a new planetary culture." Since Lindisfarne's founding as a very seventies communally-run institute in Southampton, Long Island, there have been many changes in our contemporary culture and in our global means of communication, from personal computers to telefax to Internet to World Wide Web, so part of my agenda for these next few days will be to engage in a healthy self-examination to ask ourselves if or how Lindisfarne should continue.

Stu Kauffman at home in the universe

The intellectual architecture for this particular gathering of the Fellows, as I saw it in organizing the talks—and, of course, it will unfold according to its own self-organizing dynamic in the next three days—is as follows. I will talk tonight about being "At Home in the Universe," about the process of participating in culture by extending the sensitivity of one's perceptions beyond the conventional institution's way of defining of who we are, what we are doing, and where we are going. This extension of sensitivity can be felt as a shift to a larger field of awareness than was provided by one's education or one's home institution's definition of reality. Now, of course, this shift in sensitivity, or change of horizons, can be a way of being at home in the larger universe that does not necessarily make us feel comfortable in our domestic institution, be it university or church. But this extension of horizon can be one in which all the various levels we will be exploring in the next few days do take part. Think of it as a system of nested ontologies: from Light with Arthur Zajonc, to Patterns and Particles with David Finkelstein, to Molecules with Stuart Kauffman, to Micelles with Luigi Luisi, to Genes with Susan Oyama, to Neuronal Ecologies with Tim Kennedy, to Living Machines with John Todd, to Dwellings with Sim Van der Ryn, and to Poems with Jane Hirshfield, for poems are a way of pronouncing one's sense of dwelling in place and making that kind of extended sensitivity more intimate with one's own being, because it is being grounded in language and the mother tongue. We humans do seem to carry our sense of being at home in the universe, our local address, in language. And then, finally, in a structure of *aria da capo*, we will end with David Spangler and the metaphysics of Light in spirits of Time and Place—which is another expression of this extension of sensitivity—to return where we started with Arthur Zajonc and the physics of Light. It is also appropriate to end with David, because David is the one who talked me into overcoming my fears and sense of spiritual inadequacy in founding Lindisfarne in a talk we had in 1972 as we walked along the beach near Findhorn in Scotland. Since then David has participated in Lindisfarne through all its permutations from Southampton to Manhattan to Crestone.

The missing middle, to use a phrase of our Lindisfarne Fellow Fritz Schumacher, is, of course, the shift from molecules to bacteria and living cells. So although Lynn Margulis could not be here for this gathering, and had to be in Mexico, you should insert in your imaginations the talks given by Lynn and Tim Kennedy at the Lindisfarne Fellows meeting at the Cathedral in New York in 1994. My purpose in that gathering was to show the isomorphisms in Lynn's theories about spirochete attachment and Tim's work with the discovery of Netrin, the growth cones of neurons and axon guidance.

David Spangler, Lindisfarne in Manhattan, 1978

Merle Lefkoff, Lynn Margulis, and Christopher Bamford, Santa Fe 2009

Cornelia Hesse-Honegger (with coffee cup), John Todd, Paul Mankiewicz, Mary Catherine Bateson, Pir Zia Inayat-Khan, Arthur Zajonc in foreground, Michaela Walsh and Nancy Jack Todd (right background) 2011

My role will be to start us off with culture, and then move to Light with Arthur, but also with the cultural aspects of how all these patterns unfold and contribute to our sense of identity, because Arthur Zajonc and the Fetzer Institute have been part of a conversation we have been having for the past two years about inviting a new generation into the Fellowship and Association of Lindisfarne.

And then from Arthur we will modulate from the quantum physics of light to the quantum physics of patterns of energy with David Finkelstein in an exploration of those patterns of ontology that are even prior to the unfolding—or folding—of space and time in elementary particles. Then we move to the edge of chaos and the circularity of self-organizing systems that Stuart discusses in his theories about the origins of molecular order. From Stuart we will pass to Luigi Luisi who has different ideas about the origins of life, so there is not, and has never been, a single party-line to Lindisfarne. As I have often said over these past twenty-five years, Lindisfarne is an ecology of consciousness, but not an ideology. Ecologies work through energizing difference, so we delight in these differences and the play that comes when bifurcations open up new possibilities. Luigi's micelles are an appropriate image because they are a lipid envelopment of molecular and genetic patterns of information, ones that can now be used to transport medicines into the tiny neuronal and cellular ecologies that Susan Oyama and Tim Kennedy will be discussing. Susan's work is particularly fitting to Lindisfarne because since the beginning of Lindisfarne in Southampton with Gregory Bateson's talks, we have expressed a counterweighted emphasis to the dominant culture's by stressing pattern over substance, information over matter, ecology over ideology. We have always diverged from the very American engineering approach that seeks to isolate discrete entities, take them out of their identity-forming context, manipulate them in laboratories, and then extend that control into politically dominated environments. So according to this world-view, the mind is the brain and the brain is nothing but an information-processing digital computer. The universe is nothing but aggregates of matter, and matter is nothing but aggregates of particles, quarks or genes, and these particles can be isolated in a void and re-engineered to produce systems of rational technological management and profit in place of wild, sloppy, and free ecologies. Lindisfarne has always gone against these dominant streams of force. Like a salmon swimming upstream to spawn a new generation, we have emphasized patterns of relationship, Buddhist dependant co-origination, and mutually entraining processes in which emergent domains, such as life or Gaia, cannot be taken out of the context that informs their becoming. So from Gregory Bateson to Francisco Varela to Jim Lovelock and Lynn Margulis to Susan Oyama, there has always been an interest in an alternative approach, as well as an alternative culture of science. Susan's work in *The Ontogeny of Information* has been a lonely voice crying in the wilderness of genetic engineering and sociobiology. In the midst of industrial capitalism's efforts to own the Creation through packaging genes and patenting animals, Susan has calmly voiced her critiques and objections. Hers has been a voice that has been soft and unagressive , and so not widely heard in our media culture of soundbites and our hyped-up culture of Big Corporate Science, but when it is heard in concert with other voices and instruments, from Gregory Bateson to Wes Jackson, I hope the larger "pattern that connects" can be appreciated.

Susan Oyama and Mayumi Oda, Santa Fe Meeting 2010

So, rather than jumping from micelles to neurons, from Luigi to Tim, I have suggested a countertheme that can enrich the complexity by involving

Susan's work. If we simply moved from micelles to neuronal ecologies, we could slip into packing genes and proteins in lipid bubbles in ways the large pharmaceutical companies would love to do for their own gain. Now there is no question but that Luigi and Tim's work, in Zurich and Montreal, is at the leading edge of medicine, and in his work in discovering and naming this family of proteins he calls netrins, Tim and his colleagues may have come upon ways to bind up severed neurons, cure Parkinson's disease, or understand the origins of schizophrenia in the ecologies of the interneurons; and Luigi's work may show us just how to deliver medicines exactly to the place they are needed; but unless we have a healthy sense of the distinctness of place, we shall fall into the old errors of thinking and make another mess to add streams of internal pollution to the match the external ones. That will hardly be a way of being "At Home in the Universe."

Tim Kennedy dancing Tango with Alia Wittman at Fellows Meeting, 2011

Tim Kennedy's work in exploring how axons develop along a growth cone also helps us to understand how cells can cluster through the chemistry of their membranes to become multicellular, or how neurons can associate to become neuronal ecologies. How these patterns of association move from chemically linked to membrane-bound organisms is also something Lynn Margulis has been studying in her models of symbiosis and acquired genomes. How these patterns of association become emergent domains is also something that Evan has been working on at the philosophical level. But my purpose tonight in asking Tim here from the Montreal Neurological Institute and Luigi Luisi here from ETH in Zurich is to offer a sketch of a possible future medicine. It doesn't exist yet, but it is on the horizon and I as an outsider to science can see patterns of emergence as I scan the pages of *Nature*.

Brother David Steindl-Rast and Prof. Luigi Luisi at ETH's Cortona Meeting

Part of what my work with Lindisfarne over the past twenty-five years has been all about is to try, through these conferences, to open windows to allow horizons into institutions that are made out of bricks and cement blocks and have no windows. Within these institutions, conversations are always between specialists, so it hard to see the basin and range in which Lynn Margulis, Francisco Varela, Stuart Kauffman, Tim Kennedy, and Luigi Luisi are all situated in an ecology of mind.

Now what flows nicely from Tim's work with neuronal ecologies is John Todd's work with Living Machines. As axons, synapses, interneurons, and chaperones can constellate a chemical ecosystem, so do John's cascade of organisms in a directional stream—from anaerobic bacteria to snails to plants—constellate an ecosystem of pollution-eaters. John puts the yogurt back into the guts of our body-politic so that our settlements can digest all the nasty stuff we surround ourselves with. Because John works in pattern perception and recognition, he has worked intuitively, more like a good cook than a chemist, and this has got him into big trouble with Big Science. I remember 30 years ago—before his standing fibre glass tanks and Living Machines— when John was filling up mason jars and setting them out in the sun on the front lawn of his home in Falmouth. He looked like he was canning green jellies, and he was. When you work through the mode of participation with nature rather than domination of nature as an "it," you have to work with a Taoist's sensitivity. Big Science, Baconian Science, works through separation, analysis, and control, but this other kind of science, Pythagorean Science, works through pattern recognition, imaginative articulation, and participation. Here one has to become alive and alert to recognize patterns and relationships. This is a case of being more like Barbara McClintock than Crick and Watson. These sorts of scientists tend to work more in the complexity of the field than in the reductionist controls of the lab. They see the unique in the universal context in which it derives its meaningful relationships. In an intuitive form of selection, John takes various ingredients from all around the world and brings them together—cyanobacteria and snails and sludge—and then he watches and waits. (Kibitzing from the side lines, I have been telling John for years that he should take acidothermophilic bacteria from sulphur springs and deep ocean thermal vents, for these critters that can survive in what for humans are extreme environments probably would love eating and digesting the most toxic radioactive sludges we can give them.) As the chemical exchanges of all the participants begin to loop and interact, a new emergent domain forms—a kind of loose form of immanental mind, one in which the membrane is not simply bounded by fibreglass but by the mind and the sensitivity of the Taoist scientist bringing the partners into participation. Many here will recognize that this kind of Mind extending into "pathways outside the body" was part of Gregory Bateson's explication in his great essay, "Form, Substance, and Difference." So what John has been doing is not your typical form of American civil engineering. Working as both scientist and intuitive artist in the new profession of biological designer, John is more like an architect than a laboratory chemist. But what he has designed as architecture in Living Machines is a new kind of ecological immune system for healing highly polluted environments. So the medicine for the ecology of the interneurons in the brain afflicted with schizophrenia and the medicine for the rivers and water tables of our local communities afflicted with carcinogens become occasions for new understandings of science, and this intellectual play of the Imagination has been what the Lindisfarne Fellowship has been all about in the work of three generations—from Gregory to Cisco, Susan, and Stuart, and on to the younger generation of Tim and Evan, as we saw in our twentieth anniversary conference in Crestone in 1994.

With John's ecological applications of Gregory's epistemology—an association that came directly out of the Lindisfarne conference of 1975—we can begin to appreciate that Mind is more extensive and immanental in ecologies of being, that it is not merely epiphenomenal to the brain or simply emergent from the cross-wiring of digital neural nets. If, as Stuart suggests, that order is for free in the universe, and that order comes early on and more easily present than we were led to believe, then these immanental patternings of self-organization from noise have much to teach us: they are part of an ontological culture that bridges matter and information. This culture of pattern over substance, of process over matter, takes us back to Gregory Bateson, and even further back to Whitehead and his philosophy of organism that I studied in the fifties.

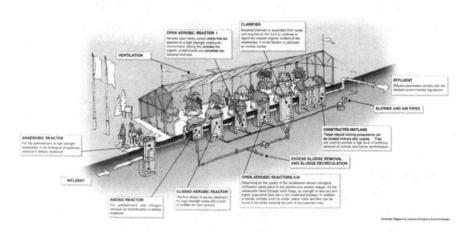

John Todd's Living Machine for Findhorn

Now John's work in developing immune systems for environments segues quite nicely into Sim Van der Ryn's green architecture and theories of ecological design. Sim has worked to create true dwellings, modes of being in place, where the architectural instrument is not simply a box or people container to keep nature out of the way of business, but a more musical instrument tuned to pulse with the natural rhythms of sun and wind. This architectural "edge of chaos" is another form of extended sensitivity, from the box to the ecology. A year or so ago, I went to a lecture Stuart gave for the Department of Physics and Engineering at Columbia University. This building is precisely one of those cinder-block boxes without windows. The classroom we were in was another cinderblock box within a box, and my wife Beatrice turned to me and said: "No wonder we have got environmental problems, this environment is just horrible." So scientists who are trained not to see, not surprisingly, grow up blind. To train these people in these environments, and then set them out into the world and expect them to design appropriate dwellings for a healthy culture is not very smart. It was precisely for these architectural reasons that I quit the environment of MIT in 1968 and went on a quest for the Holy Grail of a new planetary culture.

From Sim's work we will move to Jane Hirshfield to shift from the extended sensitivity of seeing to listening. We'll move from the reconsacration of matter in the construction of dwellings to another kind of sense of place to return to the mother tongue. If we can imaginatively appreciate how we took in language with our mother's milk—in precisely the way Wordsworth describes in *The Prelude*—to listen to poetry, then we can also begin to appreciate how poetry pronounces a connectivity to language, place, and culture—to a sense not just of dwelling, but a tradition of dwelling and traveling through space and time. Then, after an evening of poetry, we will have our board of directors meeting the following morning and consider the future of our own place and time together that we call Lindisfarne. We will close with David Spangler in a consideration of spirits of time and place as a way of imaginatively thinking about the kairos of where we are now and where we go from here as we leave this place and return to our personal forms of dwelling.

W. I. Thompson, Jane Hirschfield, and Paul Winter at the Princeton Chapel, 2013

So this is how I saw the architecture of this Lindisfarne gathering as I worked out the program in Zurich. Of course, now that we are all here, how it will go is entirely up to us as a group.

Now I would like to return to our theme of "At Home in the Universe" to consider Stuart's conclusion about reinventing the sacred for a new global civilization by reflecting on the project of Lindisfarne as an effort to work toward this end within the constraints of the kairos of the last quarter-century. "Kairos" is one of my favorite terms; it is Greek and means appropriate season of action, and just proportion. So it is both a temporal and a spatial metaphor.

Part of the original kairos of Lindisfarne was to shift ideas of both time and space by moving out of the linear sense of technological progress to retrieve a more mythopoeic sense of time. This project was expressed in my 1971 book, *At the Edge of History.* I was also concerned with moving out of the spatial containment embodied in the architecture of the modern technological university like MIT or York. So rather than spending a sabbatical at Oxford or Cambridge, I decided to visit places like Arcosanti in Arizona, Auroville in India, and Findhorn in Scotland.

Out of this *Lehr und Wanderjahr* came the founding of Lindisfarne and my third book, *Passages about Earth*. This cultural shift in the envaluation of time and space called for abandoning the technological giantism of powerful institutions like MIT, as well as the whole spirit of technological internationalism and modernization that MIT embodied during the period of the Viet Nam War. At that time, MIT felt that it was called upon to technologize the world, modernize traditional cultures abroad, and, at home, technologize the humanities by transforming the study of literature, history, and philosophy into linguistics and cognitive science. To induce artists to join the movement, the Center for Visual Studies was created, and various new electronic gnostic gadgets were offered by the Archons of the MIT Corporation to capture the enthusiasms of artist, writer, and composer. At this critical moment of historical transition, I was situated in the middle of that Vatican of the One True Catholic and Apostolic Church of Technology by serving as a professor of humanities at MIT.

The Institute at that time was being torn apart by the political conflict between the liberal technocrats who were Viet Nam hawks and the Marxist radicals who were doves. But both hawks and doves shared a faith in the power of technology and only argued over who should own the means of production. The spiritual quests of the sixties had no place there, and the crossing of Aurobindian yoga and Maslovian psychology that Michael Murphy put together at Esalen Institute seemed ludicrous to the leading liberal and radical lights of MIT. So I quit MIT in 1968, and sought to distance myself from its modernization project, and, as well, distance myself from the American Empire by going to Canada. And there at a conference at Lake Couchiching in Ontario in 1969, I heard the charismatic Ivan Illich for the first time and heard him articulate the need to create "counterfoil institutions." Illich's talk was exactly what I wanted to hear, because I had tried to set up a dialogue between mysticism and science at MIT, but I was not able to do it in their managerial culture. I was hearing a kind of silent music that had no place within the Institute, so I was searching for other spaces and times. In listening to Illich, I realized how this silent music could only come forth into sound in a counterfoil institution. One had to separate oneself from the dominant institutions of the university, the church, and the corporation.

A year or so after encountering Illich, at Professor Alastair Taylor's home near Queens University, I came upon a transmission from David Spangler that had been published in pamphlet form by the Findhorn Foundation. This little pamphlet gave voice to a disembodied presence that felt to me as if it were coming from the same source as the "unheard melodies" that I was picking up on. It spoke of the need for separation—a bifurcation—a radical move into a new world of higher consciousness. As I prepared to embark upon my sabbatical journey, I knew I would have to track this little pamphlet to its source in Findhorn. So my project became not one of a liberal's piecemeal tinkering with the dominant institutions, but a more radical project of cultural bifurcation in time and space. We did not yet speak of Strange Attractors in those days, but, in Ralph Abraham's terms of Chaos Dynamics, a new basin of attraction had appeared like a bolt out of the blue.

After returning from my trip around the world, I knew that I could not simply go back to the university and carry on with business as usual. I would have to risk it to quit the university and set up Lindisfarne as an alternative institution, as a counterfoil institution, for what the counterfoil institution could do that the university could not was to create a moiré pattern of the overlapping domains of art, science, and religion. Instead of bringing bureaucrats from the world religions together with academics, I would work to have a triple circularity of artists, mystics, and visionary scientists. This triple circularity would be the opposite of MIT's approach, because at MIT art was technological art, religion was the managerial response of ethicists to the challenges posed by technology to traditions, and science was technological invention. At MIT, the faculty was always constrained by public relations managers to find ways in which whatever we were doing in the humanities could be made to fit into the MIT technological style and image. These public relations executives were basically telling the faculty how to think, if we wanted to stay on the team. So literature became Chomsky's linguistics and cognitive science, and art became the Center for Advanced Visual Studies, which has since morphed into Negroponte's Media Lab.

But what I was looking for was not a leveling into the plane of uniformity—the sort of monocrop approach of agribusiness—but an ecological circularity in which difference was energized and accepted. My image for this was the biosphere with its triple circularity of ocean, continent, and atmosphere in which difference drives the thermodyanmic engine of Gaia. In the consilience of E.O. Wilson, he calls for the unification of all knowledge into one dominant science, but this is the fundamentalist's error that would turn the biosphere into a uniform slime of wet, gaseous sludge. This is the Titanic Archaean era out of which we have evolved, and, in the directionality of time, we should not return. My Irish icon for this triple circularity of the biosphere is the Celtic trifoil knot that is inscribed on the gate to the abbey on Iona. I felt that the importance of the circularity of the independent descriptions of art, science, and religion was to create these recursive loops of self-organization so that a new emergent domain could come forth that was not a university with a bureaucracy or an ashram with a single guru.

Religion left to itself becomes fundamentalism. Science left to itself becomes reductionism or Eliminativism—in the sense of the term used by Paul and Patricia Churchland in cognitive science. In their cognitive science, one can "eliminate" the folk psychology in which one speaks of soul or self. So science left to itself tends to implode and becomes that kind of total explanation that all too easily becomes totalitarian as it is extended over non-scientific subjects by the thought police of the technological state. The toxicity of that kind of scientific management had become all too evident to me at MIT during the Viet Nam war. But art too can become toxic. Art left to itself becomes narcissism—after the fashion of Andy Warhol, who, in an exhibition in Bern of works he did on cars for Mercedes Benz, said that the art of America is business. In the Middle Ages we had iconography, and now we have advertizing.

So any single cognitive domain—art, science, or religion—left to itself can collapse into itself and become toxic. In the nihilism of the postmodernist humanities in academe, we ended up with a sludgy and opaque subculture of anaerobic intellectuals. In eliminiativist science, uniformity replaces complexity. This is what William Blake referred to as "Single Vision and Newton's Sleep." And in religion, mythic and symbolic complexity is eliminated in fundamentalism that becomes a license to kill. Whether it is the case of an Israeli settler machine-gunning Moslems at prayer in a mosque, or a Muslim terrorist blowing up a passenger jet, or a Christian shooting a doctor or bombing an abortion clinic, we have stars that have collapsed into black holes.

Now from Stuart's discussions of criticality and the edge of chaos, we can begin to appreciate how complexity is a resource for the evolution of life, and how life emerges from conditions that are neither excessively fixed or excessively fluid. What the triple circularity allows is a topology with edges where opposites can influence or engage one another. The computer chip is not as advanced a topology as the cell, because the complex folding of proteins in a cell empowers more surfaces to come into play than is the case of a simple digital gate in a neural net. Now as Luigi Luisi has suggested to me, this triple circularity is not really between Art, Science, and Religion, but between artists, scientists, and spiritual practitioners. And this, of course, is what the Lindisfarne Fellowship is all about. A technician in a lab can be a nerd without a life or a body, but a creative scientist more often tends to be alive in more domains than one. Einstein played the violin, Heisenberg was a pianist, and Luigi writes children's stories and practices Zen. In a technical grouping, one is constrained to have only one side and to always have it engaged in the cogs of the productive machine. But in the Fellowship, one delights in more facets of reflection and listening with respect to other world-views, other ways of being "at home in the universe."

In the evolution of this triple circularity of artists, scientists, and spiritual practitioners, there is a process of cultural selection at work. Institutions tend to be dominated by alpha males who seek to reproduce themselves through graduate students. This pattern of culture generates followership and not fellowship. It is a scientific version of the High Priest in which the director of the lab has his signature on the published papers, even though his post docs have done all the work, and this growing list of publications enables the director to gain more credit and raise more funds so that he can hire more post docs to do his research for him. A high priest is a figure chosen by a bureaucracy in a dominant imperial city, but a shaman is chosen by spirits in the wilderness. A shaman comes to his power through a process of transcendental selection rather than societal selection. A village can notice that a certain child seems marked out, and this process of differentiation from the norm can initiate a process of esoteric training. What makes the Lindisfarne Fellowship different from a fraternity or club is a recognition that someone has been marked out, someone doesn't quite fit into the norm, someone has an inner complexity that doesn't live comfortably within the routines of the institutions of the high priest and his temple. In our quarter-century of activities, I would say that Gregory Bateson, Jim Lovelock, and Lynn Margulis are archetypal examples of this sort of risk-taking scientist who lives the kind of creative life we more often associate with the solitary artist or composer.

In industrial society, the artist like Blake or Beethoven took over much of the old charismatic life of the shaman, but since he or she could not heal society, the modern shaman often fell into the old role of the sacrificial victim. So you get the pattern of self-destruction and the deaths of Jackson Pollock, Mark Rothko, Dylan Thomas, and Sylvia Plath. This is the case of the artist imploding on herself and becoming toxically sick from the stagnation that comes from the lack of the healthier ecology of the triple circularity: the artist as cosmic narcissist. But if there is a self-organization at the edge of chaos in which shamanic artists, shamanic scientists, and yogic practitioners of different religious traditions come together, then a fellowship of elective affinities appears as an emergent domain, and then there is more air to breathe. Exactly opposite to the high priest in his temple or the cult leader in his sect—who consumes all the available oxygen—this emergent domain is not the realm of the alpha male surrounded by his subdominant males. This emergent domain is leaderless; it is a domain of fellowship and not followership and requires the initiator of the process to be more of a midwife than a parent.

Now we all recognize what a shamanic artist looks like, or what a shamanic practitioner of Yoga, Suf'ism, Tibetan or Zen Buddhism, or Cabbala looks like. The picture of Sri Aurobindo in his chair will suffice. But what does a shamanic scientist look like? I suppose Einstein would immediately spring to mind, and that is why I see Einstein as the Luther-like archetypal figure for the new Reformation of the post-religious era of scientific spirituality. The shamanic physicist has been chosen by the angel of physics, by what the Neoplatonists called "the Celestial Intelligences." From Pythagoras to Einstein, there is a noetic polity that extends over time and space and includes the noble dead as well as the living, the celestial as well as the terrestrial, and the shamanic scientist has a particular calling to this larger domain. He or she has an extended sensitivity that is not confined by the walls of the containing institution. Touched as they are, these people are often looked upon by their colleagues as touched in the head, so they have to learn how to hide their inner nature, because in our society they really are heretics and are in danger of being expelled from the world of science. This is not to say that some of them do not combine genius with craziness in socially impossible ways. The case of Nikola Tessla comes to mind.

When these figures are isolated and alone, they can become subject to manic inflation, seizures of paranoid cosmic synthesis, as well as depressive states. To separate genius from lunacy in solitary figures like Nikola Tessla becomes supremely difficult, and if the figure begins to attract messianic followers, it becomes harder still. But if there is a healthy fellowship, then very often the lunacy of raving to oneself can be replaced with lively conversation.

This fellowship can work for artists as well as scientists. I remember vividly the case of our Fellow Haydn Stubbing. His work now is in the collection of the Tate Museum in London, but when I first met Haydn out in the Hamptons in the early seventies, his work was being ignored and he was not treated as one of the fellas by the more famous artists in the Hamptons who were his neighbors. But when Haydn became a Lindisfarne Fellow and began to live in and through the meetings with the other Fellows, especially with the scientists, his depression left him and he entered into a highly creative period that is summed up by the two giant canvases, Iona and Lindisfarne, that are now in the Universal Hall at Findhorn. Whether he was in the pub of the Pelican Inn with Lovelock, Margulis, Maturana, and Varela, or taking Gary Snyder trout fishing in Scotland, Haydn came to life through the fellowship, and he told me so as he gave me the large painting that now hangs in St. James Chapel at the Cathedral of St. John the Divine.

Yvonne Hagen, Haydn Stubbing, Wendell Berry,
and Tanya Berry, Fellows Conference, Fish Cove, 1977

So the cultural project of Lindisfarne concerned with science and spirituality in the seventies called for moving out of the institutional space of the university to establish a counterfoil institution that could bridge the gulf between the anti-spiritual university and the anti-intellectual ashram or mindless commune of the sixties. MIT was anti-spiritual and Findhorn was anti-intellectual, so the project of Lindfisfarne was to be Madhyamika, to follow the middle path between these polarities, to supply what our Fellow Fritz Schumacher called "the missing middle."

By bringing shamanic practitioners of religion, science, and art together, a moiré pattern that wasn't singly religion, science, or art emerged. This was a culture that didn't yet exist, so I called it "planetary culture." I didn't mean international, and I didn't mean what today is called postmodernist or multicultural. My view of planetary culture was more of a feeling for an epiphany of a possible future. At the edge of history, we had come to a fork in the road: one path led to a dark age brought about by industrial pollution, and national and religious wars; the other led to a transformation of national and industrial culture. Religion with its violent fundamentalisms would be replaced by a personal mysticism in which no church or temple was needed to experience the universe as a cosmic mind. Industrial technology and capitalist economics would be replaced by ecology as the new governing science for meta-industrial settlements and symbiotic, green cities. And Baconian science would be replaced by a new Pythagorean science in which separation, reductive analysis, and control were replaced by pattern recognition, imaginative articulation, and participation.

So Lindisfarne, especially Lindisfarne-in-Manhattan—became more of a concert than a college. Like a crocus in March followed by a blizzard, Lindisfarne was too early. There simply was not the cultural or political support to create a college for a planetary culture. The gatherings of the Lindisfarne Fellows, just like this one, became a concert of intellectual chamber music or mind jazz, and not a meeting of the faculty. For brief moments, say in the Green Gulch conference of 1981, we could see out of time and glimpse what it would be like to be alive in a very different culture in a very different world. We became in Mary Catherine Bateson's words, "Our Own Metaphor," our own "Ecology of Mind." And in the literal sense of mind jazz, Paul Winter would take inspiration from his meetings with Jim Lovelock at Jim's home in Coombe Mill, create his Missa Gaia, and then perform it in Moscow before the Soviet Union melted and the Berlin Wall came down.

What has been delightful to discover with Lindisfarne is that there is an unconscious and unplanned "Association" that extends not just over disciplines but generations as well. For example, in the 1977 Lindisfarne conference on "Mind and Nature" in Southampton, I was talking to Gregory Bateson about Whitehead, and I mentioned Whitehead famous remark at a meeting in Cambridge in which he commented on Bertrand Russell's illuminating talk on Einstein by complimenting him "for not obscuring the inherent darkness of the subject." Gregory smiled down at me from his towering height and said: "Oh, yes, I remember that evening." I was astonished, as if myth had just become history, since Whitehead was part of my own high school mythic horizon, as I looked back at the intellectual culture of Europe from the world of gas stations and taco stands in L.A.

Kathleen Raine at her home in London, 2003

Another moment in which myth became history for me through Lindisfarne came when Kathleen Raine and I were discussing Virginia Woolf and Kathleen commented rather casually that she remembered the lecture at Cambridge when Virginia Woolf came and gave her famous talk, "A Room of One's Own." Through the older generation of Gregory Bateson, Kathleen Raine, and Nancy Wilson Ross—who had been a student of Kandinsky and Klee at Bauhaus—our efforts at creating an alternative movement reached back into the work of the grandparents. Emily Sellon was on our founding board of directors in 1972, and Emily, along with Fritz Kunz and their Foundation for Integrative Education and its journal, Main Currents in Modern Thought, were responsible for publishing works of a more holistic approach to science of scientists like Adolf Portman in biology and Werner Heisenberg in physics. *Main Currents* also published my very first essays as well as those of Fritjof Capra. So what we see here is a normal generational pattern that sometimes in seeking alternatives to the dominant culture of the generation of the parents, the child goes back to find inspiration in the works of the grandparents. When Owen Barfield came to our Lindisfarne conference in Crestone on the Evolution of Consciousness, I knew that I was linking our work with the work of the "Inklings," Barfield, C.S. Lewis, and J. R. Tolkien. You see this same generational pattern of inspiration at Esalen in the founding efforts of Michael Murphy, who reached back to the Integral

Yoga of Sri Aurobindo and the esoteric philosophy of Gerald Heard and his Trabuco College in Ojai.

What these examples express is a generational dynamic in which ideas get picked up, elaborated, and then played out in a new generational form. Esalen is not the yogic ashram, Lindisfarne is not Esalen, or Bauhaus, or Black Mountain. There isn't always a strict linear continuity of cultural creativity — as there was between Bauhuas and Black Mountain — and sometimes there is a caesura — a pause or silence in which a new approach comes from a different direction. Jean Gebser died in 1973, and he, along with Adolf Portman used to attend the famous Eranos conferences of C. G. Jung in Ascona in the Ticino. In 1973 I set up Lindisfarne in the Hamptons and had our first conference in the summer of 1974. These alternative forms of cultural expression are not institutional investitures; they are shamanic epiphanies of spirits of time and place. When you go to MIT or ETH, the graduate student works with his or her professor, and then the professor anoints the student and the institution enrobes them, and they go out into society to find places in other MITs and ETHs. This is the cultural process of the production of priests for temples. The shamanic epiphany, however, is much more of a "mind to mind transmission," not just the mind of a person in an institution, but the immanental Mind of this extended noetic domain.

Gregory Batesson, W. I. Thompson, Francisco Varlea,
and David Finkelstein, Fish Cove 1977

Examples of this kind of commitment to the tradition of "the pattern that connects" mind to the ecology and one generation to another would be the 1977 Lindisfarne conference "Mind in Nature" in Southampton with the Batesons, David Finkelstein, Francisco Varela, Arthur Young, and the fifteen year old philosopher Evan Thompson. Evan started out as an invisible listener at the end of the table in the dining room at Fish Cove as Gregory and Cisco went at it, from one generation to another, with a third generation getting ready to make its move. Evan began as a kid at Fish Cove, moved to becoming a student in Varela's class at Lindisfarne-in-Manhattan, then became a research assistant in Paris, and finally a co-author in Toronto.

Another performance of Cisco and Evan's work together came with the Lindisfarne Fellows conference in Perugia, Italy in the spring of 1988, and was followed by my daughter Hilary's first talk at the Fellows conference at Esalen in the summer of that year.

Evan Thompson, Francisco Varela, Hilary Thompson, and Nancy Todd with back to Camera at the 1988 Fellows Conference in Perugia and Gubbio, Italy

Thanks to the efforts of Cisco and Mauro Ceruti, we received an invitation from the very Left wing government of the province of Perugia to bring the Fellows together for a public meeting on a biological basis for design. Now "the missing middle' —Lovelock, Margulis, and Varela— that is not present here for this gathering was very much in attendance at that gathering. Nevertheless, I still think that all their ideas are still present and part of the intellectual history of this gathering. Susan was there, and Arthur as well, and this was the occasion of Evan's debut and his crossing over from Lindisfarne kid to Lindisfarne colleague as he gave his first public lecture in that beautiful Renaissance *Sala di Notari*.

Hilary's crossing over from Lindisfarne kid to colleague came at Esalen in '88. Hilary spoke on self-organization in Lacan's famous "Stade du mirroir" lecture in Zurich and related these ideas to those of Varela's on autonomy and self-organization. Hilary, like Katherine Hayles at UCLA, was trying to create a bridge between literary theory and complex dynamical systems, and Cisco was delighted. The talk was bright and humorous, and to complete the generational process, she read her poem about fathers and daughters, "Thesis, Antithesis, Parenthesis." The talk and the poem were a display of metaphysical W. I. Thompson, and Cisco, Lovelock, Bob Thurman, Susan Oyama, and Mary Catherine, and I all cracked up. So if I am retiring from the presidency of Lindisfarne with this meeting, it is because I have already passed the torch from one generation to another and can now step back and let all of you carry on in whatever way you deem appropriate.

Part of the cultural phenomenology in which the three independent descriptions of nature through art, science, and religion create a moiré pattern or emergent domain comes from the participation of historical time itself in this performance. This participation is an expression of the kairos, the appropriate season of action. But this word "appropriate" indicates that this kairos is time-bound and time-limited. So there is a larger circularity in which the kairos is situated in a greater cycle, and the ancient Taoists recognized this when they said: "Reversal is the movement of Tao." So if an artist or prophet has a daimonic sensitivity, one that shifts from the ego in its institutional location to the daimon and the Zeitgeist, then one can feel that the kairos that exalts you in a lifting wave can also leave you stranded as the wave recedes. The difference that makes a difference is time. The interpretation of historical time can exalt you in your twenties but leave you dry in your sixties, especially if you persist in holding on to the same interpretation of history. To be always defined by the Berkeley or Paris of 1968 in 1998 can be sad or tragic, depending upon whether history repeats itself as tragedy or farce. In the enantiodromias of history, the angelic can become demonic. Recall that Faust is warned by Mephistopheles that when he says: *Verweile doch, du bist so schön*," the devil can take his soul. We call this inability to move from one era to another aging, and many prophets have chosen sacrificial death as the only way for their time-bound vision to survive.

So let us consider the historical reversals of all my Lindisfarne examples. The Cathedral of St. John the Divine in New York has now, upon Dean's Morton's retirement, become once again a routine-operational Episcopal church. You won't find any of the books of the Lindisfarne Fellows in the Cathedral bookstore any longer. Bishop Greine has taken a firehose and cleaned out all the traces of our Gaia Politique. And as for Crestone: instead of becoming a meta-industrial village in which nature is scaled up and technology is miniaturized, Crestone has become a community shaped by cars, pickup trucks, roads and parking lots for all the New Age and traditional religious centers. You can have a meta-industrial village in Europe, and indeed some do exist in Denmark and Sweden, because in Europe you have trains and streetcars and a commitment to community. But in the rugged individualist culture of the American West, it is extremely difficult to create a meta-industrial village because people would rather have personal cars than public transport; they would rather have rifles instead of police, and isolated ranches instead of "big government." Nevertheless, Crestone works well for monasteries and lay retreat centers, but the cost of bringing people there makes it costly to run as a conference center.

As for the environmentalism of the seventies and eighties, even Maurice Strong has admitted publicly "The spirit of the Rio Summit has died."

Mary Catherine Batson listening to Maurice Strong,
Last Fellows Conference at Seven Pillars Academy, 2012

Even that spirit was much more corporate liberal and technocratic than the Gaia Politique articulated at the Lindisfarne Fellows meeting in Crestone in 1982. And as for the Lindisfarne Fellows meeting in Perugia in 1988, Italy has not gone Green, but has swung to the Right in the hope of meeting the German Bundesbank's demands for the three percent deficit limit for the adoption of the new currency of the Euro. And if we look around academe today, we will not see in the humanities any trace of the alternative movement of the last twenty-five years. Our Fellow David Orr's Center for Environmental Studies at Oberlin College is the shining example of an exception to the general trend. Because many of us, like John Todd, myself, and David Orr left academe in the seventies, academe returned the favor and got on with its life after divorce. It went directly from the Foucault of the sixties to the Derrida, De Man, and Gayatri Spivak of the seventies, to Hoomi Bhabha and Stephen Greenblat of the nineties. Rather than exploring contemplative spirituality, academe immersed itself in a postmodern nihilism and a new kind of Marxist materialism in subaltern studies, the New Historicism, and Queer Studies. Unfortunately, the Gay and Lesbian caucuses on most campuses were not culturally innovative, but quite conservative in wishing to gain rights and acceptance in the military, organized religion, and traditional marriage. So they simply affirmed the role and idea of the military officer, the priest, and traditional marriage and parenting. It was, ironically, Hollywood that picked up on New Age spirituality and a chic form of movie star Buddhism led by Richard Greer. In many popular films, reincarnation and life in bardo became acceptable subjects for pop culture presentations. So now we have a very American configuration in which a tight, close-minded and anaerobic academe is at one pole, and a very loose and *kitschig* New Age subculture is at the other.

To appreciate the reality of this new kairos, consider the triple circularity of religion, science, and art as the Zeitgeist rearticulates itself into fundamentalism in religion, commodity gimmickry in art, and eliminativism in science. In the sixties, Michael Murphy and I were both committed to the vision of a post-religious spirituality as prophetically announced by Sri Aurobindo.

Michael Murphy, Co-Founder of Esalen, Crestone, 1992

Mary Catherine Bateson, W. I. Thompson,
Michael Murphy, and Saul Mendlovitz 1992

Brother David Steindl-Rast, Sarah Raine, Evelyn Ames,
Paul Winter, and Michael Murphy, Fellows Conference, Crestone 1979

But now with the withdrawal of the Liberal-Welfare state in the U.S., Canada, Sweden, and Germany, the social safety net set in place during the Depression is being removed. We now live in a Bill Gates "Winners Only!" society in which the stock market goes off the charts, and our prisons begin to swell with the highest proportion of our population behind bars that we have ever had in our history. As the state withdraws, government turns to religions and says: "You take care of them." So the exercise of compassion and caring for the losers in a Winners Only society will have to come from religions, just as the decline of good public schools will also energize a return to parochial schools and fundamentalist homeschooling.

So the experimental communities of the seventies, in all their variety—Auroville, Findhorn, Lindisfarne in Southampton, The Farm, Arcosanti, Lama Foundation, Green Gulch—will become reservations for failures and dropouts from the dominant society. In a culture of dot.com wealth, they will become reservations for individual consciousness and not electronic Artificial Intelligence. What this means is that religious orders will return to succor the suckers, to care for the losers, and the postreligious spirituality of Einstein and Aurobindo will have to wait for a later era.

If we turn our attention from religion to art, we can see that rather than art becoming shamanic, after the mode of Jerzy Grotowski or Andy Goldsworthy, shamanism itself has become a consumer product in the work of people like Lynne Andrews. Deepak Chopra has become a millionaire from the sale of his videos, and spiritual ashrams have become wellness spas, and Crestone itself runs the risk of becoming a theme park of the world religions.

When we turn our gaze to science and technology, we can see that the Internet has become an externalization and simulacrum of the Astral Plane. Everything in there is now out there. In shifting his allegiance from anarchic Apple to corporate IBM, Bill Gates in the eighties paved the way for this new baroque era of wealth. The counterculture has shifted from being *avant garde* to becoming apologists for MIT's Media Lab. Think of *Wired Magazine* with its erotization of technology through drugs. The new counterfoil institutions are not really counter as much as charismatic embodiments of the new kairos. They are not the Farm or Lama Foundation with their cultural quotations of bib and tucker rural poverty, but grand baronial estates produced by the new culture of wealth—institutes like the Santa Fe Institute, this Fetzer Institute, or the new Ross Institute in the Hamptons and Manhattan.

Now it is very important to realize that each formation has its own structure of light and shadow. The counterfoil institutes as outlined by Ivan Illich in the sixties may have had an ethos of "voluntary simplicity" but they suffered from—in the immortal words of our own Joan Halifax—volunteerany. The unpaid or underpaid volunteer demanded psychic investments in the form of the role of the passive aggressive who needed contributions to their feelings of victimization. Often the move to the postindustrial community was really a cultural retrieval of the neolithic community in which matristic culture needed to assert itself through a psychodrama in which the male leader had to die to fructify the fields. So if our cultural experiments had their shadow-formation, these new and more dazzlingly brilliant institutes will also have theirs.

To appreciate this shift from the seventies to the nineties, it is worthwhile recalling the shift from the Renaissance to the Baroque. The Italian Renaissance was an expansion created by a new merchant class at a time when individual labor was valued because so many people had died in the plague of the fourteenth century. The Medici were merchants and not landed aristocrats, but as the new global economy of Europe expanded, and as the charisma of culture shifted from religion to art and science, there was a subsequent reaction in the form of the Catholic Counter Reformation and the Inquisition. The new mercantile economy was reappropriated by the aristocratic class, and the new global economy was reconstructed upon African slavery.[2] The accumulation of wealth became theatrically extravagant and architecturally exuberant. The artist shifted from being a visionary pioneer of a new culture to becoming a court painter and psychophant. This too was a culture of "Winners

Only!" so it is not surprising now that Bill Gates, possessed by this archetype, is building his own enormous Ducal estate. Appropriately, Microsoft as a company is famous for its sweatshop corporate culture and its suppression of the anarchic and individual creativity that had been characteristic of Silicon Valley in its early start-up era.

If these new global systems continue to develop in a Pacific Shift that weds American corporations to repressive Chinese authoritarian cultural forms, then this new Baroque Era may last as long as the last one, and it will be a while before another 1688 leads to another 1776 and 1789. George Santyana said that "Those who are ignorant of history are doomed to repeat it." So whether the media rich will carry on until they are guillotined by the poor will depend upon just how much history the ruling elite has studied.

A consciousness of history, by contrast, can become the occasioning agent for novelty and surprise. The Xerox machine and the *Samidzat* literature helped melt down the Soviet Union, so perhaps the Internet and the World Wide Web can help meltdown communist China so that Tibet can become as free as Lithuania. Or, perhaps, even our own Hawaii—which was taken over in an American imperial move—may find its own independent Polynesian life.

"May you live in interesting times!" is an ancient Chinese curse. And we do indeed live in interesting times. But rather than becoming bitter to curse the times and lament the passing of the idealism of the sixties and seventies, I think one should let go, bless the new kairos and give its ruling generation space to play out its own contradictions and shadow-formation. Lao Tzu did not try to become a Confucian; he left the empire, and his trace in passing was the *Tao Te Ching* he brushed on paper at the request of the border guard who would not let him pass beyond the limits of empire without leaving something behind. The gentleman-scholar withdraws from the imperial court in China, and in India, the *sanyasin* turns over the family business to the next generation and retires to become a yogi. We need these Asian models today in our American Empire.

I opened this talk by referring to Stuart Kauffman's call to reinvent the sacred in a new global scientific civilization, so let me close these remarks by returning to his sense of looking out on a new horizon. If I am right about this new kairos, and not simply getting captured by a metaphor, which is the shadow side of being a writer, then how can one engage with the triple circularity of art, science, and religion under the influence of this new Zeitgeist?

First of all, I think one should not become bitter to curse the young and say that we did it better in our day. We should not lament the age to say: "Where is the movement?", as if it always had to be the summers of '67 and '68. And I think to hold on to power like an aging Yeltsin or Kohl is to become a ghost haunting a body without being able to live in it healthfully. To avoid this sad fate, one needs to let go, give oneself completely away, and to grant to the young the power of their time. This is not a passing of the torch, which is a linear form of investiture that the professor has with his graduate students, but more of a Taoist form of active/inactivity: *Wei-Wu-Wei*. After all, we know of Lao Tzu not through his actions in the imperial court, but in the brush work of his poems in the *Tao Te Ching*, and these are the traces of his exit at the periphery and not of his presence at the center. As one lets go of the exterior kairos in historical time, I think there is an interior kairos that appears to take us on a more personal journey that can lead to an enlightened and more spiritual form of conscious yogic death.

As for the culture that remains in external historical time, this new global civilization, I think one should implement an ultraviolet shift in the cognitive domains of science, religion, and art. Here I am thinking of the bee whose vision of color is shifted into the ultraviolet end of the spectrum and can see stripes on flowers that normal humans cannot see. Since fundamentalist religion won't go away easily, and since Science is the real Church of our Technological Society, I think it might serve if scientists became more religious, in the sense of connecting the part to the whole—*re-ligare*. Just as new religious orders arose in the middle ages, new religious orders of compassionate practice within the global polity might arise to address themselves to hideous wrongs. We already have examples of this in the Fetzer Institute's commitment to holistic medicine, or in John Todd's strategies for remediation of environmental pollution, or in Sim Van der Ryn's ecological designs for healthy environments. If the scientists can shift into the ultraviolet spectrum to become more religious, I think it might serve if the religionists became more artistic. The true religion of the West is not the Church and its clergy, but art: literature, music, architecture, and painting. Where dogma can constrain or persecute, art can celebrate and liberate. As an ex-Catholic, I would rather listen to Bach's B Minor Mass than go to mass.

If in Stuart's new global civilization, scientists become more religious, and religionists become more artistic, then I think it only fitting that artists become more scientific. Art can seek to integrate what we know from science with new states of cognitive bliss in affirmations of being. My own effort in this direction over the years has been to explore this area in the form of *Wissenskunst*.

If there is a shifting toward the ultraviolet of the cognitive domains of art, science, and religion—instead of toward the infrared of religious fundamentalism, scientific eliminativism, and the corporate hypercapitalism of Time Warner and Microsoft—then I hope that no new elite will come forth to capture the reinvention of the sacred for the new global civilization. I hope the domains remain biomes in a global ecology and do not become ruling institutions in a new global ideology for a global elite managing world civilization in a Darwinian "Survival of the Wisest." In keeping with Stuart's appreciation of life carrying on at the edge of chaos, and not becoming captured either by excessive crystalization or excessive dissipation, I hope that we never completely settle down into a homey and suburban universe.

---

[1] Stuart Kauffman, *At Home in the Universe* (New York: Oxford University Press, 1995).

[2] Robin Blackburn, *The Making of New World Slavery: from the Baroque to the Modern, 1492-1800* (London: Verso Books, 1997).

Chapter 9. Conclusion:
The Economic and Cultural Relevance of Lindisfarne

Bobby Mann, founder of the Julliard String Quartet, with his Stradavarius, and Rachel Fletcher faculty member of Lindisfarne's Summer School of Sacred Architecture, Crestone, Colorado 1981

At the 1979 Lindisfarne Fellows Conference in Crestone, Colorado, and again at our Summer School of Sacred Architecture in 1981, Robert Mann, the founder of the Julliard String Quartet, gave us the gift of a performance of Bach's *Chaconne* from the *Second Partita for Unaccompanied Violin in D Minor*. After the 1979 performance in Maurice and Hanne Strong's backyard, Bobby discussed with me those exalted moments of performance in which his conscious ego just disappeared in an epiphany of transfiguration. This form of epiphany was an experience I was familiar with in my own creative process when I was giving a public talk.[1]

Giving a public lecture without reading a text or consulting your notes is the most intense form of focused thinking I have ever known. One passes up out of the clouds of personal factual knowledge into a state of intuitive *gnosis* in which one learns much more than one personally knows. When this process of take-over happens, one can feel the audience also become more focused in a single collective noetic polity. On two occasions—one at Notre Dame University, the other at a Swiss Federal Institute of Technology conference in Tuscany—people have accused me of being a Hitler, simply because that is the only example of this process of Daimonic transformation they have ever encountered through newsreels of the Forties. The disturbed and agitated man at Notre Dame said: "Anybody that can do that with an audience is a Hitler!" I responded: "You mean if you could do that with an audience, you would become a Hitler. But I do this all the time, and I am perfectly safe and have no following." When the German woman in Tuscany attacked me and also called me a Hitler, the Swiss novelist Adolf Muschg came to my defense when I began to protest to the woman's wild caricature and he interjected: "Let me respond to this, as he began to calm the woman down." Of course, the truth is—or was in those days of public lecturing now long gone—that I did not do "that" or anything with the audience. *Au contraire*, something was done to me. And it was much the same with Lindisfarne as a group.

Something took us over in silent group meditation. I was not the leader of the group, but as the one who insisted on daily group meditation merely serving as the midwife aiding a process of birth for a noetic polity. I had no followers, and, in fact, the community members were all followers of Gregory Bateson, Baker-roshi, Pir Villayat Khan, or David Spangler, and again, on the contrary, the community members were all quite vocal about my shortcomings as the spiritual leader they were looking for. In fact, they held me in low regard and resented the fact that only I could raise the money to keep us going as a cultural enterprise, so I became the negative parent, a mommy-figure of household routine providing the groceries, while the enrobed religious figures like Baker-roshi and Pir Vilayat Khan became the charismatic leaders of the seventies' countercultural movement.

As a noetic polity, Lindisfarne had moments in group-meditation, or in our conferences, when we all felt transfigured and exalted in a state of being in time that was larger than ourselves, and larger even than Lindisfarne as a group. Ultimately, the real significance of Lindisfarne resided in this shared sense of exaltation that touched and transformed the lives of those who participated in our time-bound concert of visions, ideas, emotions, and embodied minds. This personal sense of transfiguration was the *metanoia* of our noetic polity. In the stillness of group meditation after the conflicts of ego in communal living, or in the confusion and passions of love affairs that did not fit into the previous definitions of our lives, those who felt a connection to Lindisfarne experienced a moment of exaltation in which the ego dropped out of the way and something ineffable took its place.

By definition, one cannot define the ineffable, so I do not wish to try to catalogue the epiphanies and moments of exaltation as Lindisfarne's *raison d'etre*. At the core, our being together was never rational: *La coeur a ses raisons que la raison ne connait point.* I never really knew what I was doing when I quit the university, founded the Association, changed it into a community, then an institute, and then a fellowship. I was improvising as I went along— more a jazzman than a virtuoso with a written score. But because the USA is overwhelmingly a practical culture built upon the American Dream of the consumption of appliances and apps, I wish to address myself to those of us who insist on kicking the tires before they buy into the greater or lesser vehicle. I wish to focus on the economic and cultural significance of Lindisfarne in our new hypercapitalist America in which the top one percent have bought out the country in a hostile takeover brokered by the government.

In the shift from a highly polluting consumptive economy to a contemplative one of bio-cultural participation—the real meaning of our Euro-American fascination with Yoga, Suf'ism, and Buddhism—not just Detroit but jobs themselves will disappear as a source of our identity. The job as a configuration is an industrial concept. The Dark Age and Medieval monk or nun did not have a job; he or she had a vocation, a calling. The monks in "The Plan of St. Gall" had artisanal and productive crafts (including making beer for B vitamins in the winter!) but they did not see themselves as having anything so prosaic as a job.

The Stanford Parc and Santa Fe Institute economist and cultural thinker, W. Brian Arthur, has described the emergence of a new global digital economy.[2]

Beatrice Thompson, Brian Arthur and daughter
Brid Arthur at 2012 Lindisfarne Fellows Meeting

Recently, Thomas Friedman, a columnist for the *New York Times*, predicted that that the job of restaurant waiter will soon be eliminated and replaced by iPad tablets on which the customer directly chooses his menu, calculates the bill, and pays by credit card.[3] When I lived in Manhattan, aspiring actors and ballerinas supported themselves with a day job as waiters or waitresses, so this economic shift will have vast cultural repercussions. ATMs replaced bank tellers and check-in clerks at airports, and computerized language programs are replacing language teachers, and MOOCS are replacing college teachers, so soon there will be no jobs left as nanotechnologies, decentralization of production through 3D printing, and "the Internet of Things," re-structure industrial civilization.[4]   As workers are no longer needed perhaps the authoritarian neo-feudalist state of the future will have to issue Existence Licenses to protect the property-owning classes from those who are stuck in reservations of passed-over cultures where despair, alcoholism, drugs, crime, and high suicide rates prevent them from paying income taxes? Will Agamben's "state of exception" find a new way to compact the trash?

As jobs go, so goes industrial society. The days when a high school

213

education got you a job at the local plant and a tract house for life in a stable working class community are gone forever. Post World War II America is not coming back. The film *Terminator* wasn't about robots killing people; it was a political allegory about machines terminating their jobs. Small wonder Arnold Schwarzenegger went on to become Governor of California.

As industrial production miniaturizes and moves, now to China, later to India and Africa, the question for now and the immediate future is: What does the 1% think it is going to do with the 99% when it has so restructured industrial production that structural unemployment is a permanent feature of this new economy? I guess the Republicans will expect the peasants to starve and simply disappear from the horizon of their gated communities, and the Democrats will have pipe dreams of another French Revolution.

The French economist Thomas Piketty has predicted that our economy will evolve from one of producers to inheritors, and that the children of the One Percent will become a new and entrenched patrimony. What he fails to imagine is that it would not be impossible for a new FDR and a new New Deal to address itself to that situation by passing laws that restrict inheritances to ten percent and that the remaining ninety percent by default would return to the federal government to invest in public education and federal grants for research. The One Percent could escape this appropriation by designating private colleges and universities of their choice as their cultural heirs. In this way their fortunes could be returned to their alma maters and not their *alma filii et filiae*. And to recycle the funds accumulating in the blockages of the rich, a tax on financial transactions could be used to revive that old sixties notion of a guaranteed annual income to transform the structurally unemployed into students on fellowships and stipends. What Piketty does allow us to do is to rethink the dynamics of a social democracy.

A more compassionate answer to the question of the meaning of human existence is that people will move from industrial nation-states into *noetic* polities. The rich have paved the way, for they are no longer patriotic and now feel that they have nothing in common with their lower class countrymen. Someone like Mitt Romney is much more at home with a Japanese entrepreneur, an Israeli venture capitalist, or a Saudi oil prince than he is with Joe Six Pack from Detroit.

Precisely because America is no longer the source of our cultural identity—as it was in the World War II days of GI Joes—nationalism has come to be replaced by regionalism and religion. In fact, the United States is no longer united, and like the Soviet Union, it is likely to break up in the next forty years. What we see in the popularity of the Lumbaughs, Palins, Perrys,

Bachmanns, and Santorums is the distinct emergence of North American cultural zones. A Silicon Valley Californian has closer relations with China than Kansas. A New Yorker or Bostonian has more relations with Europe than with the Mid-west. We have reprised the America of the Scopes trial in which it is science vs. the Bible Belt all over again—this in spite of almost a century of cultural investments. TV has defeated public education and secured the dumbing-down of America.

The Northeast, the Southeast, the Southwest, Middle America, and the Pacific Northwest are five distinct emerging biomes. To give them cultural instead of locational tags, we could give them the Latin names of Intelligentsia, Ignoratio, Religio, Imaginatio, and Moderatio.

To stop scientific investment from being localized around MIT and Cal Tech, Democrats familiar with the backwardness of rural life like LBJ insisted that NASA invest in Houston and Huntsville, Alabama, but fifty years after this noble effort we still see a cultural divide in which places like Manhattan, Cambridge, Ann Arbor, Madison, Austin, Boulder, Chapel Hill, and Berkeley are the only places to live if you are interested in bookstores, real cafes, good restaurants, foreign movies, science, and performing arts. To live in places like Saguache County, Colorado—as I know only too well from personal experience— is to have your life reduced to a parking lot culture of no cafes, awful restaurants, Clear Channel car radio, and what is available in Walmart.

Now people of all five states of mind are spread throughout the biomes, so you have some East Coast intellectuals in the Research Triangle of North Carolina, and some zealots of the Bible Belt in the rural areas of Pennsylvania, Maine, and New Hampshire, but as some states start passing Rick Santorum's Catholic *Sharia* laws—banning Gay or interracial marriage or policing the bedrooms of the nation to insure that married couples do not commit the sin of having oral sex—you are going to see people moving into cultural zones that are more accommodating to their world-views and life-styles.

Artists and Gays have always fled our rural areas to go to places like Manhattan and San Francisco, but now we are going to see a cultural exodus in which the rural areas collapse back into black holes of Aryan Nation, junk food obesity, cigarette-smoking, and a crystal meth and heroin drug culture to relieve the boredom of rural life. From Texas to North Dakota, Idaho, Montana, and Alaska, or what Sarah Palin calls "the real America" will become an American tribal Waziristan, a "no-go zone" for the educated class of scientists and humanists.

The current cultural opposition—whether over guns or Gays—between the Heartland and the metropolitan coasts shows the fault lines of an America beginning to break up.

The rich have already moved beyond patriotism and out of the nation-state, and are no longer simply American citizens. Like Mitt Romney, they have sold off their American manufacturing holdings and outsourced their investments to factories in Bangladesh and China, and to escape U.S. taxes have parked their millions in banks in Zurich and the Cayman Islands. Being rich is a state of mind, a state of consciousness, and a patriotic fervor for national unity with the American working classes does not map onto this new cultural evolutionary noetic polity of the wealthy top one percent.

But this newly emergent noetic polity is not based upon an industrial economy of scale; it is a fractal—a bubble of consciousness in a landscape of bubbles in self-similar architectures. The noetic polity can be as small as Lindisfarne or as large as Paris.

And, of course, there will be shadow noetic polities in which the nation-state breaks up into criminal domains. The Libertarians have fantasies of armed citizens but no federal government, but they do not pay attention to just what happens in states without governments in Ciudad Juarez, Mexico, Somalia, Pakistan, and Afghanistan. A shadow-economy of organized crime, warring drug cartels, and warlords creates a new wilderness of no-go zones. We are already beginning to see the outlines of this shadow economy in the collusion of government with organized crime in China and the United States. Our War on Drugs, for example, is a scam—a faked cops and robbers game that camouflages with rhetoric the reality of price supports for the drug cartels that the punitive laws against drugs sustain.

We have already entered the period of catastrophes—of droughts and wildfires in California, New Mexico and Texas, floods and tornados in the Midwest, hurricanes and superstorms on the East Coast and the Mexican Gulf. As these events cascade with earthquakes and climate collapse with their related food shortages, governments will be hard pressed to deliver services and this social collapse will further increase the growth of war lords, gang armies and vigilantes, and criminal polities. The Dieback of humanity predicted by Wes Jackson and other ecologists and social forecasters will begin. As resources such as clean water—thanks to fracking—and healthful food grow scarce, nation-states will compete with one another, and corrupt governments will turn nations into crime polities and crime polities into sub-nations. Notice how China and the USA have converged. China is *de jure* communist, and the USA is *de jure* democratic, but they both are *de facto* one authoritarian and plutocratic system in which a "Deep State" rules through a combination of corruption and organized crime.

In this new world of each against all, human identity will not be based upon anything as stable as a job or patriotic fealty to a large nation-state. In the prehistoric *sanguinal* polity of the tribe, identity was based upon kinship and blood relations. In the *territorial* polity of history—whether city-state or empire—identity was based upon location within boundaries. In the *noetic* polity, identity is based upon states of consciousness—tiny and immediate for some, vast and planetary for others.

Teenage boys join gangs because it provides them with an immediate sense of belonging, one that is often stronger than the sense of belonging provided by broken families and communities. My forty years of work with the Lindisfarne Association was an effort to provide a sense of belonging that came from my vision of "planetary culture" in which meditation replaced religious doctrine and political ideologies with an inner identity coming from the direct experience of a unique/universal, atman/Brahman, relation of an I with a Cosmic Mind. Call it God or Buddha Mind, or whatever term your *sadhana* requires, but this Cosmic Mind is a self-similar architecture of bubbles of consciousness from cells to galaxies. During its phase of life as an intentional community in Southampton and New York, I noticed that most of the people attracted to Lindisfarne came from broken or dysfunctional families. Paradoxically, we were isomorphic to the teenage gang that provided "an alternative culture." Lindisfarne was a noetic polity in which identity was based upon an ecology of consciousness and not upon an ideology or a cult following manipulated by a charismatic guru.

Consciousness emerged in evolution by pushing more and more processes into unconsciousness. I don't need to know how my liver is doing when I am writing a poem. I do want to know how my body is feeling when I am making love, so consciousness is a floating attractor, variously contacting other organic formations when it needs to. What we see going on now in the world is that the economy is being pushed from the consciousness structure of identity into the unconscious of the ecosphere.

This transition is, of course, like all historical transitions, a painful one. Money has ceased to circulate and has accumulated at the top 1% of the population as the source of wealth has shifted from industrial production to financial transactions. To make money in this world, one has to have money, and one simply cannot earn enough money to buy the chips to play at the tables in the casinos of high finance by saving as a wage earner.

To end the pain for the 99%, money needs to shift from a liquid currency to a gas, an atmosphere that one has to take for granted in the very act of breathing.

Various saints over the centuries, from St. Francis of Assisi to Mahatma Gandhi to Mother Teresa, have tried to effect a shift in our conscious system of identity by refusing to own things or accumulate wealth. In phase changes there are always a few individuals who effect the shift in state ahead of the mass; they are like the Cooper Twin electrons that effect the shift from conducting to superconducting in a metal.

History is slow and sloppy as a temporal process, but eventually the mass catches up. At first there are only a few isolated individuals, say artists in the Italian Renaissance or scientists in the Scientific Revolution, but soon the whole medieval civilization makes the transition from feudalism and religion to art and science in modern civilization.

Of course, there are always holdouts. Foragers resisted agriculture, tribal nomads resisted cities and empires, and now Islam resists the Great Satan of global hypercapitalist civilization. In the sacking of Baghdad in 1401, Tamerlane proved that holdouts could do a lot of damage, and, indeed, hold up civilization for centuries. But today Baghdad is not Mongol. And neither is it American, since baby Bush's project of enforced capitalistic modernization failed as much as Tamerlane's project of nomadic tribalization.

Marshall McLuhan claimed "the sloughed-off environment becomes a work of art in the new and larger environment." The Findhorns, Lindisfarnes, and Aurovilles of the seventies were the new interactive works of art in the invisible environment of jet travel and electronic hyper-capitalism. With the job no longer providing people with a sense of meaningful identity, they will begin to self-organize into intentional communities like Findhorn and Auroville. Since I was an intellectual, the Lindisfarne Association became a gathering of scientists, artists, and contemplatives. Because I did not wish to carry on like the guru of a cult, Lindisfarne was a more democratic complex adaptive system—a fellowship and not a followership. But others, like Richard Baker-roshi of the San Francisco Zen Center, were not so restrained and Zentatsu Baker-roshi presented himself as an enlightened figure who deserved to have all his needs and desires provided for by the contributions of the community.

Wendell Berry's idealized early twentieth-century monogamous family farm can also be seen to embody this Hegelian dialectic of *aufheben* in which the sloughed-off environment becomes a work of art in the larger and invisible environment. In an age of agribusiness and Big Pharma joining to produce tasteless artificial chemical milkshake foods like *Soylent*, the family farm becomes a boutique farm providing real food for upscale restaurants like Alice Water's Chez Panise—in other words, a work of art in the larger American environment of fast food drive-throughs that are no more than gas stations for humans.

Wes Jackson and Wendell Berry at the last
Lindisfarne Fellows Conference in 2012

The scientific work of Wendell Berry's good friend Wes Jackson and his Land Institute in Salina, Kansas has enriched the soil underneath Wendell Berry's idealized family farm. In Wes's work in shifting agriculture from a monocrop of annuals to a polyculture of perennials with grains that restore the prairie instead of exporting it into the sea of the Gulf of Mexico, he has created new grains for a new global society.[5] In the presentations of Lindisfarne Fellows, Wes Jackson, Wendell Berry, John Todd, and Lynn Margulis, the Fellowship achieved the cross-fertilization of ideas that I had hoped for in bringing diverse thinkers and doers together.

The seventies intentional communities were like the mitochondria with their ancient DNA that moved inside the eukaryotic cell—as described by our Lindisfarne Fellow the microbiologist Lynn Margulis—and went to work as little energy farms inside a larger molecular and genetic information system. So in the transition from value as a liquid currency of Money to a planetary biospheric gas, we are going to have to miniaturize all the previous economies (foraging, farms, and factories) inside our new planetary economy and ecosphere.

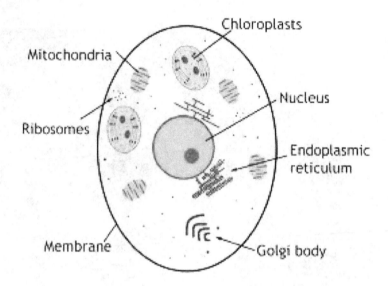

Here our Euro-American cultural fascination with Buddhism is telling, and what it tells us is that compassion is now more important than competition. In the Protestant Ethic and the Spirit of Capitalism, as explored by the sociologist Max Weber, or in the Gospel of Wealth, as exemplified by Baptists John D. Rockefeller—Senior and Junior—wealth was a sign of God's blessing on the pious. That Protestant world-view is now becoming so caricatured in the 1%'s indifference to the 99%, that it is showing signs of being in a state of cognitive dissonance and crisis. The fears of the Rick Perry's, Ted Cruz's, Sarah Palins, and Michelle Bachmans of conservative politics express this sense of anxiety that the great age of white American rural Evangelical Protestantism is disappearing in a tsunami of multicultural planetization.

The new challenge is one of distribution, because now in the etherealization of money,[6] only Goldman Sachs is manipulating "the difference that makes a difference" in micro-time transactions. Therefore, I see the tax on financial transactions that Hazel Henderson has called for as critical, because it would create a fund with which to award "fellowships" and start-up funds to more people than just the bankers, and allow people to live in these noetic polities.

The Tea Party and the Libertarians as well as the Occupy Wall Street demonstrations around the world were indications that third and fourth parties are emerging—in a meiosis-like cellular process—from the early industrial formations of Tory and Whig, or Republican and Democratic.

In anthropological terms, the Libertarians are a classic "revitalization movement" (see A. F. C. Wallace's 1956 defining paper in the *American Anthropologist*)[7] that appears whenever the old "mazeway" of a culture's movement through space and time is put under stress or threatened with erasure. In my 1985 book *Pacific Shift*, I called this movement of rural White Protestants "the Ghost Dance of the Rednecks." The first Ghost Dance of the Redman was a response to the railroads that Brian Arthur describes as having created the new American economy.

Now the Robber Barons like the Koch Brothers want to return to a Victorian economy of a class of serfs with no trade unions, public health, environmental protection, or public education, and they are willing to spend 100 million dollars on attack ads against liberal social democrats to convince the stupid to vote against the commonweal.

The Koch brothers represent another "revitalization movement" of the Gilded Age's industrial capitalism, a movement that indicates that Business also feels threatened with cultural erasure by a new international scientific elite. The businessman's denial of global warming and climate collapse is *prima facie* evidence of this fear.

The Tea Partiers and Libertarians see global warming and health insurance as deceits used by the intelligentsia to scare the populace into socialism with new and massive systems of government control. Given the hideous evil perpetrated by psychologists at McGill University and economists at the University of Chicago working for the CIA that Naomi Klein describes in her book, *The Shock Doctrine*,[8] these fears of the populace are not unfounded or paranoid. But this union of the confused and unemployed populace with the top one percent of the wealthiest disturbingly recalls the convergence of the masses and the I. G. Farbens and Siemens corporations working together to forge the fascist concept of the State in the Great Depression of the 1930s in Germany.

From my point of view as a liberal arts college graduate in the Humanities, these evils first described by C. S. Lewis in his novel *That Hideous Strength* and then more factually chronicled by Naomi Klein, the pretensions of the Social Sciences in their philosophically ignorant efforts to classify their ideological works as a rigorous science after the models of physics and chemistry were exposed. Whether it is the case of Professor Donald Ewen Cameron at McGill, or Professor B. F. Skinner at Harvard, or Professor Milton Friedman at the University of Chicago, it is the case of delusional specialists responsible for the torture and deaths of millions from the orphanages in Romania to the dictatorships of Chile and Argentina.

The contempt for the 99% by the wealthy 1% does have historical precedents. Imperial Rome gave us *latifundia* and bread and circuses; the Middle Ages gave us rituals and faith in the Great Chain of Being that bound peasant and lord together. The Enclosure Acts ended that relationship and gave us the market system, replacing crofters with sheep in the Highland Clearances and giving us market-based genocide in the Irish Famine. Nassau Senior, the first Chair of Economics at Oxford—ironically then called "moral science"—said at high table: "The trouble with the Irish famine is that not enough of them died."

If we are becoming a global noosphere of transnational interconnectivity—as Brian Arthur argues—one consequence is that all wars now become forms of suicide bombing. The toxic weapons we used in the first Gulf War with Papa Bush, and the depleted uranium artillery shells we used in the second Iraq war with Baby Bush, have proved toxic to our own soldiers and they have returned home with more than Post-Traumatic Stress Disorder.

The response of the Military-Industrial complex to this new vulnerability has been the use of drones, and soon will be robotic instruments for teleporting violence.

In this noosphere, we all use the Internet and the digital infrastructure; even terrorists use the Internet to recruit new followers. Unfortunately, both governments and terrorists are now becoming similar. "We become what we hate." The President can now declare a U.S. citizen to be a terrorist, or merely a terrorist sympathizer, and kill or imprison him or her indefinitely without due process of law. Authoritarian America and authoritarian China are now converging into one system of anti-democratic governance as our joined economies become a mutually dependent system, but one closed to any system of management except control from the top. The recognition of this political transformation is what is really behind the recent globalization of movements as different as the Arab Spring, Occupy Wall Street, and Ron Paul's Libertarian attack on our imperial military foreign policy.

It would now appear that industrial and service economy "jobs" are disappearing at the same time that international currencies like the Euro are in crisis and public universities like Berkeley and community colleges everywhere are being stripped of funds, so that they cannot take up the slack by employing the unemployed. We seem headed for a crisis greater than the Great Depression. The solution, it would seem to me, is not a propping up of the old economy through government bailouts of the Big Banks, but an entire restructuring of our dysfunctional industrial civilization.

On human terms, I fear this is not possible. *Homo sapiens* is just not that sapient.

Earth Day began in 1968 and Maurice Strong organized the Stockholm Conference on the global environment in 1972 and helped to create the United Nations Environmental Program—the year I founded the Lindisfarne Association. But the environmental movement was followed by forty-four years of corporate obstruction with Reagan, the Bushes, the Clintons, and now even Obama. I am afraid that we are in for a catastrophic environmental transition and a massive dieback, unless national governments can come up with something that is not Business as usual. Germany and the U.S. came out of the Great Depression through war. As William James suggested, we need to come up with the moral equivalent of war.

The new digital economic infrastructure suggests to me that the old industrial economy is now going through a process of miniaturization in which, as Brian Arthur shows, productivity goes up, but unemployment goes up as well as jobs simply do not come back on the scale once characteristic of industrial society.

In the industrial revolution, prefigured by the change in infrastructure brought on by the Enclosure Acts, agriculture was miniaturized as a new and smaller content within the structure of the new industrial society. Sheep replaced crofters and the dispossessed agricultural laborers migrated to a nineteenth-century North America emptied of aboriginal peoples by small pox and the army, and to the new cities and slums of the Industrial Revolution.

After World War II, many Americans—I among them—took part in a second wave of migration from the old industrial Rust Belt to the West Coast where first the aerospace industry, then the electronic industries and service economy absorbed them with their government-supported expansion of the defense industries for the Cold War.

Now in the digital revolution, factories and work forces are miniaturized, and industrial cities such as Detroit seem unlikely to spring back to what they were in the post World War II era. And, as Brian Arthur points out, the service economy of office workers, bank tellers, and teachers is contracting while the population is still expanding.

In the first contraction of agricultural and the second expansion of industrial society, art became a new economy as it was extended from the aristocratic to the middle classes. Where chamber music was once played in the large homes of the aristocracy, large symphony halls took their place, galleries proliferated for the new medium of canvas paintings for upper middle class homes, and the popular author, such as Charles Dickens, became a celebrity supported by a vast readership.

In the second contraction of the industrial and expansion of the service economy, education replaced art as the new superstructure. The University of California became the largest public university system in history, but it was simply the top of the pyramid of state universities, community colleges, and good public school systems. The critic as Professor in a collective became more important than the archetypal solitary Romantic Artist. Roland Barthes proclaimed the death of the author with his or her system of author-ity. Derrida's philosophy of *différance* may not have adequately described the literary work, but it certainly described the new monetary system that Nixon introduced to replace Breton Woods. Value became a mercurial fluid and not a stable solid. The solitary visionary of a Beethoven or a Blake became a thing of the past, and the Romantic Artist became replaced by the Rock Star or the Celebrity. The Celebrity is, however, a mirage, as it requires an atmosphere of hot air to produce and maintain its ephemeral illusion of individuality.

Now economic value has become an atmosphere and *not* a fluid currency, but we still treat money as if it were a currency that flowed through channels, and so we are experiencing a crisis of money and credit in which one percent of the population becomes the accumulating reservoir of money.

So it would seem to me that it is not just industrial productivity that is experiencing a process of miniaturization; it is the whole economy that is being miniaturized in a larger emergent structure. The economy is like a system of continents within the planetary atmosphere—which means that money should not be stored in the one percent at the economic stratosphere, but should be inhaled by everybody to sustain the life of a new planetary civilization.

But what seems to come between emergent civilizational economies are plunder economies and Dark Ages. If one reads Caesar's *Gallic Commentaries* and Tacitus's *Germania*, one realizes that what later became the European aristocracy was first simply a protection racket. Raiders on horses would take slaves home to do the work, while they increased the number and scope of their raids and drunken feasts. They soon found that if they took everything from the farmers, the farmers would starve, and they themselves would have no crops to plunder the next year. So the man on a horse coerced the farmer into an agreement; he would protect him from other raiders, if he agreed to give the lion's share of his harvest to him. Out of this arrangement, the Plunder Economy evolved into the next economy—feudalism based upon land tenure and oaths of fealty. The myth of blue bloods and the divine right of kings was the mythological system that grew up, like kudzu around a telephone pole, to cover the old protection racket of the Germanic and Celtic barbarians.

Bucky Fuller said that the first people to think on a planetary scale were the pirates. Piracy was the next Plunder Economy that came at the shift from land-based economies to mercantilist and capitalist ones. Queen Elizabeth used the pirates and privateers like Francis Drake to help her break the power of the land-based barons and contribute to the growth of trade that supported the Tudor monarchy.

What we see now with Mitt Romney's Bain and Company and Goldman Sachs is the new Plunder Economy in which the hostile takeovers of American factories and their subsequent closures and selling off of their parts is followed by a reinvestment in factories in China and Indonesia. Then the profits from these overseas investments are deposited in banks in Switzerland and the Cayman Islands to avoid American income tax. These enormous profits are then used to make huge donations to the Republican Party to energize a hostile takeover of the federal government so that tax cuts and special allowances can protect these corporate raiders from government controls and regulations, as well enabling them to buy ads to convince the electorate that the Republican Party is patriotic. So far this scam has worked and the electorate has been stupid enough to vote for these corporate con men like Romney who are simply robbing them. This new American Plunder Economy is the transition between our present hypercapitalism and a postnational global ecology of noetic polities, of which only a few will be scientific.

Recently, headlines in newspapers and the Web have shown how corporate entities like Apple Computer have more cash on hand than the federal government. The Occupy Wall Street movement was a recognition of this fact of life. As their signs said: "We are the 99%." Although the OWS movement was often criticized for lacking a coherent ideology, it was precisely its lack of an ideology that was its uniquely relevant characteristic, its *arête*. This New Left movement expressed an ecology of consciousness, an affirmation of diversity, and not an ideology characteristic of the industrial thinking of the 1930s. As they said in the one page hand out given to me and the visitors and supporters at Zuccotti Square:

> Occupy Wall Street is an exercise in "direct democracy." We feel we can no longer make our voices heard as we watch our votes for change usher in the same old power structure time and time again. Since we can no longer trust our elected representatives to represent us rather than their large donors, we are creating a microcosm of what democracy really looks like. We do this to inspire one another to speak up. It is a reminder

to our representatives and the moneyed interests that direct them: we the people still know our power.

Although Obama pretended to be sympathetic to the occupiers of Wall Street, he was more their cause than their colleague. When Obama orphaned the liberal progressive wing of the Democratic Party, he formed the New Left by leaving it out in the cold.

Following President and First Lady Hillary Clinton's deregulation of Wall Street with the advice of their viziers Robert Rubin and Larry Summers, Obama chose to continue the shift to the right in which the Clinton Democrats became what used to be the Rockefeller Republicans. When Larry Summer's disciple Timothy Geithner was put in charge of bailing out the banks—thus encouraging the reckless and high risk-taking speculations that caused the crisis of 2008—Obama created the new corporate culture in which the banks were too big to fail. For investors, this new culture—as Paul Volcker pointed out (*New York Review of Books*, November 24, 2011, p. 75)—meant that their profits would be private, but their losses would be reimbursed out of public funds. Risk-taking no longer had any risks. Small wonder that nothing changed in the behavior of Goldman Sachs *et alia* in which they paid themselves large fees from companies they raided and ravaged.

This New Left Green movement was neither socialist nor communist, for those ideologies were expressions of twentieth century industrial thinking. Communism was the category-mistake that sought to eliminate all differences to appropriate all property by the State. But a weather system, as well as an ecosystem, works through the thermodynamics of difference. Too much can give us a hurricane, too little can give us a drought. What is needed now is not a cascade, or mudslide, but an energizing of interruptions of flow through a system of terraces. Nature works through pulses of light and dark, hot and cold, not a uniform extension of sameness. Mars may have once been a living planet, but when it lost its magnetic field, it lost its atmosphere, its weather, its ecosystem of pulses.

Earth's magnetic field allowed life to evolve and cell membranes to form. What is needed now is an economic magnetic field to protect difference and pulsation. What is not needed is the extremes of obscene wealth and abject poverty, for that would be like having a continental weather system of only floods and droughts—a weather system that we are already experiencing as industrial climate change continues to bear down on us.

Whether the Tea Party may like it or not, the only entity positioned to generate a magnetic field is the federal government. Its task is now to redefine and create the system of terraces for the circulation of money. The Banks will not do it; the government of ordinary businessmen refuses to do it. So the difference engine that will drive the emergence of the new system will be ecological catastrophes.

In the meantime, it would seem to me that I am merely rediscovering the wheel—the very old idea of a Guaranteed Annual Minimum Income, first proposed by Thomas Paine at the beginning of the shift from agrarian to industrial society, and later advanced by such thinkers as John Maynard Keynes, Robert Theobald, Daniel Patrick Moynihan, and Hazel Henderson.

Maurice Strong and Hazel Henderson at the
1992 Lindisfarne Fellows conference in Crestone, Colorado

I enjoy my Social Security check each month and use it as a fellowship to support my writing and research. Social Security is not welfare, but an insurance system that I paid into throughout my working career. I am sure that some young people—after the manner of Jobs and Wozniak who worked in the garage that saw the birth of the Apple computer that challenged the rule of IBM—would use their GAI fellowships with equal imagination.

The small tax on financial transactions that Hazel Henderson has been calling for— or the global tax on capital that Thomas Piketty has been calling for—seems to me to be the source of funds to support a Guaranteed Annual Income. A financial transactions tax could become the system of terraces that can step down the abundance at the top that threatens to break like the faulty dam it is and drown us all in the collapse of money as a cultural system. Or, to change the metaphor from our Lindisfarne Fellow John Todd's observations on terraces in Java to our other Lindisfarne Fellow Lynn Margulis and her comments on planetary Gaian evolution and cyanobacteria, it is the slight outgassing of oxygen through photosynthesis that got rid of the toxic methane atmosphere to give us the beautiful blue sky that— unlike Beijing—we still enjoy for the time being.

Looking back as a cultural historian, I now believe that the United States came to a fork in the road in the election of 1998, and in the choice between George W. Bush's neo-conservatism and Al Gore's *Earth in Balance*, it confronted its last chance to avoid the catastrophes we are now going through. The Islamic State, or ISIS, is a direct consequence of Bush and Cheney's invasion of Iraq.

"*Tout commence en mystique et finit en politique*," Charles Péguy wrote in *Notre Jeunesse*. Lindisfarne was the *mystique* and Jerry Brown and Al Gore were the *politique*. Governor Brown came to the Lindisfarne Fellows meeting of 1980 at the Green Gulch Zen Farm in Marin County, California. Brown was familiar with the issues of pollution and climate change that Lindisfarne had been discussing since 1975, and he appointed Lindisfarne Fellows like Gregory Bateson, Rusty Schweickart, and Sim Van der Ryn, as well as the Lindisfarne Scholar-in-Residence for 1975 Tyrone Cashman, to his administration. But the U.S. dismissed Brown as "Governor Moonbeam" and elected Governor Reagan to its Presidency in 1980. Had Al Gore chosen to challenge the unconstitutional interference of the Supreme Court in the election of 1998—in which he held the plurality of votes—we might have avoided the disastrous policies of the Neocons that gave us the trillions of dollars War in Iraq and the incalculable number of deaths we are still experiencing there, as well as the slow catastrophe of irreversible climate collapse we have now entered. But through the mass entertainment industry of sports and politics, and the industrial cheerleadership of Reagan, the Clintons, and two Bushes, the consumers bought their energy intensive McMansion houses and gas-guzzling tank-like SUVs and closed formations into right wing corporate industrial politics, Christian religious fundamentalism, and the fake electronic community of *Facebook* that enabled the Deep State more effectively to keep track of them all and monitor their thoughts. It gives me little satisfaction to think in this my last book "we told you so." When the *New York Times Magazine* reporter Ted Morgan wrote about our 1975 Lindisfarne Conference in the February 29, 1976 issue he asked: "What if they are right?" The Times reporter provided people with a chance to move from *mystique* to *politique*, but people sipped their coffee, turned the page and went to work on Monday to carry on with business as usual, and in 1980 voted for Reagan who claimed pollution came from trees.

The consciousness of a system can change the system, but the Congress of the United States now chooses to repress consciousness of the crisis of industrial civilization and to deny climate change and science in general.[9] So now rather than creating our destiny we will have our fate thrust upon us. The transition from one world to another is going to be more breakdown than breakthrough. The sky has turned on us, and what was the ground of our being has now become the horizon of our undoing.

---

[1] See https://archive.org/details/WilliamIrwinThompsonE1

[2] "The Second Economy." (W. Brian Arthur, *McKinsey Quarterly*, October, 2011).

[3] Thomas Friedman, "Average is Over," OpEd column, *New York Times*, January 24, 2012.

[4] See Jeremy Rifkin's utopian pitch for *The Zero Marginal Cost Society, the Collaborative Commons, and the Eclipse of Capitalism* (New York: Palgrave Macmillan, 2014).

[5] See Wes Jackson's excellent newsletter for the Land Institute, *Land Report*, especially Number 110, Fall, 2014, "Perennial grains draw world interest," p. 4.

[6] http://www.wildriverreview.com/Column/Thinking-Otherwise/January-6-2011/William_Irwin_Thompson

[7] A. F. C. Wallace, "Revitalization Movements," *American Anthropologist*, LVIII (April, 1956), pp. 264-28

[8] Naomi Klein, *The Shock Doctrine* (Picador: New York, 2007).

[9] (http://www.rense.com/general64/du.htm)

For a positive suggestion on integrating science into democratic government, see my "Catastrophist Governance and the Need for a Tricameral Legislature" in *Self and Society: Studies in the Evolution of Culture* (Imprint Academic: Exeter, UK, 2009), 137-143.

Appendix

1. "Lindisfarne, the Founding of a New Educational Community," from *Change: the Magazine of Higher Education*, May, 1973.
2. "Re-membering the Forms of Emptiness: Dedication of the Haydn Stubbing Paintings in St. James Chapel, the Cathedral of St. John the Divine, New York City, November 5, 1988."
3. "The Lindisfarne Chapel," Crestone, Colorado, 1992.
4. Roster of the Lindisfarne Fellows, 2012.

1. The Lindisfarne Association: the Founding of a New Educational Community[1]

Upon his retirement from the United Nations, Secretary-General U Thant said that from where he stood he could see that the world has only the seventies in which to redirect the drift of events or face the disintegration of civilization. If we are facing a return of the Dark Ages, as many scientists fear, then it is natural that Western thinkers fall back upon the tradition of the monastery school as a way of preserving civilization. In the years since World War II we have built countless new universities and experimental colleges, but still the cultural disintegration goes on; in fact, in many cases civilization now has to be protected from the universities. The spirit of the sixth and seventh-century monasteries of Iona and Lindisfarne cannot be so easily packaged into a new technocratic institution, for the older institutions grew out of a vision that had the strength of opposites held in tension. That vision was at once conservative and anarchist. It was conservative in that the monks sought to preserve the old Graeco-Roman knowledge; but even in passing it on, they changed it by their touch. The old knowledge became powerfully compact as it became a content in the new larger structure of Christian civilization. The old classical scrolls became the new illuminated manuscripts of the Book of Kells and the Lindisfarne Gospels. The old classical intellectual became the new physically laboring monk. What leftists now admire in Mao's China is that part of the heritage of the Christian civilization they ignore.

The vision was anarchist because it grew out of the circumstances of the primitive Irish Church. The Roman Church was based upon imperial ecclesiastical bureaucracy; each urban center had its bishop who was responsible to Rome. But in Ireland and Scotland there were no towns; there was only the still savage countryside with its monastery citadel. Unprotected by any imperial system of power, the monastery rested in its savage space upon the visionary power of its abbot, who from the point of view of the hierarchy was nothing more than a common priest. A bishop was a prince of the Church; he was the skilled minister of power who helped make the Church more Roman than Catholic. But the abbot was more shaman than priest; his power came from within and not from the investiture of his office. With each monastery presided over by its own abbot, the Irish Church was held together by nothing stronger than a historical vision and a culture in which authority was cherished as much as power was distrusted.

The monastery schools were thus the very antithesis of Roman bureaucracy. The Roman Church in England under Augustine was the Church of Peter, but the Irish Church in Scotland under Columba and Aidan was the Church of John—a Church of an anarchist kind of Christianity that went back to an era when authority and power were kept separate in the figures of Christ and Caesar, and not bent together in the empire of the papacy. Through the vision of men like St. Columba and St. Aidan, Europe was able to survive the Dark Ages that separated classical from Christian civilization. The Ionas and Lindisfarnes they founded were tiny seedlings, but when they were transplanted later by Alcuin and Charlemagne, they developed into the universities upon which the whole growth of European civilization was based.

The sixth century is gone but the Dark Ages may be coming back.[2] Now more than ever we need the strength of cultural institutions like the Church and the university, but now more than ever they lack the very visionary strength we need. The Church has become a museum, and the university, which Plato founded, has ended up in Plato's cave. The best of the teachers and students are dissatisfied; the worst are happy in their expertise—an expertise in shadows cast upon the wall. It is time to move outside in search of a different kind of light.

To move outside of institutions, it will be necessary to move outside their patterns of consciousness and experience. The domination by power does not represent the only failure of the postwar multiversity. Like a rich city that produces so much that it suffocates in its own pollution, the university now produces more information than its center of gravity can support. With 36,000 books published every year in the United States alone, and with more than a million scientific papers published in the world at large, the knowledge factories are trapped in their own contradictions. When there were only a few hundred books at the heart of Christian or classical civilization, a reading of "the Great Books" could make an intelligent man learned, if not wise. But now that we are in postcivilization, we cannot depend on merely civilized techniques of learning to answer our crisis. New modes of consciousness must be developed (or recovered?) as education moves toward integration at a higher level of order. As the classical scroll was to the illuminated manuscript, so now the book must become to the illuminated mind. Books must become powerfully compact as they become a content in the new larger structure of planetary civilization. If we are to have another Lindisfarne, it must be a transformer in which the energy of man's cultural evolution is stepped up to another level. The transformational disciplines of the great universal religions, such as Yoga, Zen, and Sufism, must themselves become transformed as they become part of the new truly universal Catholicism we need if there is ever to be a planetary civilization on Earth.

When the ordinary individual finds himself becoming lost in complete cultural disorientation, he must either leap upward to imaginative integrations on a higher level of order or descend to subrational levels of insentience. For an alarming number of people in our culture (perhaps as many as 35 million in North America), the chemicals of alcohol, marijuana, amphetamines, barbiturates, tranquilizers, opiates, and psychedelics provide an immediate escape from the dilemma of consciousness. It is useless to expect education to deal with this problem. Education is part of culture; if the culture is failing, the education system will fail along with it. All the welfare workers, psychiatrists, ministers and educators cannot deal with a cultural problem in which social work, psychology, organized religion and education are primary expressions of the failing culture. Chemical addiction is one part of our cultural entropy, and the structures of the old culture cannot deal with it in terms of its institutionalizing techniques.

But if the problem lies in the basic nature of culture, so does the solution. The genius of religion has always been the recognition that the transformation of the individual is inseparable from the transformation of human culture. The Lindisfarne Association, which we are now organizing, is intended to be one place in which the individual can overcome his sense of cultural disorientation in postindustrial civilization by gaining a new sense of the role of the single human consciousness in the emerging planetary transformation of mankind. Once we have a sense of the whole curve of human evolution, we have precisely that sense of the meaning of human existence which is missing in most of our occupationally oriented business and educational corporations. The Lindisfarne Association is simply one perspective on this whole curve of cultural evolution.

Our first concern will be to understand the nature of our emerging planetary culture and to work out forms of activity that flow out from that understanding. The problems of this new culture are far too important to be left in the hands of think tanks, task forces of civil servants and cadres of technical experts who too often think in terms of computer models rather than spiritually and aesthetically patterned ways of human life. The Association will critically survey the work of all these think-tanknicians, futurologists and behavioral modifiers who have such grand designs on human culture. Our commitment will be precisely to those spiritual dimensions of culture that are ignored by such groups as Les Futuribles, the Hudson Institute, and the Club of Rome. The Association will be acutely interested in contemporary world affairs and will offer its resources and facilities to the New York-based Institute for World Order's program of study in problems of pollution and international law. By sponsoring seminars, lectures, and conferences in cooperation with the Institute, the Association hopes to silhouette its work with the individual residents against a wider horizon.

The second major concern of the Association will be in the generation of new forms of knowledge and education appropriate to the new planetary culture. In our end is our beginning, so the end of Western Civilization involves a turn of the spiral of time back to the Pythagorean world view that lies at the very base of Western culture. In the attempt to integrate science, religion, and art, the Association will follow the lines of thought developed by Whitehead and Teilhard de Chardin and continued today by such physicists as Werner Heisenberg and C. F. von Weizsäcker and their Research Foundation for Western Science and Eastern Wisdom in Starnberg, Germany. In this country, we will support the work that the Center for Integrative Education has been carrying on for the last quarter of a century. The Association will support its magazine, *Main Currents in Modern Thought,* and support through the award of fellowships the work of those junior and senior artists, scientists, and scholars who are working along the lines of thought shared by the Association and the Center for Integrative Education. Through the work of the Center in integrative principles for curriculum design, the Association hopes to develop an educational way of life appropriate to a truly planetary culture.

As society changes, so do forms of knowledge, disciplines, and whole educational systems. In the nineteenth century the problems of the new industrial society generated the new science of sociology, and the work of Marx, Engles, and Durkheim provided a new way of knowing man. Now that we are living in a technetronic society that flows over all the boundaries of the old industrial nation-states, it is becoming clearer that new forms of knowledge are needed to help us reinterpret the world. In an attempt to answer this need, the Director of the Association will not simply be an administrator but will continue his research, writing, and lecturing in the phenomenology of culture. The director will offer a course on "The Transformations of Human Culture," that will serve as one perspective on the whole development of human culture from the hominization of the primates to the planetization of mankind. As a form of knowledge, the course itself will strive to approach the level of mythology in that it will seek through artistic means to become a performance of the very reality it seeks to describe. In this sense, the course will represent the director's own attempt to move from *Wissenschaft* (science) to *Wissenskunst* (knowledge as an art form). This lecture series will provide one explanation of the Association's work to the residents and will lay a foundation for the work of the fellows along their own lines of synthesis and integration.

The third major area will be concerned with the way in which our planetary culture and our new forms of education affect the individual transformation of consciousness. At a university the program of residence is instruction within the informational disciplines of the sciences and humanities: the hypothetical-inductive method for the former and the hermaneutic of textual exegesis for the latter. At Lindisfarne the program of residence will include instruction in the transformational disciplines of Yoga, Buddhism, and Sufism, as well as in an effort to rediscover the esoteric schools of thought of our own Judeo-Christian traditions. Each resident will select one seminar/ workshop in a particular discipline of his or her choosing, and then will begin to compose a dedicated daily way of life, a *sadhana*, that is in harmony with his own particular personality and character. For the period of residence, the individual will work with one of the fellows and the other members of the seminar/workshop. A program of residence in Yoga, for example, would involve daily physical exercise (Hatha Yoga), meditation, and seminars in discussion of philosophical texts. As an integral part of this sadhana, each person, and this means everyone, including directors, will contribute two hours a day to the housekeeping chores of the community labor in running the Association. A typical day in the life of a resident might be as follows:

7:00 Exercise and meditation
8:00 Breakfast
8:30 Communal work
10:30 Communal tea
11:00 Seminars
12:00 Lunch
1:00 Seminars, workshops, private study, crafts, play.
4:00 Hatha Yoga or Tai Chi
5:00 Communal Tea
5:30 Dinner
7:00 Concerts, lectures, films, group sessions, drama.
10:00 Evening meditation

To support this program of residence there will be fellows qualified to give instruction in the various transformational disciplines. In addition to these instructors in Yoga, Zen, and Sufism, fellowships will be awarded in science, art, and the humanities in cooperation with the Center for Integrative Education. Each fellow will be responsible for one seminar/workshop of ten residents, and each fellow will be expected to be in residence at the Association. For the first year of full-time operation, the selection of fellows might be in these areas: hatha Yoga, Tai Chi, Raja Yoga, Buddhism, Sufism, mathematics, music, physical science, psychology, and the humanities.

The Association will grant no degrees, diplomas, or certificates of residence. It is committed to the separation of authority from power and it does not in any way wish to involve itself with the status system of American higher education. The standards of achievement will be the natural ones of individuals working for self-mastery. There will be no formal means of examination and evaluation, no grades, colored robes, degrees of initiation, titles or other institutional appurtenances. If, at the end of a period of residence, an individual wishes to apply to a university, he or she may ask a fellow or one of the directors to write a letter of reference. Such a letter will be the only document that a resident will be able to take away with him after his stay at the Association.

Because many of the people attracted to the esoteric teachings of religion have had a history of drug experimentation, it is inevitable that some of those who may wish to come to Lindisfarne will be concerned about drugs and the drug culture. In order to be accepted at Lindisfarne, however, the individual must have given up the use of drugs and be able to see the wisdom in choosing another method for the expansion of consciousness.

Those who feel that there is a place for the moderate and informed use of drugs in personal transformation are advised to seek out other centers, but those who have had a history of drug use or chemical or alcoholic addiction and now wish to move their lives in Lindisfarne's direction will be welcome. In many ways, we feel that those who have failed to relate to postindustrial society are often, paradoxically enough, uniquely open to enculturation in the emerging planetary civilization. As Yeats has said: "Nothing can be sole or whole/That has not been rent."

Nevertheless, Lindisfarne will not be a therapeutic community or a college, for we are not so much interested in training or retraining people for life as in bringing them to life. We are not merely interested in preparing the young for what their elders think is their destiny, but we are interested in bringing people together at the critical turning points of life. Individuals at these turning points begin to ask all over again the very basic questions of human identity: "Who am I? Where do I come from? Where am I going?" At these turning points, they are not critically concerned with success and job training but with the very basic meaning of their own movement through life-time. They are concerned not so much with "what to do" as with "how to be." By bringing people together at all of these points of life, we are moving away from the youth reservation of the university and the geriatric reservation of the Church. With all the generations present, with the sacred and secular held in balance, Lindisfarne will not have the rarefied qualities of an institute, think tank, or ashram, the self-indulgent qualities of a growth center, or the escapist qualities of a rural commune. In short, the Lindisfarne Association will be a unique form of higher education here and abroad.

Postscript, 2006

Actually, this model for daily life worked out pretty well. Were this model to be combined with the evolution of consciousness curriculum I designed for the Ross School in East Hampton,[3] New York, to serve in place of the 1950s University of Chicago Great Books curriculum, I would say that with realistic funding, Lindisfarne could serve as the model for a new liberal arts college — along the lines of Bard College in New York or Hampshire College in Amherst, Massachusetts. And if the college were to be combined with a kindergarten to secondary school, then the educational community would be complete.

The balance between work and study, meditation and Tai Chi or hatha yoga was effective. And what also gave the community a particularly wholesome way of life was the presence of the three generations. Lew and Eva Balamuth and the retired Episcopal Bishop, Chandler Sterling served in the roles of grandparents or Elders. Chandler created an organic garden that had a centering role in our life, and Lew Balamuth led a weekly discussion group on Gurdjief's vision of esoteric Christianity. A school was created for the four children of the community, and with a good faculty to student ratio of six teachers to four children, the kids enjoyed a program of learning and communal labor with the adults that no large school, public or private, could match. And the group meditations together were profoundly moving. The deeply centered silence became palpably solid, as if an angel had entered the room and taken up the truly esoteric position of our hidden teaching fellow in residence.

David Kaner, Sylvia Channing, students of the Ross School, Courtney Ross, Founder of the Ross School, Ralph and Ray Abraham at the 2010 Lindisfarne Fellows Conference at the Upaya Zen Center in Santa Fe, New Mexico, 2010.

The experience of being a student at Lindisfarne was worthwhile, and many used the time as a space in which to redirect their lives. They went on to become professors of Philosophy, Literature, and Buddhist studies, as well as editors, literary agents, and practitioners of alternative medicine in acupuncture. Their time spent at Lindisfarne was not a waste.

The main problem, of course, was money. Most colleges, such as Williams, Amherst, or my own Pomona, had been founded by religious congregations, so they could draw off other sources of funds and were not dependent upon tuition. Without a church congregation, or wealthy alumni, there was simply no way for Lindisfarne to support itself through student tuition — especially for the small numbers of students we had. The only funds we had was a loan from Jean and Sydney Lanier to make the first payment on the mortgage for the property on Fish Cove in Southampton, New York, and small grants from Trinity Church, the Rockefeller Brothers Fund, the Lilly Endowment, and the Erwin Sweeney Miller Foundation to pay the stipends of the first group of teaching fellows. After a year and a half of running as a school, we switched to becoming a communally run institute and began to concentrate on the development of the very successful conferences we had held.[4] We became what Harpers magazine called "a summer camp for intellectuals."

Like other cultural experiments before it such as Black Mountain College, Lindisfarne became a concert of ideas and a performance art of the Zeitgeist, but it also became totally dependent upon my fund-raising, and though others tried to step in to help me, they were not able to raise funds. Normal institutions, like Harvard or Princeton, can have development officers who are able to raise funds, but wealthy donors who become interested in temporarily interesting groupings such as Lindisfarne, tend only to want to have meetings with the founder. So Lindisfarne survived as long as I could raise funds — which I did for twenty-five years. But sooner or later, whether you are trying to raise funds as a dancer-choreographer for your dance company or a cultural philosopher for your institute, you burn out. Institutions with interlocking boards of directors in capitalist society can raise enormous funds to create endowments, but what Ivan Illich called "a counterfoil institution" has a harder time doing this. In a self-fulfilling prophecy in which donors feel the new cultural project is only likely to be charismatic and interesting for a brief period of relevance, they give funds for three-year grants for specific projects, but shy away from endowing the enterprise and making it stable and sustainable.

2. Re-membering the Forms of Emptiness

Dedication of the Haydn Stubbing Paintings in St. James
Chapel, Cathedral of St. John the Divine, New York City,
November 5, 1988.

The philosopher asks himself: Why is there something rather than
nothing? For the philosopher the very act of questioning seems to be a
noble quest, a way of creating a path, as Heidegger phrased it, "into the
clearing." But painters do not ask the question; they present the perception
that occurred in wonder before the intellect could respond with the question
framed. For some painters the original perception in which Being is not taken
for granted is re-created in the work of art and becomes the re-presentation
of the moment in the clearing. Newton Haydn Stubbing was one of those
painters whose silences of color astonished the viewer with the inexplicable
appearance of Being, which, because it had no reasons, could not respond to
questions with answers.

To frame a question, the mind needs to remove itself in a distancing of
knowing from being, but a painting, especially one of Haydn's paintings, is
the kind of presence that draws thinking back into being. The binary, logical
world of the object in containing space dissolves into a presence that is empty
of definitions but full of relationships in all the dimensions in which colors
form. These opening silences of light become the space of another time, a time
of re-collection in which we re-member, re-connect, re-touch, as the world of
the ego's conventional construction is brought to a sky where *things* can no
longer tolerate being designated. The object, which, only a moment before we
had mistaken for a thing, becomes an epiphany, a moment of divinity in which
the fallen world of objects chained down into lines of egocentric perspective is
gathered back into a clearing in which the stars echo in the rocks. This is our
heritage of Being that we inherit as beings, but we have forgotten and thus
can no longer hear the music of the stars echoing in the stones. And perhaps
for our postmodern era, suspended as it is between materialism and nihilism,
so like a desperate New Yorker out on the ledge of an impersonal skyscraper
but suspended above his own highly personal abyss, it is not always pleasant
to recall, for the recollection tells us just how much we have lost. Sometimes
the few who do not remember can never again surrender to the conventionally
inhabited world. These tormented souls, such as Nietzsche, Van Gogh, or
Rimbaud, if they cannot re-member, would rather dismember: better the

black reality of the void than the illusionary substance of matter.

The art of Haydn Stubbing is neither a social expression of our postmodern culture, nor an infantile nostalgia for some preverbal mind the foetus had in the womb; it is the Buddhist face we had before we were conceived. In this re-membering, the English painters have been sometimes helped by the English poets. Wordsworth, starring at a blind beggar leaning against a milestone and holding a sign on his chest for the passer-by, was stopped for a moment to wonder who was really the blindman that carried his history written over his heart in ciphers he could not read. Wordsworth would call those intensely visual moments "spots of time." The paintings of Haydn Stubbing are also, quite literally, spots of time.

There are no people or societies in Stubbing's paintings, for the fundamental society that he presents is more basic than a scene of social commentary or societal rage. His is an art that re-members our identity and does not simply stamp our temporary passports with visas that permit us to live and work in an alien land. Social commentary in art has a very perishable relevance, but the kind of art that touches the horizon of Being is not about the edge between the personal and the social; it is itself the shore between something and nothing.

Yes, I realize that I am being old-fashioned and romantic, that what I am saying about art works very well for Wordsworth and Rilke, for the apples of Cezanne, the water-lilies of Monet, or the stars of Van Gogh; but it does not work so well for the tableau of Kienholz, the tabloids of Lichtenstein, or the constructions of Tuttle. But here today in St. James Chapel in the Cathedral of St. John the Divine, we all recognize that we are not staring at a wall in the Whitney, and that what has brought us together is a re-membering of more than ourselves in this space and time. This art that blesses us has its own contemplative power and no amount of holy water that we in the company of priests could cast on these canvases could make them holier than they are. So we are here today in our smaller society not to commemorate or to consecrate, but to give thanks for the re-membering in the mystical body of mind and nature that Stubbing presented to us.

The paintings that are all about us are suspended horizons of groundlessness. Literally, the colors matter. Haydn's colleague in the Lindisfarne Fellowship, the neurophysiologist Francisco Varela, has studied and written about the perception of color. Varela has come to the conclusion that color vision is not an impression made by a subject reporting on an object in the "outer" world; rather, color vision is a performance of the nervous system with the entire body in concert, and all the elements that we might wish to single out as "red" do not come in as signals at the same time; they have to be orchestrated by the brain to perform the phenomenon we call "red." Where then is the hard edge between the inner and the outer, perceiver and perceived, subject and object, between mind and nature? It is there in Haydn's paintings, there in that performance of groundlessness in which "form is not different from emptiness, emptiness is not different from form."

The words I choose to accompany Haydn's groundless landscapes come from the Buddhist *Heart Sutra* and are chanted by the monks in the zendo as the appropriate accompaniment to meditation. Haydn liked to call his work "open-eyed meditations," and the phrase is good, for in the immanental world of Zen, one does not meditate with closed eyes. In the transcendental world of Hinduism, one closes one's eyes to the world of *maya*, of illusion, and tries to escape through yoga from the limitations of the merely physical body. Haydn's work is neither transcendental nor immanental, but is, rather, the shore between these two modes of being in a body, where the two interpenetrate as objects dissolve into clouds and clouds solidify through color. His landscapes are not portraits of "nature" sitting majestically in the light, but portraits of consciousness. As with zazen, Haydn's open-eyed meditations bring us to the edge of knowing, and there along the immediate horizon of the eyelids, darkness endures in artful compassion for everything that comes to light.

3. The Lindisfarne Chapel, 1992

Although we had a dedication ceremony for the beginning of the project of creating a Lindisfarne meditation chapel in Southampton in March of 1976—a ceremony in which the High Lama Nechung Rinpoche and the Hopi Spokesman for the Tribal Elders Thomas Banyaca along with Janet McCloud of the Seattle Indians took part, I could not begin the construction of the chapel until we had moved from the Hamptons to Crestone, Colorado. At the entrance to the Lindisfarne Chapel I placed a small notice that I wrote in 1992 to explain my ideals for a post-religious spirituality that is not based upon ritual or one culture's iconography:

The Lindisfarne Chapel

"Be still, and know that I am God." Psalm 46:10

"The tranquil night,	La noche sosegada
At the time of the rising dawn,	En par de los levantes del aurora,
Silent music,	La musica callada,
The supper that refreshes,	La cena que recrea y
And deepens love."	enamora.

St. John of the Cross

The Lindisfarne Association is a fellowship of artists, scientists, and religious contemplatives devoted to the study and realization of a new planetary culture for our new global civilization. The Christian-Buddhist dialogue and collaboration have been major parts of Lindisfarne's work since its founding in 1972, and the Crestone Mountain Zen Center was founded at a meeting of the Lindisfarne Board of Directors at the Cathedral of St. John the Divine in New York City in 1988.

The Lindisfarne Chapel, which is still under construction and not yet officially open to the public, has been conceived and designed as an interfaith sanctuary for silent meditation; it is intended to be a sacred space rather than a religious place, and therefore is meant to be more an invocation of the future than an evocation of the past. This chapel has been created in a time of religious warfare all over the world, and so it is critical to the survival of humanity that a space be brought into being in which differing religions can come together. You will notice that there is no iconography that makes one tradition feel at home but another feel out of place. In spirit, the chapel follows the principles of "No decoration, only proportion; no iconography, only geometry." The stone ring embodies the presence of the elemental powers of Earth; the baked bricks of the floor embody the human realm of the transformed nature that is culture; the geometrical lattice of the dome embodies the interweaving of the Celestial Intelligences associated with the angelic and boddhisativic realms, and the skylight embodies the center in which the elemental, human, and angelic realms come together to create a vessel for the pure light of Emptiness at the center.

Guided by the principles of the Perennial Wisdom of the past, the designer, W. I. Thompson, the architects Keith Critchlow and John Barton, and the builders Michael Baron and Robert Van Iwaarden, have worked to create an expression of the sacred geometry that underlies a seashell or a sunflower, a Christian cathedral or a Buddhist temple. But just as an understanding of geometry underlies the perception of specific concrete forms, so does the experience of contemplative silence underlie the various traditions of ritual and prayer. The Lindisfarne Chapel is not intended to be a temple for religious rituals or a theatre for the performing arts, and if someone enters this space with this secondary purpose in mind, we only ask that one honor the primary purpose of the space with a few moments of silent meditation before turning to song or movement.

1992-2014

When I returned to Crestone in 1992 to live in the log cabin that Laurance Rockefeller had generously built for me, I resumed work on the Lindisfarne Chapel and Laurance contributed again to its construction. Around this time the Zen monks took to calling the Chapel "the dome," and although I corrected them continually and said this was as offensive to me as if I were to call their Zendo "the box," they persisted. To this day, they insist on calling it the Lindisfarne Dome on their website, which is doubly annoying since it disregards the fact that while Keith Critchlow designed the dome, I designed the Chapel as a whole and redesigned the floor. When I was away from Crestone because of intense allergies to pinyon pollen and pine sap, these American and German converts to Japanese Buddhism openly expressed their discomfort with the idea of a chapel within their midst and treated the structure as if it were a barn for guests to sleep in overnight in sleeping bags, or to rent out to groups who wished to use if for classes in movement therapies and religious dances, meetings, or performances.

Au_{16}

I had envisioned a skylight based upon the atomic structure of gold (Au_{16}), and planned to have the triangular panels capable of being opened to vent the space because it became quite hot in the summers. I planned to use only the top half of this structure as the skylight, with the flat facet of one triangle of clear glass facing the sky so that the stars above could be visible at night.

Design for Lindisfarne chapel Skylight

In order to respect the line of the curvature of the dome, I planned that the structure would not rise too high or be so large as to disrupt the overall form. Because of my illness from dehydration and kidney failure in 2007, I was never able to implement these plans and had to leave Crestone, first for the hospital in Alamosa, and then for a month's hospitalization in Santa Fe.

When the Lindisfarne Chapel was left entirely to the management of the Crestone Mountain Zen Center, the monks returned to calling it the Lindisfarne Dome, and Baker-roshi's wife—Mary Louise Baker—an ETH Zurich-educated architect—took over the design of the skylight. Mrs. Baker did not know of Lindisfarne's program in sacred architecture or its summer schools for architects, and relied solely on her excellent training in a distinguished Swiss school renowned for its post-Bauhaus, highly rational industrial style. Mrs. Baker, no doubt in respect for Baker-roshi's preference for all things Buddhist, redesigned the skylight so that the whole chapel now has the look of a Buddhist Stupa in Tibet or Nepal. Her shift in design has worked very well, and the change from green to brown for the tiling of the roof harmonizes with the beige structure of the stucco entrance and the whole building sits very nicely against the backdrop of the mountains. Mrs. Baker's installation of trapeozoidal-shaped lights at the conjointure of the beams, however, reverses the movement of the eye from upward to the crown of light to downward in a sense of Zen's grounding—as opposed to a New Age, ungrounded arc of transcendence. I had planned invisible track lighting that would subtly highlight the celestial geometry of Keith Critchlow's dome at night, so as to balance the strong elemental and chthonic energy of the compression ring with its stones taken directly from our land and the culturally transformed earth of the bricks set into the floor in the pattern of the logarithmic spiral of the core of the sunflower so beloved by Keith Critchlow. In other words, all the elements of the Chapel were designed to embody the cosmology of Lindisfarne, but when I left there was no one to oversee the project, and since the Zen monks were only in affinity with Buddhist architecture, they looked upon the "Dome" merely as a commercial asset and redesigned it as a stupa to serve its new Zen Buddhist sangha. An interfaith chapel was simply too Christian and "New Age."

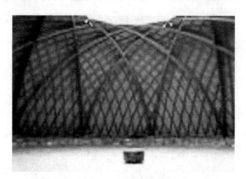

Before

After

I now realize that I and my cultural projects with Lindisfarne were "out of timing" for a world recommitting itself to religions both in the conversionary zeal of the suburban American Zen monks who tried to be more medieval and Japanese than the Japanese themselves, and the anti-modernist zealots around the world who were recommitting themselves to new fundamentalist extremes in Judaism, Hinduism, Christianity, and Islam. So the "Lindisfarne Dome" is well renamed, because it is no longer a chapel for a practicing community, but a public and neutral space that supports the Crestone Mountain Zen Center's summer guest program.

The Roster of the new
Lindisfarne Fellowship for 2012 was:

- **Ralph Abraham**, Director, Visual Mathematics Institute, Santa Cruz, California.www.ralph-abraham.org/
- **Brian Arthur**, Economist, Santa Fe Institute, New Mexico. http://www.santafe.edu/~wbarthur/
- http://www.polarisventures.com/
- **Christopher Bamford**, Author and Publisher, Great Barrington, MA. http://www.lindisfarne.org/
- **Mary Catherine Bateson**, Emerita Prof. of Anthropology George Mason Univ., Fairfax, Virginia. http://www.marycatherinebateson.com/
- **Nora Bateson**, Cinematographer, Nelson, British Columbia, Canada.
- **Wendell Berry**, Poet and Farmer, Port Royal, Kentucky.
- **Evan Chambers**, Chair of Composition, Associate Professor of Music, University of Michigan at Ann Arbor. http://www.music.umich.edu/faculty_staff/bio.php?
- **Bruce Clarke**, Author, literary critic and cultural historian, Professor of English, Texas Tech University, Lubbock, Texas. http://www.faculty.english.ttu.edu/clarke/
- **Richard Falk**, Emeritus Professor of International Law, Woodrow Wilson School, Princeton, NJ. Santa Barbara, CA.
- **David Finkelstein**, Physicist, Georgia Inst. of Technology, Atlanta, Georgia. http://www.physics.gatech.edu/people/faculty/dfinkelstein.html
- **Joan Halifax-roshi**, Anthropologist and Abbess, Upaya Zen Center, Santa Fe, New Mexico. http://www.upaya.org/roshi/
- **Hazel Henderson**, Author & Economist, St. Augustine, Florida.http://www.ethicalmarkets.tv/
- **Cornelia Hesse-Honegger**, Artist, Zurich, Switzerland. http://www.wissenskunst.ch/en/biographie.htm
- **Jane Hirshfield**, Poet/Author, Mill Valley, California. http://www.barclayagency.com/hirshfield.html
- **Vivienne Hull**, Co-founder, Whidbey Institute, Whidbey Island, Washington. http://www.whidbeyinstitute.org/
- **Wes Jackson**, Botanist & Co-Director, The Land Institute, Salina, Kansas. http://www.landinstitute.org/

- **Pir Zia Inayat-Khan** is the spiritual leader of the Sufi Order International and founder of Seven Pillars House of Wisdom, New Lebanon, New York. www.sevenpillarshouse.org.http://www.sufiorder.org/
- **Stuart Kauffman**, Director of the Center for Biocomplexity and Informatics, University of Calgary, Alberta, Canada. http://www.ucalgary.ca/ibi/kauffman/
- **Tim Kennedy**, Molecular Biologist, Professor of Neuroscience, McGill University, Montreal
- **Merle Lefkoff**, Political Scientist and Founder of the Madrona Institute, Santa Fe, NM and San Juan Island, WA. http://www.www.madrona.org
- **James Lovelock**, Chemist, Coombe Mills Laboratories, Devon, England. http://www.ecolo.org/lovelock/
- **Amory Lovins**, Physicist, Rocky Mountain Institute, Snowmass, Colorado. http://www.rmi.org/
- **Luigi Luisi**, Polymer Chemist, Professor, Universita degli Studi di Roma Tre. http://www.plluisi.org/grl_luisi.html
- **Paul Mankiewicz**, Ph.D. Biologist, Director of the Gaia Institute, New York City. http://www.gaiainstituteny.org/
- **Laura McClanahan**, Artist, Glen Gardner, NJ.
- **Robert McDermott**, Author, Professor, California Institute of Integral Studies, San Francisco California. http://www.ciis.edu/faculty/mcdermott.html
- **Saul Mendlovitz**, Emeritus Prof. of International Law, Rutgers Univ., Rutgers, New Jersey. http://catalogs.rutgers.edu/generated/nwk-law_0406/pg5500.html
- **James Parks Morton**, Interfaith Fellowship, New York City. http://11thhouraction.com/ideasandexperts/jamesparksmorton
- **Dulce Murphy**, Director, Esalen Institute-Russian Exchange Program, San Francisco, Calif.
- **Michael Murphy**, Author & Founder of Esalen Institute, Big Sur, California
- **Natasha Myers**, Dancer and Anthropologist, York University, Toronto, Canada, http://www.arts.yorku.ca/anth/nmyers/
- **Mayumi Oda**, Artist, Kealakekua, Hawaii. http://www.mayumioda.net/
- **David Orr**, Prof. of Environmental Studies, Oberlin College, Ohio. http://www.oberlin.edu/envs/faculty_pages/orr.htm

- **Susan Oyama**, Emerita Prof. of Psychology, John Jay College, City Univ. of New York
- **Dorion Sagan**, Author, Science Writers, Amherst, Massachusetts. http://www.sciencewriters.org-
- **David Spangler**, Author, Issaquah, Washington. http://www.Lorian.org.
- **Brother David Steindl-Rast**, Author, & Benedictine Monk, Benedictine Grange, West Redding, Connecticut. http://www.gratefulness.org/brotherdavid/index.htm
- **Joy Stocke**, Founder and Editor of the Wild River Review, Princeton, NJ. http://www.wildriverreview.com/index.php
- **Maurice Strong**, Founder of the United Nations Environmental Programme
- **Neil Theise**, MD., Faculty of Medicine, Albert Einstein College of Medicine and Beth Israel Hospital, NY. http://www.neiltheise.com/
- **Evan Thompson**, Professor of Philosophy, University of Toronto, http://individual.utoronto.ca/evant/
- **W. I. Thompson**, Author & Founder of the Lindisfarne Association. Portland, Maine.
- **Robert Thurman**, Prof. of Religion, Columbia Univ. New York. http://www.bobthurman.com/biography.shtml
- **John Todd**, Institute for Natural Resources, University of Vermont, Co-Founder of New Alchemy & Ocean Arks, Falmouth Massachusetts, http://www.toddecological.com/
- **Nancy Jack Todd**, Author & Editor, Co-Founder of New Alchemy and Ocean Arks, Falmouth, Massachusetts, http://www.oceanarks.org/
- **Rebecca Todd**, Dancer, Choreographer, Cognitive Scientist, the University of Toronto, Canada.
- **Sim Van der Ryn**, Architect, Sausalito, California,
- http://www.ecodesign.org
- **Michaela Walsh**, Founder of Women's World Banking International, New York, walshmich@gmail.com.
- **Paul Winter**, Musician, Director of the Paul Winter Consort, Litchfield, Connecticut, & Cathedral of St. John the Divine, New York, http://www.livingmusic.com/
- **Arthur Zajonc**, Prof. of Physics, Amherst College, Massachusetts, www.arthurzajonc.org

[1]Originally published in Change: the Magazine of Higher Learning, Vol. 5, No. 4, May, 1973, 44-48.

[2]When I wrote this in 1973, India had a population of 500 million; now it has a billion and has become a public health disaster, despite its Silicon Valley transplants. And if China continues in its Western style of industrialization, and the citizens exchange their bicycles for automobiles, you can say goodbye to the blue sky of the planet. But even before this crisis becomes manifest, China will face a water crisis and it too will likely implode in a massive public health crisis. Small wonder that the urbanologist Jane Jacobs has written a new jeremiad on the coming dark ages. (See Dark Age Ahead: New York, Random House, 2004). Jacobs moved to Toronto from New York at the end of the sixties and worked to stop the Allen Expressway and the general Los Angelization of Toronto. She and the whole NDP neighborhood community movement failed and the Tories worked to bring the unbridled capitalism of Thatcher and Reagan to Ontario. The social democracy of Canada is now just as threatened as American society is under Bush.

[3]See W. I. Thompson, Transforming History: A New Curriculum for a Planetary Culture (Great Barrington, MA: Lindisfarne Books, 2009) and "The Cultural Phenomenology of Literature" in Light Onwords/Light Onwards: Living Literacies Text of the November 14-16 Conference at York University (Toronto: The Coach House Press, 2004), 158-185; also, W. I. Thompson, "Literary and Archetypal Mathematical Mentalities in the Evolution of Culture" in Self and Society: Studies in the Evolution of Culture (Exeter, England: Imprint Academic, 2004), 35-50.

[4]See Earth's Answer; Explorations of Planetary Culture at the Lindisfarne Conferences, ed. M. Katz, W. Marsh, G. Thompson (New York: Harper & Row/Lindisfarne. 1977).

CPSIA information can be obtained
at www.ICGtesting.com
Printed in the USA
LVHW020412020622
720196LV00013B/986

9 780936 878867